Urban Hunters

Eurasia Past and Present

General Editors

Catriona Kelly
University of Oxford

Douglas Rogers
Yale University

Mark D. Steinberg
University of Illinois

Urban Hunters
Dealing and Dreaming in Times of Transition

Lars Højer and Morten Axel Pedersen

Yale UNIVERSITY PRESS / NEW HAVEN & LONDON

Published with assistance from the Mary Cady Tew Memorial Fund.

Yale University Press books may be purchased in quantity for educational, business, or promotional use. For information, please e-mail sales.press@yale.edu (U.S. office) or sales@yaleup.co.uk (U.K. office).

Photographs are by the authors except as indicated.

Set in Adobe Garamond and ITC Stone Sans type by Newgen North America, Austin, Texas.
Printed in the United States of America.

Library of Congress Control Number: 2018962996
ISBN 978-0-300-19611-5 (hardcover : alk. paper)

A catalogue record for this book is available from the British Library.

This paper meets the requirements of ANSI/NISO Z39.48-1992 (Permanence of Paper).

10 9 8 7 6 5 4 3 2 1

Contents

Acknowledgments

Many people have contributed a great deal to this book's completion. First of all, we would like to express our deepest appreciation and gratitude to our friends and acquaintances from Ulaanbaatar, without whose seemingly unlimited hospitality, knowledge and assistance this book would never have materialized: Zhenia ("Jenya") Boikov and his family; Bayarmaa Khalzaa and her family; B. Otgonchimeg and her family; Burmaa Nyamaa (and her mother, Bulgan Nyamaa, and aunt Tungalag Nyamaa, our initial contacts with Mongolia), as well as Sasha, Bolor, Olga, Sasha, Oyunaa, Nadia, Ruslan, Denis and many others. A special thanks to our Mongolian *düü* Jenya: dear friend, gatekeeper, key informant, research assistant and much more for both of us over more than twenty years.

We would also like to extend a special thanks to our *bagsh*, Caroline Humphrey, who supervised both our doctoral theses in Cambridge and has since then been an unremitting source of inspiration and support. We would also like to express our gratitude to Joel Robbins for providing much of the inspiration that first led us to formulate this book's critique of postsocialist studies, but also for being such a generous and encouraging friend. In addition, we wish to thank the following scholars, collaborators and friends for discussions, questions, comments, recommendations, advice and much more: Chima Angadike-Danes, Andreas Bandak, Franck Billé, Mikkel Bille, Barbara Bodenborn, Lauren Bonilla, Joseph Bristley, Uradyn Bulag, Mikkel Bunkenborg, Manduhai Buyandelger, Jens Bønding, Giovanni da Col, Anneline Dalsgaard, Veena Das, Gregory Delaplace, Bumochir Dulam, Rebecca Empson, Krisztina Fehervary, Esther Fihl, Martin Demant Frederiksen, Liz Fox, Munkh-Erdene Gantulga, Zsuzsa Gille, Bruce Grant, Jessica Greenberg, Signe Gundersen, Charlotte Haslund-Christensen, Michael Haslund-Christensen, Ghassan Hage, Mette High, Martin Holbraad, Birgitte Stampe Holst, Deborah James, Kåre Jansbøl, Niels Reedtz Johansen, Benedikte Møller Kristensen, Regnar Albæk Kristensen, Stine Krøijer, Anja Kublitz, Gaëlle Lacaze, James Laidlaw, Mette My Madsen, Ida Sofie Matzen, Hiro Miyazaki, Aude Michelet, Hanne Mogensen, Ida Nicolaisen, Finn Sivert Nielsen, Morten Nielsen, Dastan Nigamet, Otgonbayar, Serguei Oushakine, Libby Peachey, Lise Røjskjær Pedersen, Gustav Peebles, Charles Piot, Rebekah Plueckhahn, Camilla Ravnbøl, Tomasz Rakowski, Adam Reed, Stine Simonsen Puri, Anna Rauter, Morris Rossabi, Steven Sangren, Frank Sejersen, Shürentsetseg, Vera Skvirskaja, Marissa Smith, David Sneath, Charles Stafford, Marilyn Strathern, Katie Swancutt, Anna Tsing, Hürelbaatar Ujeed, Uranchimeg Ujeed, Michael Alexander Ulfstjerne, Henrik Vigh, Christian Vium, Huan Wardle, Hedwig Waters, Alan Wheeler, Susan Whyte, Rane Willerslev, Alexei Yurckak and Astrid Zimmermann. In addition, Morten would like to thank colleagues and students from the Department of Anthropology at the University of Copenhagen (especially members of the Anthropology of the Future reading group and the Advanced Anthropological Theory and the Anthropology of the Future classes) for their valuable inputs over the years, and Lars would like to thank colleagues at the Center for Comparative Culture Studies and at the Department of Cross-Cultural and Regional Studies at the university for providing a highly stimulating research environment. We are extremely grateful also to the two anonymous reviewers for their thoroughness and incisive and helpful comments, as well as to Douglas Rogers and the two other original series editors of Eurasia Past and Present, Catriona Kelly and Mark Steinberg, for taking on and supporting the project. Thanks also to Bayarmaa Khalzaa for linguistic assistance; to Flora Botelho, Steen B. Kelså, Elaine Bolton, Dina Dineva and Bob Land for helping prepare the manuscript for publication; and finally to William Frucht, Karen Olson and Mary Pasti at Yale University Press.

Fieldwork was conducted by Morten in Ulaanbaatar as well as in the cities of Darhan and Erdenet during the summer months of 1995, 1996 and 1998 and from January to February 2001, June to August 2003, February to October 2004 and June to September 2009. He would like to thank the Danish Research Council for the Humanities for funding a postdoctoral project on Mongolia's urban markets, as well as the Danish Film Institute and the Danish Research Council for the Social Sciences for economic and institutional support. Apart from numerous shorter (less than a month) research stays in Ulaanbaatar between 1998 and 2017, Lars carried out fieldwork in Ulaanbaatar during summer and/or autumn in 1995 and 1997, and then again for several months in 2006 and for five to six weeks in 2007. He would like to express his gratitude to the Danish Research Council for the Humanities for funding his postdoctoral research on exchange, protection and insurance in Mongolia's new trading cultures from 2005 to 2008, when the main research for this book was carried out.

In addition, we would both like to extend our gratitude to Dronning Margrethe og Prins Henriks Fond, Kong Christian X's Fond and Ebbe Munchs Mindefond for financially supporting our first "expedition" to Mongolia together in 1995–1996. This, along with the moral and institutional support we received from our former teachers at the Department of Ethnography and Social Anthropology at Aarhus University, and the Ethnographic Collection at Moesgaard Museum, Aarhus, was when it all started and when we first got to know several of the main characters in this book.

Drafts of the different chapters in this book have benefitted from the questions and comments received in numerous contexts, including: the Encounters of a Postsocialist Kind panel at the European Association of Social Anthropology, Vienna; the Economies of Fortune and Luck conference at King's College, Cambridge; the Freedom, Creativity and Decision Conference at CRASH, Cambridge; the workshop Anthropological Engagements with Hope at the University of Copenhagen; the End of Transition? conference at the University of Aarhus; the Antimonies of Vagueness conference at the University of Copenhagen; the Megaseminar on Problems of Change and Continuity at Sandbjerg, Southern Denmark; the workshop Conceptualizing Network/Chain and Comparison at the Danish Institute for International Studies, as well as invited presentations at the Department of Anthropology at Cornell University; the Mongolia and Inner Asia Studies Unit at Cambridge University; the Harriman Institute at Columbia University; the Department of Anthropology at Brunel University; the Department of Anthropology at the University of St. Andrews; the Department of Anthropology at University College London; the Department of Anthropology at the London School of Economics; the Center for Russian, East European, and Eurasian Studies at the University of Michigan; and the Russian, East European, and Eurasian Center at the University of Illinois at Urbana-Champaign.

In Chapters 1, 4, 5 and 7 and the Conclusion we have drawn on the following already published works: sections of Pedersen's chapter "Incidental Connections: Freedom and Urban Life in Mongolia" and Højer's chapter "Apathy and Revolution: Temporal Sensibilities in Contemporary Mongolia," both published in B. Bodenborn, M. Holbraad and J. Laidlaw (eds.), *Freedom, Creativity, and Decision: Recovering the Human Subject* (Cambridge: Cambridge University Press, 2017); sections of our cowritten article "Lost in Transition: Fuzzy Property and Leaking Souls in Ulaanbaatar," published in *Ethnos* 73, no. 1 (2008); sections of Pedersen's article "A Day in the Cadillac: The Work of Hope in Urban Mongolia," published in *Social Analysis* 56, no. 2 (2012); sections of Pedersen's article "From 'Public' to 'Private' Markets in Postsocialist Mongolia," published in *Anthropology of East Europe Review* 25, no. 1 (2007); sections of Højer's article "The Spirit of Business: Pawnshops in Ulaanbaatar," published in *Social Anthropology* 20, no. 1 (2012); and sections of Højer's article "Troubled Perspectives in the New Mongolian Economy," published in *Inner Asia* 9, no. 2 (2007). We thank the publishers of these works for permission to draw on them.

Finally, we would like to express our deep gratitude to our parents, Karen Højer, Knud Højer and Ellen Pedersen, who made our first trip to Mongolia in 1995 possible and have been a tremendous support throughout. And above all, we wish to thank our wives and children for their enduring love and support: Kimiko, Sophie and Ines (Morten), and Mette, Peter, Karl Emil and Johanne (Lars).

Note on Transliteration

Except for widely used spellings of well-known historical names, such as Genghis Khan, the following system has been used when transliterating from the Mongolian Cyrillic alphabet:

А	a	Л	l	Х	h
Б	b	М	m	Ц	ts
В	v	Н	n	Ч	ch
Г	g	О	o	Ш	sh
Д	d	Ө	ö	Ъ	"
Е	ye	П	p	Ы	y
Ё	yo	Р	r	Ь	'
Ж	j	С	s	Э	e
З	z	Т	t	Ю	yu
И	i	У	u	Я	ya
Й	i	Y	ü		
К	k	Ф	f		

While we have, in the case of some Mongolian words (for example, *hashaa*), followed Sneath (2000: viii) in adding a Roman "s" to the end of Mongolian plural forms when they appear as an integrated part of an English sentence, we have in the case of words that are used very often (such as *chyenjüüd* and *shaarigchid*) retained the Mongolian plural forms in English sentences as is.

Our transliteration of Russian terms follows the Library of Congress system.

Urban Hunters

Introduction

In 2004, there were, supposedly, only two Cadillacs in Mongolia. One of them, a black and beautiful if somewhat battered 1970s model with arching curves and white leather seating, belonged to Hamid. (All personal names used are pseudonyms.) Like many people we came to know in Ulaanbaatar during our fieldwork before and after the turn of the millennium, he gave the impression of someone who refused to give up. Born in the former Soviet Republic of Azerbaijan, and with a colorful career behind him, including a spell as an oil engineer in Saddam Hussein's Iraq, he had arrived in Ulaanbaatar in the early 1990s for business purposes and ended up settling there. Due to a number of ill-fated trading adventures, Hamid and his female partner were living in poor conditions, crashing in the homes of friends (or rather, the parents of friends, for few of them had their own place, even though they were well into their thirties), while spending the days in relentless pursuit of new business opportunities or chasing people who owed them money.

The car itself was a node in an informal socioeconomic network spread out across relatives, friends and acquaintances of the sort that has become so widespread in Mongolia since the collapse of state socialism in 1990 (see, e.g., Sneath 1993; Humphrey and Sneath 1999; Pedersen 2007a; Pedersen and Højer 2008; Plueckhahn and Bayartsetseg 2018). Indeed, among the handful or so of men and women in their thirties whose lives we have followed and sometimes become involved in since 1995, a significant proportion of an average day in their lives had become dedicated to tracking down people who owed them money or looking for potential creditors from whom they could borrow money themselves (often to pay back money they already owed to others). This was despite the fact that it seemed to be the exception rather than the rule that loans were repaid, especially within the agreed time frame and in full. There would usually be a remainder that was not returned, a remainder that was simultaneously a source of worry and hope. Debtors' failure to pay, in turn, diminished creditors' ability to pay back their own debts, thus generating additional remainders (as well as additional worries and hopes) across the city of Ulaanbaatar ad infinitum.

The Cadillac had first been given to Hamid as collateral for a large sum of money owed to him by one of his acquaintances, who had asked for a loan to open a small restaurant selling *shashlik* (kebabs) on one of Ulaanbaatar's big shopping streets. Unfortunately, the *shashlik* adventure turned out to be unsuccessful, and all the money was lost. So, when Morten met Hamid in 2004, he had become stuck with the Cadillac. The car was not complete: some vital parts of the engine were missing, which the unfortunate Uzbek had originally given as collateral to yet another of his many creditors. Since Hamid had not been able to raise the necessary cash to retrieve the lacking engine parts, he had, in fact, never used the Cadillac during the several years it had been in his possession. Instead, it was being stored at the gritty premises of a used-car salesman in Ulaanbaatar's industrial wastelands, where Hamid would invite his friends for Sunday excursions, a sort of urban picnic that involved dusting, cleaning, polishing and admiring the car while sharing, with never-fading enthusiasm, dreams of future prosperity and beautiful women galore

The story of Hamid and the others was far from unique. Like so many other places in the postsocialist and, indeed, the postcolonial world—in particular the countries of the former Soviet Union (Nielsen 1987; Burawoy and Verdery 1999; Berdahl 2000; Nazpary 2002; Shevchenko 2009; Ghodsee 2011; Kruglova 2016; Rakowski 2016)—a large share of Ulaanbaatar's population had, for much of a fifteen-year period, not known whether they would still have a job the next day (perhaps the state farm, the factory or the school was about to close down due to "structural reforms"). Nor did they have access to reliable information about what their salary would buy them a year, a month or sometimes even

Periurban Ulaanbaatar (2011)

a week ahead (subsidized food, transport and utilities were another target of "shock therapy") or, indeed, whether whatever savings they might have would be available the next day (during the 1990s, several Mongolian banks closed down as the owners fled the country, and over the next decade a number of savings and loans cooperatives went bust, sometimes accompanied by accusations of fraud). While the multifarious ramifications of postsocialist transition and neoliberal reform were felt and experienced by everyone in Mongolia (for two overviews, see Bruun and Odgaard 1995; Plueckhahn and Dulam 2018), the sense of crisis and radical change was especially acute for people like Hamid and his friends, who belonged to a cohort of young (or sometimes not so young) men and women between the ages of twenty and forty around the turn of the millennium.

For many people in Ulaanbaatar, and for members of this generation in particular, life in the "age of the market" (*zah zeeliin üye*) and "democracy" (*ardchilal*) involved a scramble to secure enough money, fuel and food to get by until the next day. Particularly vulnerable were the hundreds of thousands of migrants who had given up their pastoralist life due to recurrent natural disasters, lack of economic opportunities and rising rural poverty (Sneath 2003; Bruun and Narangoa 2006) to settle in shantytowns of fenced yurt (*ger*) and wooden-shack compounds (*hashaa*) that had always encircled Ulaanbaatar's Soviet-built center but which, from 1990 onward, expanded to form a veritable slum city.[1]

Indeed, the scale and intensity of economic, political and societal change that Mongolia underwent following the collapse of state socialism in 1990–1991 was radical and extraordinary, even in comparison to other postsocialist countries (Rossabi 2005: 48). Inflation skyrocketed, reaching 52.7 percent in 1991 and 325.5 percent in 1992 (National Statistical Office of Mongolia 2005: 122), and economic growth and net incomes stalled as, within a few years, Soviet economic support was exchanged for support from Western countries, Japan and the international financial institutions, which had very different ideological aims. According to this (for lack of a better word) neoliberal agenda, socialism was within a few years to completely disappear, and the market was to fully replace it—and in the no-man's-land between these two purported systems was the so-called transition: an exception and aberration defined purely in terms of what it was not. Yet, real people inhabited this transitional no-man's-land, many of whom faced economic hardship, even lack of basic necessities, and since few had been prepared for this situation, parents found themselves without a sense of direction on which they could imagine their own and their children's future.

This book explores how, for many people from Hamid's generation—the men and woman who came of age just before and after the collapse of state socialism in 1990–91—transition became a way of life. As their country as a whole became stuck in what was supposed to have been a temporary transition from one societal form (state socialism) to another (market capitalism), radical change became an omnipresent part of people's lives. Far from representing a passing and external condition, virtually every arena of their lives (their families, their friends, their jobs and, indeed, their own selves, or, in the words of some of them, their "souls") was subject to repeated ruptures. Torn between the socialist age and "the age of the market," our Ulaanbaatar friends were, as one of them sometimes put it in English, "lost" in transition (see Chapter 1)—not so much in the sense of being mute victims of transition, but more in the sense of being overwhelmed, captivated and seduced by radical change. More than adapting (or trying to adapt) to, or for that matter resisting (or trying to resist) change, they had embodied or could we say become possessed by it, for they had internalized the temporality and the moralities of transition to such an extent that it became their own subjectivity.

Accordingly, while the concept of transition is often invoked as a temporary instability between two stable orders (authoritarian socialism and democratic market economy), this study explores what happens when rupture acquires a logic of its own. Indeed, goes our central contention in this book, the forms of social agency and economic subjectivity we witnessed in Ulaanbaatar around the year 2000 cannot be adequately accounted for by existing social-scientific theories of human agency and social practice. What is needed is not just an ethnography but a theory of social agency in contexts of rapid change, which takes transition seriously as a distinct human predicament imbued with unique social forms and temporal logics. The central argument of this book is that our friends dealt with the change, not by trying to anticipate and thus neutralize or control it, but through a *systematic unwillingness to plan* that called to mind hunter-gatherers, who also seem "to live in the present, with little thought for the future and little interest in the past" (Day et al. 1999: 2). As we are going to argue, this analogy between hustling and hunting is more than metaphorical: there are real similarities between how certain people in Ulaanbaatar generate and share resources in the postsocialist city and ways of obtaining and distributing resources among hunting peoples across the world, including Northern Mongolia, where we both have worked previously (Højer 2003, 2004, 2019a; Pedersen 2001, 2007b). By chronicling the hopes and the hardships, and struggles and aspirations, of a handful of young Ulaanbaatar men and women whose lives we followed closely from 1995 to 2010, we aim to theorize "urban hunting" as a sui generis social practice that may be found across different regional and historical variations.

So, while the book is in many ways a classical anthropological monograph that seeks to describe "the social life of some particular region of the earth during a certain period of time" (Radcliffe-Brown 1952: 4), it is also an attempt to theorize, in new and hopefully convincing ways, what seems to be a more general feature of human life. For the fact is that far from representing a unique postsocialist or Mongolian generation, Hamid and the others belonged to a global cohort of dispossessed men who are unable, and perhaps unwilling, to amass the necessary wealth and resources to set up a household and commit to the long-term goals and horizons of conventional social reproduction. Instead, our Ulaanbaatar friends—much like the millions of restless unmarried men struggling to make a living in West Africa's cities (Vigh 2006; Piot 2010) and indeed the millions of young (as well as not so young) Europeans and Americans who are now facing a permanent "life in debt" (Han 2012; see also Papailias 2011)—were stuck in the strange temporal horizon of permanent crisis: what was supposed to have been a temporary state (youth, the transition from socialism to capitalism, indebtedness, etc.) turned out to be a chronic condition. This book, then, is an ethnography, as well as a theory, of the opportunities and challenges of life during times of transition. Our objective in tracing the multifarious reverberations—as well as the gradual sedimentation and institutionalization—of radical change across disparate arenas of postsocialist life is to account in a novel way for the nature of social agency within contexts of rapid societal change. In addition to contributing to scholarship on Mongolia and postsocialism, then, we wish to outline "a general theory of hustling" that takes transition seriously as a universal predicament with distinct temporal logics and social forms.

FIELDWORK AMONG FRIENDS

The ethnographic data on which this book is based has been gathered over the course of multiple periods of fieldwork in Ulaanbaatar in the period from 1995 to 2010, among a group of informants and friends mostly shared by the two authors. Indeed, it is no coincidence that we refer to these informants as "friends," for the book is the outcome of our long joint friendship with a number of young (and now not so young) Ulaanbaatar inhabitants, mainly a group of ethnically mixed Mongolians and Russians/Ukrainians whom we have known since the mid-1990s when we first visited Mongolia together as students. During the 1990s and early 2000s, we used to hang out with them—communicating in English, Mongolian and sometimes Russian—en route to what we, rather naively, still used to consider "the real field" in Northern Mongolia. However, partly following our involvement in a documentary film project in Ulaanbaatar (*The Wild East: Life of an Urban Nomad* [Haslund-Christensen 2002]), and partly because of individual research trajectories, our attention increasingly turned to Ulaanbaatar and its markets, traders, pawnshops and other so-called informal economic sites and arenas. Accordingly, from the late 1990s onward, each of us independently of one another conducted several long swathes of fieldwork especially in this but also in other Mongolian cities (notably Erdenet and Darhan). In this process, our friends turned into some of our most important informants and gatekeepers. Eventually, we came to the conclusion that, rather than each trying to write a book about our common friends, in which we would have to work hard to distinguish between both our ethnographic data and our anthropological findings, why not instead coauthor a monograph in which we could draw freely and fully on the almost four years we have in total spent with these people (some of whom we regard as among our closest friends) as well as the almost two decades over which we have now been following their lives.

In referring to some of our key informants as friends, or in one particular instance even as a so-called dry (nonconsanguineous) younger brother (*huurai düü*), we do not wish to suggest that our relationships with these people have been purely affectionate and altruistic and devoid of "economic" or other op-

Hanging out (1995)

portunistic considerations. Although the concepts of "friend" and social or economic "resource" are often seen as incompatible (see, e.g., Rabinow 1977: 29,
142)—and while equality is often posited as a necessary condition for friendship
in Euro-American contexts (Rouner 1994)—our relationship with our friends
and key informants was mediated through loans (mainly from us to them),
payment for research assistance, and gifts (clothing, money, vodka, meals, cigarettes, etc.). In that sense, however, our relationship with them was not so
different from their relationship with each other. After all, they obtain loans

from each other all the time, too—often without paying them back and hardly ever on time—just as they eagerly engage in sharing and spending any surplus money available to any one of them. They, too, ask one another for help, smoke each other's cigarettes and share bottles of vodka procured by friends. Friendship does not necessarily preclude "mutual exploitation," as Crick and others imply (1992: 176), nor are mutual economic ties necessarily the opposite of friendship. Far from posing a challenge to the genuineness of our social obligations and emotional attachments (or the epistemological status of our ethnographic data), therefore, our friendship-cum-economic relations with informants were an opportunity for gaining genuine ethnographic insight into their relations with each other. The muddy and awkward imbrications between the affective and the opportunistic in our liaisons with these informant-friends are thus part and parcel of our object of study: forms of relatedness during times of transition in which "the social" and "the economic" are complexly intertwined.[2]

In addition to these questions concerning the multifarious nature of social relations with and among informants in postsocialist and other contexts (see also Watson 1992; Bell and Coleman 1999), there is also another sense in which our focus on and reflection about "friends" link up with our argument. We are referring to the (hard-learned!) lesson that the openness and fluidity of social relations in urban milieus in general and those subject to radical transition in particular make it even harder than otherwise to retain the traditional anthropological and sociological fetish of closed communities within which relations are fixed and across which new intimacies and antagonisms cannot develop. Indeed, this is one of the key insights we wish to convey in this book: that a central feature of the social life of transition consists of recurrent ruptures and discontinuities in social networks, plans and dreams of the future—along with the resulting possibilities for new opportunities and imaginaries, including those arising from friendships with scholars "from abroad." To substantiate this observation and its ramifications on scholarship on postsocialist as well as other societies in transition, we now present a more detailed outline of the book's central argument.

POSTSOCIALIST AND POST-POSTSOCIALIST ANTHROPOLOGY

In the early 1990s, Katherine Verdery famously asserted that the "startling transformations" of previously existing socialist policies would provide social scientists with a "remarkable opportunity" (1991: 419) and were "veritable laboratories for all manner of subjects" (1995b: 3). Anthropology, she predicted, would have a major part to play in the study of such transformations, and the collapse of state socialism would suggest a range of new research questions (Verdery 1991: 419, 432). In making these predictions, Verdery anticipated the rise of anthropological studies of postsocialism—a new regional as well as thematic subfield of the discipline with which everyone is today familiar.

One of the major preoccupations and widely recognized contributions of postsocialist anthropology has been its critique of so-called transition discourse. According to this standard critique, the neoliberal and largely Western metanarrative of postsocialist transition, which was advocated and implemented by foreign advisors and many indigenous policy makers in the 1990s, assumes that a smooth market economy will—inevitably—replace the inefficient planned economy of the past, just as real democracy automatically will take the place of one-party rule. Much in line with the modernization paradigm of the post–Second World War (Ferguson 1997), and unilinear theories of social, cultural and economic evolution in general (Morgan 1985 [1877]; Spencer 1904 [1860]), it is postulated that history has one direction and will eventually "end" (Fukuyama 1989), and that "culture and superstition" (read: socialism and planned economy) are unnatural "traditional" barriers to the natural realization of market economy and democracy.

Anthropology has indeed been vehement in its critique of this approach (for a major contribution, see Burawoy and Verdery 1999). For one thing, many anthropologists have asked, it may be that socialism was the longest and most painful route from capitalism to capitalism, as an Eastern European joke would have it (Verdery 1991: 419; 1996),[3] but if a market economy is the natural state of affairs, how come we lost track of it? Another key anthropological objection to such transitology discourse has been its implicit or explicit assumptions of unilinear progress, that is to say, the fact that the dominant neoliberal metanarrative of progress and development and growth assumes a clearly defined beginning (social*ism*), a chaotic but finite interlude between two (the transition) and a fixed endpoint (capital*ism*). Postsocialist anthropology has deconstructed these assumptions by scrutinizing the discourse about transition as a cultural system in itself, which influences the way policies are formulated and academic analysis is made (Burawoy and Verdery 1999; cf. Englund and Leach 2000). Other scholars have questioned the purported uniformity and homogeneity within and between different socialisms (Hann 2002: 8; see also Humphrey 1998; Verdery 1995a; Vitebsky 2005; Yurchak 2006). It cannot be assumed, the argument goes, that Cuban and Mongolian socialism are one and the same thing, for socialism itself did not appear out of nowhere but emerged in specific contexts that were dissimilar from one another. While obviously deeply influenced by Moscow and the Soviet Union, socialism had an ambivalent, complicated or encouraging attitude to national specificity (Bulag 1998; Kaplonski 1998; Raman and West 2009: 7–9), and different cultures, traditions and histories of socialism emerged in different nation-states and regions. Accordingly, while revolutionary socialism, according to Karl Marx, "would draw its poetry 'only from the future,'" twentieth-century revolutionaries "inevitably had to build on the materials bequeathed to them by their predecessors" (Raman and West 2009: 5). The Bolsheviks in the Soviet Union, for example, drew on capitalist and tsarist forms (Raman and West 2009: 5–6), and communal ideals in state socialist Mongolia resembled presocialist regimes of collective ownership (Sneath 2002). Moreover, heterogeneity arose inside the systems themselves. Economic and cultural policies changed throughout the socialist period, and while informal economies, parallel cultures, hidden transcripts and ambivalent discourses may not always have thrived, they at least existed (see, e.g., Humphrey 1994, 1998; Watson 1994; Yurchak 1997, 2006; Raman and West 2009). In sum, socialism itself was "wrought with contradictions, discrepancies, and competing realities behind what seemed to be a rigid totalitarian system" (Buyandelgeriyn 2008: 238).

This general anthropological concern for contextualized specificity and difference—that there were a multiplicity of different socialisms formed by historically generated particularities within and discrepancies between different local political, religious and cultural traditions—has strongly influenced anthropological understandings of postsocialist transition. It has been demonstrated, and we ourselves have taken part in demonstrating, how perceptions of market economic trade are embedded in socialist moralities, and how new sociopolitical forms have emerged from the ruins of old socialist—and presocialist—structures (see, e.g., Verdery 1996, 2003; Mandel and Humphrey 2002; Humphrey 2002a, 2002b; Kandiyoti 2002; Wheeler 2004; Hann 2007; Pedersen 2007a; Højer 2012). Foreign capitalist enterprises, such as US factories in Poland, have been shown to be molded in relation to local socialist values and practices (Dunn 2004), and organizational forms have been found to be built "*not on the ruins* but *with the ruins* of communism" (Stark 1997: 36, emphasis in original). In short, the lesson taught by anthropologists to other scholars of postsocialism may be encapsulated in the important message that societal forms cannot appear ex nihilo, and since nothing happens in a cultural vacuum, postsocialist social life does not mark any radical break with a monolithic precapitalist past. For, in Caroline Humphrey's apt phrase, there has not been, and never will be, "a sudden and total emptying out of all social phenomena and their replacement by other ways of life" (2002a: 12).

In recent years, a number of scholars have tried to take stock of the original program of postsocialist anthropology first set in train by Verdery and later refined by Caroline Humphrey, among others (see, e.g., Hann 2007; Buyandelgeriyn 2008; Raman and West 2009; Henig and Hamilton 2010; Thelen 2011; Dunn and Verdery 2011). In doing so, a number of suggestions have been put forward to replace "postsocialism" with new and more up-to-date terms such as "post-post-transition" (Buyandelgeriyn 2008) or "enduring socialism" (Raman and West 2009) as part of a more general questioning of the lasting relevance of a research paradigm based solely on the trope of "transition" and "rupture." Yet, it seems to us, that while these sophisticated attempts aimed at developing a "post-postsocialist" anthropology are important contributions in their own right, they have largely been based on a similar set of tacit assumptions concerning a stipulated continuity of social and cultural forms as discussed above. For instance, in a review article, Buyandelgeriyn (2008) repeats the critique of transition theory and, following Tökés (2000), labels it a novel form of evolutionism, and she further points to the importance of cultural difference and the multiplicity of postsocialist experiences. Preexisting socialist practices and cultural differences "engulfed the transition" (Buyandelgeriyn 2008: 236), and "the vast majority of research shows that the market economy in non-Western contexts operates much more on the basis of the rules of the local cultures, kinship, and community rather than the rules in force in Western contexts" (2008: 245). In stressing the variety and unpredictability of postsocialist trajectories, not to speak of the uncertainty of lived experience in times of transition (see also Buyandelgeriyn 2007; Kideckel 2008), she asks anthropology to move beyond "post-transition," in the sense of a tangible threshold between two states and a predetermined developmental route, and introduces the concept of "post-post-transition" to stress the necessity of destabilizing if not entirely doing away with the idea of transition.

Raman and West raise a similar critique in their introduction to the edited volume *Enduring Socialism* (2010). By demonstrating how even the most ardent proponents of a market economy mimic "socialism's apathy for the past" by imitating precisely what they most vehemently oppose, they expose how socialism and capitalism are part and parcel of the same logic of modernity and rupture (Raman and West 2009: 2; cf. Humphrey 1992; Buck-Morss 2002; Højer

2009). Raman and West further expose the futility of assuming the existence of a radical difference between socialism and capitalism (and more generally between past and present social and cultural forms) by comparing various economic institutions from the socialist period and its aftermath, showing how all these cases, in different ways, constituted a hybrid amalgamation of state and market. Mixed political-economic forms such as the so-called New Economic Policy introduced by the Communist Party in the early USSR, they argue, were and still are the rule rather than the exception in actually existing socialism and capitalism. Accordingly, expressions such as "mixed forms" and "enduring socialism" may serve to complicate easy distinctions and stereotypes (2010: 9) and allow for a closer ethnographic exploration of the complex assemblages that societies and political economies comprise. "The idea of the 'post,'" as they put it, "is in many ways the bane of our time" (2010: 10).

So, if Raman and West can be said to go beyond the first generation of post-socialist studies, it is mainly by denouncing the concept of transition even more strongly than their precursors (2010: 13) by focusing more intensively on, and searching more eagerly for, "continuities between diverse 'postsocialist' presents and their corresponding socialist and presocialist pasts" (2010: 15). In a similar same vein, Buyandelgeriyn's critique of transition theory's metanarrative and her focus on divergent postsocialist trajectories, localities and experiences—while highly important in its own right—is also very much in line with anthropology's original postsocialist paradigm; in fact, if anything, Buyandelgeriyn's and other recent anthropological writings on former socialist societies put an ever greater emphasis on historical contextualization and social, cultural and political continuity than the first generation of postsocialist studies associated with scholars such as Katherine Verdery, Caroline Humphrey and Chris Hann. In short, the lasting ethnographic and theoretical contribution of much postsocialist anthropology can, to an overwhelming extent, be boiled down to a systematic and often highly relevant and timely questioning of the dubious and ethnocentric assumption that market capitalism and liberal democracy would automatically blossom in a pure form. Relative continuity has been demonstrated where the market reformers, and much transitology discourse, have instead preached radical discontinuity. Notwithstanding that numerous ethnographic studies in postsocialist settings have highlighted fractures, transformations and ruptures in sociocultural forms and the irreversibility of change (e.g., Stark 1997), the default anthropological understanding has been that "strong threads of continuity . . . mark even the most dramatic of social ruptures" (Hann 2002: 5; cf. also 2007: 5).

TAKING TRANSITION SERIOUSLY

While we obviously find the above lines of inquiry crucially important and can testify to the many varied insights that such ethnographic critiques of conventional transition discourse have generated, they nevertheless give rise to a critical question in relation to this particular study: Where do such studies leave "transition" itself as an ethnographic object and theoretical concept? And to what extent does the previous anthropological scholarship about postsocialism enable us to understand the life of our Ulaanbaatar friends? At the heart of the postsocialist (and post-postsocialist) anthropological paradigm sketched above, we saw, lies a more or less tacit premise about the basic continuity of social and cultural forms. Old institutions and forms of livelihood always hold sway in one way or another, it is generally assumed. To be sure, social, political, cultural and existential forms may fragment and become changed, or they may integrate with new such forms and assume different shapes, but there are no clean ruptures with the past, which is always "carried on" into the present, no matter whether people themselves share this basic sense of continuity or not. This is what Joel Robbins (2007), in an influential critique, has described as anthropology's "continuity thinking":

> [A]nthropology has largely been a science of continuity . . . I mean by this that cultural anthropologists have for the most part either argued or implied that the things they study—symbols, meanings, logics, structures, power dynamics, etc.—have an enduring quality and are not readily subject to change. This emphasis is written into theoretical tenets so fundamental as to underlie anthropological work on culture from almost all theoretical perspectives . . . Given its strength, the most common and satisfying anthropological arguments are those that find some enduring cultural structure that persists underneath all the surface changes and, in the last analysis, serves to guide them and determine the sense they make—a sense that, in spite of whatever elements might be part of it, should still be one displaying some continuities with those of the past. (9–10)

Following Robbins, our diagnosis is that postsocialist anthropology—and social and cultural anthropology more generally—has been unable or at least unwilling to imagine the possibility that radical breaks can happen, even when the people studied have themselves emphasized a sensation of rupture in their lives and of severance from the past (although see, e.g., Humphrey 2008b). Instead, anthropologists working in the postsocialist world have, often with good reason, emphasized how old institutions have endured in new contexts, how networks from socialist times have been extended into the present, and how people themselves have sought to overcome the uncertainties of transition by creating a sense of meaningful coherence through different kinds of narratives drawing on existing cultural resources. While we consider such approaches valuable, necessary and often convincing, it also seems to us that they share a blind spot. By systematically treating "transition" and "change" as something that has to be explained away, both the first established generation of postsocialist anthropological studies and the second generation of post-post-postsocialism anthropologists have led to a methodological and theoretical shortcoming. For while it remains a vital anthropological task to make connections between past, present and future social forms visible, the proclivity to "continuity thinking" in postsocialist anthropology has meant that the potential distinctiveness of life in transition has been ignored. Radical change as "a way of life"—a sui generis phenomenon in and of itself characteristic but not unique to postsocialist contexts—has become black boxed and largely invisible. It is precisely this ethnographic and theoretical lacuna that the present study is intended to fill.

The problem is, of course, not that the vast body of existing anthropological scholarship on postsocialism has ignored history, change or any other context of transition, far less the experiences, narratives and uncertainties of different subjects subjected to it (after all, that is just what good ethnography is supposed to do). The problem is only that "transition" as a sociocultural form in and of its own right has, with few notable exceptions, not been fully explored or properly theorized in postsocialist scholarship. It is true that Chris Hann, as part of his general questioning of postsocialism as a viable concept, has mentioned Robbins and his critique of continuity thinking (Hann 2007). Yet while Hann acknowledges the purchase of this critique for postsocialist anthropology, he is also rather quick to stress that "many outcomes . . . have been shaped by . . . intangible continuities" (2007: 6) and more generally emphasizes the importance of history and of specifying what he calls the "differential rates of change" (2007: 7). Another, more concerted attempt to take transition seriously has been made by the sociologist Olga Shevchenko (2009). Echoing some of the recent anthropological literature on "crisis as context" (Vigh 2009; more on which below), she makes the important observation that "a crisis may be perceived not as an isolated occurrence, but as a routine and unchanging condition. In such circumstances, the crisis evolves from a singular and alien happening into the very stuff of everyday life, the immediate context of decisions and actions and, after a certain point, the only reality with which individuals have social and cultural tools to deal. Crisis may become the default expectation that organizes people's priorities and desires, as well as the benchmark against which they measure their successes or failures" (Shevchenko 2009: 2). As she goes on to suggest, a chronic crisis may become the very essence of a community's identity, a mode of living and a way of self-imagining without which the community is inconceivable. In order to assess these patterns in their complexity, then, one has to explore them for their own sake and not merely in terms of their deviation from some past standard" (Shevchenko 2009: 3).

Taking our departure in these important critiques of what might be called the fetish of continuity prevalent in postsocialist scholarship and beyond, one of our chief ambitions in writing this book is to instill a strategic dose of "discontinuity thinking" in scholarship on former state socialist and indeed other societies in transition. Rather than seeing transition as a process only *mediated* by cultures of socialism and/or previous traditions or institutions, we wish to take transition seriously also as a "culture" in its own terms that is imbued with its own set of dynamics and indeed "logics." In line with existing conventions within postsocialist anthropology and beyond, we agree that our informants' lives cannot be properly understood with reference to a single discontinuity (the collapse of socialism). Unlike most postsocialist anthropologists, however, we do not think that Ulaanbaatar social life can be theorized only as a continuity, endurance or evolution of past forms either. Rather, for our informants, the one rupture became many ruptures. Their only continuity was discontinuity, if you like, for transition had become a permanent way of life for them. So, while we challenge continuity thinking for ignoring rupture and radical change as a form of life, we also challenge (neoliberal) transition discourse for reducing transition to an interlude in time, an irreversible process between two states. Transition, we submit, is also imbued with its own temporality, sociality and indeed distinct "culture," and our friendship with Hamid and the others put us in a privileged position from which to explore this fact.

It is thus our contention that many (though by no means all) of the events that occurred during our fieldwork in the company of our Ulaanbaatar friends add up to an identifiable social and cultural form, which, to paraphrase Oscar Lewis, reflects a set of "common adaptations to common problems" (1968: xliii) that often "develop when a stratified social and economic system is breaking down or is being replaced by another," namely, in the case at hand, the transition from state socialism to liberal capitalism. Like Lewis' "culture of poverty," this "culture of transition" is characterized by various "interrelated social, economic and psychological traits" (1968: xliv), ranging from "low income, lack of property ownership, absence of savings, absence of food reserves in the home, and a chronic shortage of cash" to "a strong present-time orientation with relatively little ability to defer gratification and to plan for the future, a sense of resignation and fatalism, a widespread belief in male superiority" (1968: xlviii).[4] Nevertheless—and this is where we depart from Lewis—what we refer to as the "culture of transition" is not a mere adaptation to the powers that be (the market, the state, the ruling classes), nor does it amount to "a stable and coherent way of life which is passed down from generation to generation along family lines" (1965: xliii). Rather, we propose that the overarching social and political-economic environment within which this transitional culture took place was *itself* subject to radical change and transition.

Of course, time hardly stood still in the socialist period (though see Verdery 1996: 39–57). In Mongolia (Empson 2006; Pedersen 2011) and elsewhere (Grant 1995; Rogers 2008), experiences of crisis and discourses of change—a "poetic of unfinished reconstruction" as Ssorin-Chaikov has aptly described it (2003: 113)—were endemic to state socialist everyday life, notably but not only during its last decades (Yurchak 2006; Shevchenko 2009). Yet, we submit, the severity of rupture and the pervasiveness of change that have been such characteristic and intense features of postsocialist transition (and possibly other contexts of radical change) cannot just not be posited as "a heightened form of change to be found in all forms of society" (Hann 2007: 6). What is more, our contention is that this extreme sense of rupture at the heart of the experience of transition can only be explored by taking issue with the dominant theory of time within anthropology, namely the largely tacit assumption that the world comprises "things that change" and that it is "time that does the change to them." Taking transition seriously, we propose, involves posing some different but equally hard questions, such as: how might time *itself* be different in contexts of transition?

THE TWO TIMES OF TRANSITION

Consider again Robbins' critique of continuity thinking in the anthropology of Christianity and beyond. "This assumption of continuity," he writes, "is in turn related to assumptions about the nature of time and belief that support it. Christian ideas about change, time, and belief are based on quite differ-ent assumptions, ones that are organized around the plausibility of radical dis-continuities in personal lives and cultural stories" (2007: 6–7). More precisely, continuity thinking operates with a "homogenous, empty time . . . *in* which things happen but not *to* which things happen" (2007: 12; emphasis in original). This is opposed to what Robbins—borrowing a term from Walter Benjamin (1968)—describes as the messianic model of time, in which sudden eruptions of revolutionary ruptures "make the continuum of history explode" (Benjamin cited in Robbins 2007: 12). Indeed, for Robbins, Christianity is all about such radical breaks, both in the form of a past rupture ("conversion") and an antici-pated radical future one ("the day of judgment"). With the advent of Christian culture, he convincingly argues, "something does not just happen *in* time, but rather happens *to* it" (2007: 12).

Might our Ulaanbaatar friends' lives also revolve around a concept of time that is as qualitatively different from the image of time as an empty "container" of events, which is so common within anthropology, including, as we have seen, its postsocialist variant? And could it be that the radical discontinuities discussed by Robbins can be recognized in Hamid and the others' experiences of their lives, too, despite the fact that hardly any of our friends are devoted Christians? We think so. While few if any of them had been baptized and several of them identified themselves as Buddhists (see also Chapter 6), all of our friends felt they had experienced major ruptures in their lives that had changed their lives from one moment to the other, and to which they were always referring back in constant but futile attempts to fully understand their circumstances and those of others. Yet there seems to be a major difference between the transitional life that we have witnessed and recorded in Ulaanbaatar and the messianic time of Christianity described by Robbins. Robbins' messianic time gives rise to singular ruptures that, crudely put, create a new homogeneous—and predictable in the sense of teleological—time horizon (from conversion to judgment). The time of transition, on the other hand, is constantly forced outside of itself, exploding history again and again.[5] We follow Robbins, then, in criticizing perspectives—in the anthropology of Christianity and postsocialism alike—that take transition to be somehow external to the cultural forms that affect it. However, we also want to suggest an understanding of time where transition *itself* is in transition. Here, a single transition has exploded into a multitude of ruptures, and social and physical space is likewise characterized by heterogeneity and discontinuity. To substantiate this point, consider an example.

Once, Kolya, one of the main protagonists of this book, had to arrange a trip to Karakorum, the old capital of the Mongolian empire, for two European tourists in his capacity as self-made tour guide and translator. He needed a car and a driver, and was relying on a Russian friend in this regard. The friend's car, however, had broken down and was in need of repair, and Kolya needed to make further calls to secure a (cheap and reliable) driver for the next day's trip. His father-in-law was supposed to have returned from the Gobi desert but had not done so, and for some reason, after making a few calls, Kolya assumed that his partner would find the necessary driver. Kolya was calm, not at all worried by the prospect of failing or running short of time, and he went off to play pool in a bar in the neighborhood for a couple of hours in the late afternoon. Realizing later in the evening that his partner had not found a driver, let alone looked for one, he went home to fetch his long list of contact phone numbers.

For some reason—and to his great surprise—it was nowhere to be found, so, as a last option, he called the owner of a guesthouse, who managed to book a driver for the coming day. Kolya, however, now realized that the trip would cost him more money than he was going to make. This, however, was the least of his worries, because it also turned out that he had already received—and spent— every single US dollar paid for the trip! So how was he now going to pay for the driver? Two options presented themselves: obtain a loan from a friend or acquaintance or owe the driver money, thus pushing the problem into a future that did not disturb his present too much. "Anyway," he proclaimed, "who knows what the future will bring?" (In the end, he did manage to find a driver by paying him with money borrowed from a friend, namely Lars.)

So, whereas according to Rebecca Empson, people in northeastern Mongolia in the late 1990s were "not living in a way that they consider[ed] to be 'transitional'" (2011: 24), for our friends, on the contrary, change itself featured as a prominent regularity in their everyday lives.[6] As such, we here seem to be faced with an even more radical sense of discontinuity and rupture than the "messianic" case that Robbins discusses. For Kolya and the others, it was not just that a different future *could* materialize at any moment, as is the case with Robbins' Christian millenarians. Rather, many potential futures constantly *did* present themselves in a given moment following a temporal logic that seemed to work "independently of the causal thrust of the present" (Robbins 2007: 12).[7] Thus it was not only a clear sense of direction that had been lost in the aftermath of Mongolia's postsocialist rupture but also the very need for actions to be directed by a predictable future more generally (where loans had to be repaid, appointments kept, salaries saved up, etc.). We thus agree with Verdery that postsocialist realities comprise the collusion of "two differently constituted temporal orders" (1996: 37), socialism and capitalism, but only with the important qualification that this collusion in Ulaanbaatar became invested with its own temporality, namely an accidental or "jumping" logic according to which all kinds of unconnected circumstances made social and economic reality fundamentally irregular and unpredictable. Here, transition emerges as a sui generis condition of social life that is not confined to a single revolutionary moment or to an exceptional period. On the contrary, transition comprises all the reverberations of an original rupture that has melded into a generalized state of unpredictability. Transition has come to have a life of its own.

Thus there were two times of transition in Ulaanbaatar around the turn of the millennium. On the one hand, there was the revolutionary and irreversible rupture instigated by the collapse of state socialism and the introduction of capitalism and democracy in 1990, when, to paraphrase Robbins,

Second Ring Road (2006)

"one temporal progression was halted or shattered and another [was] joined. It [was] this kind of thinking about the possibility of temporal rupture that allow[ed] people to make claims for the absolute newness of [their] lives" (2007: 12). But in addition to this irreversible and inherently discontinuous transition from one form of society to another, radical change itself also became a durable fact of life in Ulaanbaatar's age of the market: rupture became a mode of social life in the sense that virtually everything (physical structures, debts and savings, social relations of obligation, infrastructure, etc.) was subject to constant failures and breakdowns—which is just another way of saying that, from the perspective of our friends and other people from their urban cohort, transition meant that it was not only "times" but also "change" itself that was changing. In short, the very question of "what change is" became subject to perpetual transition and transformation.

But how does one live in such radical change: What, if any, are the tactics and the strategies by which people find their way through contingent landscapes in permanent transition? Is it possible at all to speak of ways of procuring, distributing and consuming resources in such a context of chronic crisis, and if so, how might we go about theorizing these transitional practices in anthropological terms? To answer these questions, we need to take issue with some of the most cherished theories and most deeply held assumptions concerning what constitutes meaningful social action and individual as well as collective agency within anthropology and cognate disciplines.

APPARENTLY IRRATIONAL OPTIMISM

As our introductory example of Hamid and his Cadillac indicated, far from being uncertain about their lives, our Ulaanbaatar friends came across as strangely, if not downright unreasonably, optimistic. Instead of expressing the deep uncertainty, marginalization or apathy reported from so many postsocialist and indeed postcolonial contexts (Lewis 1968; Nazpary 2002; Vigh 2006; Ferguson 1999; Lindquist 2005; Buyandelgeriyn 2008; Kideckel 2008; Oushakine 2009; Piot 2010; Han 2012; Frederiksen 2013; Greenberg 2014; James 2014; Rakowski 2016), he and our other friends came across as surprisingly hopeful. Their repeated experiences of failure—of supposedly lucky days turning sour, of loans to business partners that were never returned—were not being translated into what seemed to be the only sensible conclusion, namely that they were subject to the dehumanizing forces of global capitalism and neoliberal de- and reregulation in their most predatory form (Comaroff and Comaroff 1998; Tsing 2005; Friedman 2007; Povinelli 2008, 2011; Biehl 2004), and that there was really not very much they could do about this state of affairs (short of instigating radical political change—an "Ulaanbaatar spring"?—which never seemed to have crossed their minds). Nor did they succumb to a self-defeating "shocked subjectivity," mimetically reproducing the shell shock of postsocialist transition through passive behavior (Friedman 2007).

So, and somewhat to our surprise, it gradually dawned upon us that the optimism of Kolya and others was not driven primarily by promises of future capitalism (or what some Mongolian politicians later would coin the new Mongolian "wolf economy") propagandized by the Mongolian government as well as by international organizations and bilateral donors more generally (see Empson 2014). Nor did it take the form of common (n)ostalgia motivated by hopes of returning to the (retrospectively idealized and reified) "stability" of socialism, let alone a deep past associated with the medieval Mongolian empire and other symbols of national greatness and permanence (see Humphrey 1994, 2002b; Kaplonski 2004; Højer 2018, 2019b).[8] Relevant as these explanations might be when trying to anthropologically understand and analyze new forms of social agency and economic imaginaries in Mongolia and elsewhere in the postcolonial and postsocialist world, adopting them wholesale entails the risk of losing sight of the distinct temporal and social dynamics born from—and characteristic of—life in transition. For far from accepting that the best they could aspire to was pragmatically to muddle through the hardships of transition by navigating the uncertain and increasingly dire horizon of radical change the best they could (Vigh 2006; Wasquant 2007), Hamid and the others stubbornly acted as if tomorrow would be a better day by engaging in new business adventures in the apparently irrational belief that profit would wash up at their feet from the ebb and flow of broken promises, failed deals, default payments, and all too serious threats.

This "apparently irrational optimism" flies in the face of prevailing social scientific accounts of social life premised on the strategic manipulation of the dialectics between societal structures and individual agency, including so-called practice-theory (Bourdieu 1977; see also Sahlins 1976; Ortner 1984). Urban hustlers such as our Ulaanbaatar friends always represented a thorny issue for Pierre Bourdieu since their presence in the world suggested that some people were unable, and perhaps unwilling, to "be practical." "Subproletarians" was the term he deployed to denote such people, many of whom could be found just outside Paris, in the poverty-stricken *banlieues* that surround this and other French cities. According to Bourdieu, the problem with subproletarians is that they have no "practical sense of time" and thus no "disposition to see objective potentialities on the present structure" (2000: 213). More precisely, he lamented, "[t]he often disorganized and even incoherent behaviors . . . by these people without a future, living at the mercy of what each day brings and condemned to oscillate between fantasy and surrender, between flight into the imaginary and fatalistic surrender to the verdicts of the given, are evidence that, below a certain threshold of objective chances, the strategic disposition itself, which presupposes practical reference to a forth-coming . . . cannot be constituted" (2000: 221).

There is little doubt as to how Bourdieu would have responded to the case of our Ulaanbaatar friends—namely as perfect examples of subproletarian subjects, who, while "locked in the present, kno[w] only the free-floating indefinite future of [their] daydreams" (1979: 50). From this perspective, Hamid and the others were not just apparently irrationally optimistic, they *were* irrationally optimistic. When Hamid invited his friends for another afternoon of collective daydreaming inside his Cadillac—or when Kolya and the others were hanging out, for hours and sometimes even days, in bars or in Internet cafés waiting for a chance to strike a new deal—this would for Bourdieu have indicated a suspension of the normal human "disposition to see objective potentialities on the present structure" (2000: 213). Instead of making "strategic dispositions" based on their "objective life chances," our friends at first blush fitted Bourdieu's account of the subproletarian fatalist. After all, they also seemed to "oscillate between fantasy and surrender" by delving into what on the face of it seemed to be utopian daydreams and unrealistic "business" propositions that appeared to suggest that they suffered from a "generalized and lasting disorganization of behavior and thought"—"as if, when nothing was possible, everything became possible, as if all discourses about the future—prophecies, divinations, predictions, millenarian announcements—had no other purpose than to fill what is no doubt one of the most painful of wants: the lack of a future" (2000: 226).

Yet, as much as the lives of our Ulaanbaatar friends on first appearances lived up to this rather gloomy (and patronizing) description, there is also something that does not add up. After all, it was not exactly the case that "nothing was possible" for young working-class people in Ulaanbaatar around the millennium. There were, arguably, plentiful nonskilled jobs to get back then: as security guard, waiter, or (if one had a license) minibus driver or chauffeur for the rich, however unattractive these were due to their long working hours, meager pay, and almost total lack of job security (see Bruun and Odgaard 1995; Morris 2001). If we stick to Bourdieu's vocabulary, there were "real demands" for unskilled labor in urban Mongolia in the year 2000; it was just that our friends did not want to accept that these "objective chances" represented their only, as it were, subjective chances. At first glance, then, it seems that our friends did not want to be practical! Or, more precisely, they did not want to be practical in the *practice-theoretical* sense. That is, they *were* practical, but in a way that differed qualitatively from the theory of practice propagated by Bourdieu and a whole generation of practice anthropologists. For the same reason, we submit, their "apparently irrational optimism" can only be understood if we make recourse to an alternative concept of human agency and a different theory of social practice, where the experience that "everything is possible" is not dismissed as a mistaken assessment of one's "objective chances" or as lacking "feeling for the game."

Before beginning to formulate this alternative theory of practice, we need to take a closer look at certain metaphysical assumptions concerning the nature of temporality and agency that undergird the practice-theoretical paradigm. More precisely, Bourdieu's model rests on two implicit assumptions concerning the nature of social contexts or fields, neither of which squares well with urban Mongolia around the turn of the millennium, especially not with the postsocialist generation to which our Ulaanbaatar friends belonged (see Chapter 1). The first assumption inheres in Bourdieu's own habit of anthropological "continuity thinking." We are referring to his well-known description of social practice as a "game" with corresponding "rules," "fields" and "tactics" (1977) and, on a more basic level, the underlying idea that society reproduces itself in ways that can be partly anticipated and thus acted upon by differently positioned individual agents. Over recent decades, this rigid concept of social context has been subject to anthropological critique and modification—for instance, in Henrik Vigh's theory of "social navigation" (2006), which represents a sophisticated attempt to improve Bourdieu's practice-theoretical model by accounting for how different agents navigate ever-shifting social landscapes by "moving within movement" (Vigh 2006, 2009).

The second assumption about the nature of social context in Bourdieu's work has not been subject to the same degree of anthropological scrutiny and critique (although see Hodges 2008). We are referring to the fact that, for Bourdieu and other practice theorists, the future still tends to be conceived of as a sort of vista—a *space* of possibility in the form of the "horizons of a temporally extended present" (Gell 1992: 223). The problem about this deep-seated practice-theoretical assumption is precisely that it "uses a metaphor based on space to explain a process that takes place in time" (Robinson 1953: 255, cited in Maurer 2002: 27) in order to stress—in "riverine imagery" (Hodges 2008: 401)—how the present "flows" unceasingly and seamlessly into the future. This tacit metaphysical assumption, stipulating a sort of primordial spatiality and thus also an a priori continuity to social context (that is, an imagined stability pertaining not to single contexts but to what constitutes a context as such), lies behind the core practice-theoretical premise that a given agent is able to anticipate his actions with "practical reference[s] to a forth-coming" (Bourdieu 2000: 221) and thus optimize the life chances afforded to him by the social world. Even in many of the most recent and sophisticated renderings of practice theory, such as Henrik Vigh's (2006, 2009), something remains fundamentally predictable, namely an anticipatory future orientation. Vigh writes, for example, that "trying to anticipate 'what is coming' and attuning action accordingly is what is at stake in social navigation, as action is plotted, and tactics are generated" (2009: 431). Even in Vigh's motile seascape of ever-shifting social relationships, then, people are preoccupied with "making sense," "clarifying," "adapting," "anticipating" and "assessing possibilities of action" (2009: 422–424). Indeed, much as in Bourdieu's original theory, the skilled social navigator is obsessed with the forthcoming—that is, with "constantly . . . predicting and foreseeing the unfolding of the political and economic environment" (Vigh 2009: 422)—to such an extent that the unpredictable arguably becomes the (predictable) ground on which one behaves tactically. It is therefore of little surprise that Vigh is more concerned with criticizing Bourdieu's notion of (stable) "fields" (as "landscapes" *on* which people move) than with fundamentally questioning the concept of "game" and its "tactics" as such. Thus the divergence between practice theory and social navigation is, in Vigh's own wording, mainly "located in the speed and acceleration of change"—in the quantity rather than quality of change, if you like—whereas tactics, strategies and plans, however short-term, still remain at the heart of people's endeavors. Valuable as Vigh's model may be for understanding social agency within certain contexts of hardship, it still leaves undertheorized how people act in relation to the future in transitional milieus that are not only changing but where *change itself changes* in the sense that rupture—and not flow—is the ground. Here, the "anticipatory forthcoming" itself becomes prone to rupture, and social agents downplay approaches to the future based on anticipation, predictability and foreseeing. Instead, they anticipate rupture and act in "jumps."

This is precisely the challenging situation that Kolya and our other friends found themselves in; challenging, that is, not just in ethnographic terms, in the sense that it was difficult for them to live in radical transition, but also in theoretical terms in that it is hard for us, as social scientists, to analyze and explain what it means to do so. As Kolya would sometimes say, "Life is life, sometimes things change." In being forced to "anticipate" (or could we say *un-ticipate*) the accidental (the sudden disappearance of a salary, the failure of people to keep appointments, the fleeing of debtors overnight, the lack of insurance, etc.), our Ulaanbaatar friends seemed extremely reluctant to tame the future by planning, even to a point where thinking of the future too concretely and trying to imagine how one might intervene in, change and "outsmart" the future was feared to invoke misfortune (see Højer 2003, 2004, 2019a). Which is precisely the point: our friends' lives were so unpredictable that their actions were often neither tactical with reference to short-term horizons nor strategic in the form of long-term goals set with reference to more expansive future vistas (see de Certeau 1984; Castoriadis 1987). Rather, as we shall now explain, they had perfected a temporal attitude that enabled them to engage with the unexpected in ways reminiscent of (but not identical to) the alleged "presentism" of hunter-gatherers.

Bourdieu is by no means the only social scientist who has attempted to explain (away) the apparently irrational attitude toward the future among "sub-proletarians" and other people who "live in the present." A whole number of anthropologists working in different contexts around the world, including James Woodburn (1988), Michael Stewart (1997) and perhaps most famously of all Oscar Lewis (1968), have discussed how different marginalized peoples and groups (ranging from hunter-gatherers to Romas and working class urban youth) all share a "presentist" or "fatalist" attitude to time, which sets them apart from the more dominant groups surrounding them. According to the editors of the excellent volume *Lilies of the Field: Marginal Peoples Who Live for the Mo-*

ment" (Day et al. 1999), to "live for the moment" can be understood as a ritualized practice that, in defiance of the powers that be, turns "the short term into a transcendent value" by "displacing the present from its organic link to past and future" (Day et al. 1999: 21; cf. Bloch 1977). More precisely, Day, Papataxiarchis and Stewart suggest, what brings together "the pleasure of the markets in Hungary, Madagascar, London, and Poland, and of moving through the town in Brazil, the elevated spirits of Greek and Gypsy conviviality, and the happiness of the Huaorani siesta" is the fact that they "are all existential properties of the present . . . Through disconnecting the short from the long term, an 'atemporal' present is constructed" (Day et al. 1999: 21). But is that really what Hamid, Kolya and the others were spending their days on? In defiance of the uncertainties generated by the transition from socialism to capitalism, were they "living in the present, with little thought for the future and little interest in the past" (Day et al. 1999: 2)? In fact, we argue in this book, far from negating the passage of time and being oblivious to the future and the past (as both Bourdieu and the editors of *Lilies of the Field* in different ways have it), our Ulaanbaatar friends' attitudes to life in transition were often characterized by an *exalted awareness* of the potentials of the future. In that sense, it would be more accurate to say that they were "living for the moment," that is, constantly leaping in and out of a multitude of potential futures (of prosperity, different kinds of lives, business ventures, etc.), than to say that they were fatalistically confined to "living in the present" (Day et al. 1999: 2), as many hunter-gatherers and other marginal peoples are imagined to do. Crucially, the object of these dreams and hopes was, however, not *the future* as a spatialized horizon of tactical projection (as in the practical-theoretical model), but rather the *many potential futures* figured by, and made actual through, the moment (cf. Pedersen 2012; Krøijer 2015). As we are going to show in the chapters to come, people would thus leap into (or *had* to leap into) suddenly emerging futures—in their dreams or for real—without taking the intermediate steps that a successful tactic, gradually evolving toward its future goal, would. Rather, Kolya and the others would optimistically reach for a goal before they had made the "calculations" for getting there. Some of them would literally jump on a train to go to Ukraine to establish a different life (ignoring the many intermediate steps to be taken to reach this goal, such as obtaining a visa; see Chapter 1). Others would act on an impulse and travel to China to do business (ignoring meticulous planning and the many potential hurdles on the way; see Chapter 4), and yet others again would suddenly buy land (without being much concerned about getting everything settled in terms of ownership beforehand; see Chapter 4)—or they would all of a sudden obtain a loan for an expensive mobile phone (or a Cadillac!) without having any clear plan for how to pay it back (Chapter 7).

This, then, is how our friends were practical; far from "living in the present," they had developed the capacity and the propensity to inhabit a sort of "deep moment" that contained multiple potential futures that they could plunge into, in their dreams or for real. Which, in turn, captures the problem with practice theories: they rest on an over-spatialized and single-layered temporal ontology, which, among other problems (see Hodges 2008; Laidlaw 2014),[9] reduces "the potential" to "the possible," and "the moment" to "the present." In fact, one may even suggest that it would have been detrimental for Hamid and Kolya to be practical in Bourdieu's sense. For had our friends been able or willing to form "realistic hopes" by turning "wishful thinking" into "credible thoughts" (Appadurai 2004), they might have muted their capacity for eliciting invisible potentials of the moment (and, hence, the future) by limiting themselves to the visible possibilities of the present.

Far from representing one dodged attempt after another at applying a failed "practical sense," the repeated failure (but also occasional success) of things to work out in our friends' lives emerges as the result of a deliberate, and sensible, temporal orientation that might be called the work of hope (see Chapter 7). And it is precisely in this respect that their apparently irrational optimism constituted an alternative, non-practice-theoretical practice. Far from evincing a lacking awareness of time and an imprisonment in the present, living in the moment allows for an exalted awareness of its potentials—the tiny but innumerable cracks through which the promise of another world shines.

URBAN HUNTING

We can now move on to another central proposition in this book, namely that the attitude of our urban friends toward their urban environment is not just superficially similar to but *formally analogous* to that of hunters and gatherers, as described in classic as well as recent ethnographic studies (see, for example, Turnbull 1961; Meillassoux 1973; Ingold 1980; Woodburn 1982; Hamayon 1990; Brightman 1993; Bird-David 1999; Willerslev 2007; Suzman 2017). Indeed, the moment one puts aside, for heuristic purposes, the undeniably huge differences between the two environments and contexts at hand—the crowded post-socialist city and the sparsely populated alpine taiga or tropical forest—then several striking analogies become visible and call for further investigation and comparison.

We are not the first scholars to notice this. Tomasz Rakowski makes a similar argument in his acclaimed ethnography of "the degraded" in postsocialist Poland (2016). "Much as," Rakowski observes with reference to Colin Turnbull's classic work, "the Pygmies can endlessly divide and classify tree bark, for instance, with regard to its application, taste, appearance, and smell, so too can [two of his homeless interlocutors] divide and waste rubber" (2016: 218). Indeed, Rakowski argues, drawing on Tim Ingold's Heidegger-inspired approach (2000) and Levi-Strauss' notion of "the science of the concrete" (1966), "[t]his special form of ecology, of being in the environment, of acquiring and collecting materials of all sorts, is thus, at the same time, a practical and cognitive activity, and a hunting/gathering skill in managing postindustrial, ready-made resources, like those found in nature" (2016: 220). Rakowski's Polish ethnography (which only came to our attention during the final stages of preparing this book) has much going for it, and in several respects forecloses some of the findings we have reached in our own work on Mongolia. Nevertheless, there are also noteworthy differences between our respective conclusions and the data and theories used to reach them. For Rakowski, postsocialist hunting and gathering as a unique "being in the environment" is restricted to the people at the very bottom of society—it is a last-resort alternative to which the homeless and other "degraded" turn when there are no other "means of survival" (2016: 38) in the harsh and unforgiving environment of neoliberal reform and increasing commodification.[10] On our account, conversely, "urban hunting" does not so much apply to a particular class or segment of people, although there are certainly communities and contexts (such as our friends at the time of our fieldwork) in which the practices and discourses that concern us in this book are more prevalent and dominant than others. But our argument also departs from Rakowski's in a more basic sense that revolves around the way in which we theorize what we take to be sui generis social, economic and temporal logics pertaining to the phenomena, which we refer to as "urban hunting."

Our point is thus not simply that urban hustlers, like many rural hunters, tend to share their spoils according to egalitarian norms and moral economies (including what Nikolas Peterson has dubbed "demand sharing," 1993),[11] or for that matter, that, like hunters in Northern Mongolia when searching for wild animals, our friends spent most of their time waiting for hours and sometimes days, for the right moment to "kill." On a more fundamental level, our point is also that neither hunters nor hustlers, in Mongolia or elsewhere, are in a meaningful way practical in Bourdieu's (sedentary, Fordist) sense of the word.[12] Instead, as we have suggested, Ulaanbaatar's hustlers around 2000 were practical in an alternative (nonsedentary, non-Fordist) way, which we aim to explore and theorize in this book. For, as we shall now further substantiate, rather than being practical in the anticipatory, pessimistic and risk-averse way theorized by the practice theorists, our friends were practical in the presentist, optimist and risk-prone manner characteristic of hunters in search of prey.

At the heart of the issue is the intense unpredictability and the distinct temporal horizon that is characteristic of the two extractive practices and resource environments of hunting and hustling. True, hunting takes years of apprenticeship and experience to perfect, which means that some hunters are better at finding and killing game than others (much in the same way that good hustlers know where to position and comport themselves in order to increase their resource base [see Chapters 3 and 6]). Still, no matter how experienced the hunter, there appears to be a *fundamentally irreducible element of unpredictability* to the flow of resources in a given hunting environment. Yet hunters tend to have confidence in their environment's ability to provide game, at least at some point in the future (see, e.g., Bird-David 1990, 1992; Ingold 1996; Sahlins 1974: 2; Willerslev 2007: 31–35). Again, this is not to say that hunting—whether in its conventional form or the urban variety we are concerned with here—involves a happy-go-lucky and laissez-faire attitude in which the hunter does little more than wait passively for the next opportunity to extract resources to present itself. On the contrary, to be a good hunter (in the dual sense of being good at hunting and at excelling in being the kind of person whom a hunter is ideally supposed to be) requires concentration, endurance and patience. One needs to stay constantly alert, not vis-à-vis a continuously rolling future that can be anticipated and perhaps planned ahead (as in the case of some agricultural and especially factory work), but with respect to the sudden eruptions of intensity, bursts of action and changes of trajectory that characterize the tracking and killing of prey in Northern Asia and elsewhere. It is this constant fluctuation in the flow and availability of resources that we propose is formally identical among rural and urban hunters—not because they share a cultural tradition (although this may indeed be the case in Mongolia or Siberia), but because the relationship between "predator and prey" is imbued with similar temporal dynamics in the context of hustling and hunting. Hence the title of the present section—and the title of our book.

"[T]he essence of hunting," Tim Ingold has suggested (1986: 91), "lies in the prior intention that motivates the search for game."[13] Indeed, one of the important anthropological contributions to the interdisciplinary field of hunter-gatherer studies (a field that has often been dominated by discussions about "optimal foraging theories" [Smith 1983; Guenther 2007] and other more or less evolutionary and sociobiological premises and approaches) is the insistence that hunting as an activity cannot be reduced to the act of killing prey alone or so-called practical know-how and techniques (ranging from knowledge of the forest and its different species of animals and plants to specialized technologies such as traps) involved in preparing, organizing and executing a successful hunt. On the contrary, as scholars such as Ingold and Willerslev have argued (Ingold 2000; Willerslev 2007), to be a good hunter is not only a question of being "practical," at least not as long as the latter is defined in opposition to "the symbolic" (Ingold 2000; cf. Leach 1976). Superior huntsmanship among Siberian peoples also comprises an extremely wide range of seemingly nonpractical activities such as sacrifice and magic (Chaussonet 1988; Hamayon 1990), as well as dreaming (Willerslev 2004a). In fact, as Willerslev has argued based on his fieldwork among Yukaghir hunters, "the dreaming self, far from taking a break from the demands of coping with reality, sets out in search of meanings that will help it to accomplish concrete objectives in waking life" (2007: 175–176).

Much the same, we suggest, goes for the array of activities and imaginations that our friends lumped together under the common denominator of "business." Among other things, "doing business" included endless and seemingly pointless driving around the postsocialist city and its periurban slums; visits to Buddhist astrologers to map out one's "luck" (*hiimor'*) and "life-force" (*süld*); and, indeed, the countless hours they spent in each other's company in defunct cars and other unlikely places engaged in individual daydreaming (*möröödöl*) and collective hoping (*naidvar*) (more on which in Chapter 7). This, then, is what we are trying to convey by pairing and comparing "dealing" with "dreaming" in this book: the ethnographic fact that, far from representing two opposing activities, practices of dealing overlapped with and were indistinguishable from practices of dreaming during times of transition. To paraphrase Willerslev, Kolya and the others didn't see "the two worlds [of dealing and of dreaming] as opposed, but . . . as mirror images of each other" (2007: 176). Of course, they were perfectly able to differentiate between different mental states, including dreaming and daydreaming. Yet, it is an ethnographic fact that in different parts of the world ranging from the Siberian *taiga* (Willerslev 2004a) to inner-city Cairo (Mittermaier 2011), in certain situations, "the line between sleep and wakefulness . . . is of little relevance to [one's] interlocutors," in the sense that it allows these people to "think through other imaginations . . . to rupture and expand [their] own" (2011: 6). However, it was not all forms of dreaming that were invested with this quasi-occult capacity. On the contrary, the "dreams that mattered" (cf. Mittermaier 2011) were the shared hopes and collective aspirations made with others, and seldom the private fantasies and daydreams people lapsed into in solitary introspection.[14]

This, then, is why it would be ethnographically problematic to insist on an overly rigid distinction between the putatively "real practice" of dealing on the one hand and the seemingly symbolic imaginary of daydreaming on the other. Rather, dealing and daydreaming, and more generally economic practices and cosmological imaginaries, are two intertwined modes of the single pragmatics of urban hunting. Indeed, this is what most days in our friends' lives boiled down to: dealing and dreaming, in different combinations and with varying degrees of emphasis. They were simultaneously dealing and dreaming when hanging out, for hours and hours on end, in cafés, restaurants and bars waiting for "business" to happen, and they were both dreaming and dealing when seated in cars cruising around the city sharing cigarettes and making extremely detailed plans about how to make "profit" (ashig) without doing "boring work"; just as they were at one and the same time dealing and dreaming when, following the failure of another profit to materialize, they solicited guidance from Buddhist lamas and shamanic practitioners in Ulaanbaatar's market of occult entrepreneurs. In Ulaanbaatar around 2000, dealing and dreaming had become so mutually intertwined that it made little sense to distinguish between them. Both activities were equally part of what might be called the "total social fact" of urban hunting. Far from merely representing yet another counterintuitive icing on an already apparently irrational cake, our friends' propensity for daydreaming—and, more generally, for "wasting their time" on all sorts of seemingly superfluous activities—were basic features of a nontactical extractive technique whereby "profit" and other resources were allowed to "pop out" of a deeply transitional milieu. Nevertheless, these two basic modes of transitional life can be ethnographically described and anthropologically analyzed as separate activities, as reflected in the way in which the remaining chapters of this book are organized.

So, when we say that our friends' attitude toward time and resource generation from their surroundings was comparable to hunter-gatherers, it is meant as more than just a nice metaphor. There were real similarities between the manner in which our friends extracted and shared "profit" from the postsocialist city and the modes of obtaining and distributing resources found among groups of hunter-gatherers studied by anthropologists, including Tanzania's Hadza (Woodburn 1988) and Siberia's Yukaghirs (Willerslev 2007) and Evenki (Ssorin-Chaikov 1993) and, indeed, Eastern Mongolia's Buryats (Empson 2012), Northern Mongolia's Darhads (Pedersen 2001) and Dukha (Kristensen 2007,

2015; Pedersen 2009) and Central Mongolia's Halh (High 2017). As some of Ulaanbaatar's most accomplished urban hunters, Hamid, Kolya and the others had perfected the skill for extracting resources from the city by systematically "reap[ing] without sowing" (Day et al. 1999: 4) and continually "mak[ing] demands on people to share more but not to produce more" (Bird-David 1990: 195). And far from a subproletarian flight into the imaginary and the unrealistic, and for that matter an extension of rural traditional nomadic culture into a modern urban setting, the social practices of waiting, hanging out, dreaming and hoping were important and quite respectable ways of acting in times of radical societal change.

A HUSTLER-GATHERER CONTINUUM

By way of closing, we wish to make one thing absolutely clear. In titling this book *Urban Hunters*, and in insisting that the notion of hunting is to be understood as much more than just a nice metaphor, we are emphatically *not* seeking to make any essentialist or otherwise homogenizing claim concerning either what kind of persons our interlocutors are, or the nature of the complex social, economic and political reality with which they were confronted during the time of our fieldwork. To be sure, not everyone in Ulaanbaatar around the turn of the millennium was an urban hunter who spent the day in a half-broken Cadillac and on other seemingly irrational acts of dealing and dreaming, and our friends were obviously also capable of being practical in the practice-theoretical sense in those situations and contexts where their future horizons were sufficiently predictable. Nor, to be sure, were all or even most of our friends and interlocutors more generally men, though we may have given this impression so far in this introduction. Leaving aside, for the time being (but see Chapters 2 and 4), the fact that many of our female friends and interlocutors (and Mongolian women more generally) in some sense adapted more easily to the times of transition than did their male peers (see, e.g., Benwell 2009; Buyandelger 2013), the category of "urban hunters" is by no means restricted to the male gender. In fact, as especially Chapter 4 makes clear, some of the most extreme instances of "living for the moment" and of "apparently irrational optimism" could be found among women at the time of our fieldwork.

Far from postulating the existence of and organizing our account around a single sociological type (a reified and essentialized construct one could call "man the urban hunter," with a nod to classic hunter-gatherer studies and subsequent feminist critiques hereof, see, e.g., Slocum 1975), then, this book is concerned with an array of extremely diverse persons and activities evincing to various

Ulaanbaatar women (2007)

degrees traits that may be deemed urban hunting–like. There is a continuum of postsocialist persona who in different ways are all engaged in acts of "hustling and gathering" in the messy orchestration of social life known as Mongolia's age of the market. Much in line with the flexibility associated with hunter-gatherers, these were people who—in different measures and combinations with other modes of social agency—anticipated unpredictability, took things as they came, embraced momentary opportunities and allowed (day)dreams to expand their horizons and to optimistically gauge the future. In fact, it is possible to identify a handful of different urban hunter/hustler persona, who occupy different positions or stages on the axis suspended between the two poles of, on the one hand, urban hunters, such as our friends, who spend much of their time dealing and dreaming, and the "normal people" with their "normal lives" that are often held up as an idealized bourgeois counterpart to our friends' predicament, on the other. This is not the place to describe in detail the different persona inhabiting this continuum; that is a task that is better left to the chapters to come. Suffice it to say that the ethnographic journey that is assuming its beginning in the next chapter shall take us from (male) pickpockets and other petty thieves operating in the crammed alleys of Ulaanbaatar's black markets to ambitious (female) flour traders and other entrepreneurs trying to control and monopolize the flow of goods in and out of these same venues; just as we shall recount the tragicomic tale of two brothers and their mistaken business adventure in Ukraine, and chronicle the successful attempt by a third brother from the same household to become a successful businessman capable of not just making big money from almost magically fast deals but also of saving up at least some of the profits thus gained for both domestic consumption and long-term property investment. We shall also follow a young woman on her business ventures into little-known waters, such as the pork-fat trade across the Chinese border, just as we shall see how another woman tried to carve out an introverted island of Protestant existence amid the sea of transition.

So, instead of restricting the "urban hunting" designation to a certain kind or group of people or a certain time and place, it is much more ethnographically accurate and analytically germane to broaden its usage to refer to a diverse range of persons, practices and milieus, which in different senses and to different degrees subscribe to the political-economic characteristics and the social and temporal "logics" that we have outlined above. This is precisely what we shall do in the seven ethnographic chapters that make up the rest of this book, which are organized with this overarching message concerning a broad continuum of urban hunters in mind. The chapters that follow have thus been put together with a double purpose in mind. On the one hand, each chapter conveys a sense of the multitude of socioeconomic forms and multifarious ways of coping with life in Ulaanbaatar around the turn of the millennium. But on the other hand, each chapter also homes in on various kinds and techniques of urban hunting that our friends cultivated, and sometimes perfected, in the course of the two decades spanned by our account. To heed this challenge, each chapter uses both individual autobiographies and extended case studies to illustrate a broader argument about life in permanent transition. Indeed, the book is organized in such a way that our key informants/friends play a central role in all chapters, thus ensuring that our argument is personified by, and related to, concrete individual lives while also meeting the wider goal of outlining a general theory of hustling that remains faithful to urban Mongolian people's experiences of the postsocialist age of the market.

So, as much as this study pays particular attention to urban hunting as a distinct mode of economic practice and social agency during times of transition, this does not—of course!—mean that our friends or anyone else in postsocialist Mongolia was incapable of being practical in the more conventional, practice-theoretical sense. Nor does it mean there were not many men and perhaps especially women who were very adept at and spent much energy on managing the uncertainties and hardships of transition through well-known forms of tactical agency. What our focus on urban hunting *does* reflect, however, is a concerted attempt to take transition seriously as a sui generis phenomenon and, indeed, an unsolved anthropological puzzle that calls for an alternative account of social agency. Indeed, as we have sought to indicate, while urban hunting was and may still be a prominent feature of social life in urban Mongolia and other former socialist countries, it may also be identified within a range of other historical or contemporary contexts, such as the deprived suburbs of post–financial crisis Europe or the war-torn postcolonies of sub-Saharan Africa. In this sense, our ambition for this book goes beyond contributing to postsocialist studies alone.

Chapter 1 Lost in Transition?

When democracy came, my father's life somehow stopped. Back in socialist times, he had dreams. He was working for the national railway company, he went on holiday with his friends, and went fishing with his sons. Now, all he does is sit in front of the TV, always tuned to Russian stations. My parents were completely lost. A lot of families suffered like this. They had plans back in socialist times and then suddenly the transition came and there was a lack of products. They were just workers—that's all. Back in socialist times, a trader was seen as a bad person. It was sort of low. A good person was a socialist person, a working person. Those involved in trade were cheaters. They knew what democracy was, what money was. So they already had a capitalist mind.

Such were the words of Kolya, the second youngest of four brothers in an ethnically mixed Ukrainian/Mongolian family from Ulaanbaatar and one of our main protagonists in this book. Kolya's family used to live quite comfortably under socialism, but as this passage makes clear, their entire way of life was severely disrupted by the advent of "democracy" and the "market economy" in 1990. According to Kolya,

Mother and son (1995)

his father first and foremost "believed in himself," yet at the same time, one could hardly imagine a more socialist man. The son of a Mongolian father who had been educated in Ukraine and worked in the headquarters of Choibalsan, Mongolia's "Stalin" and uncontested leader from 1939 to 1952, and a Ukrainian mother who—for a while—worked as a cook for the same Choibalsan, he had been left behind in Mongolia at the age of fourteen when his family moved to Ukraine. While he had worked as a welder for the National Railway Organization since then, that is, during the whole socialist period, he had never felt entirely at home in Mongolia. He was a small and lively man, but on festive occasions, one would often see him raise his glass and tearfully burst into melancholic Ukrainian songs. Yet he was also a proud worker who felt utterly at home in his profession and who was a staunch believer in the collectivist ideals of communism. Indeed, a primary producer of *infrastruktura*, Kolya's father in many ways represented the ideal worker (*ajilchin*), who was on the cusp of Mongolia's path toward the bright and progressive future of communist modernity. The daughter of a herdsman from the southern steppes, Kolya's mother worked in a well-funded nursery which, in characteristic state socialist fashion, was run by the state railway organization. Unlike her husband, her parents were both Mongolian, and she had a number of relatives in Ulaanbaatar and several rural provinces. Like her husband, however, she was a firm believer in the socialist system and had lived her entire life within its seemingly predictable framework.

The future—understood as "the horizon of the projection of the self into an imagined future" (Friedman 2007: 435)—of the household had been perfectly on track: the two parents would become older, retire and eventually pass away, and their four sons would take over from them within the system, perhaps even assuming their father's honorable profession. This was a time, it seems, "when the path between present and future was, simply, planning" (Collier 2011: 5). By the mid-1980s, however, the pillars of this horizon had slowly begun to crack with the introduction of the Mongolian versions of *glasnost* and *perestroika*. Much as the country had copied the USSR in its path toward socialism, it also mimicked the Soviet Union in its undoing of it, at least until the early 1990s (see Kaplonski 2004: 48–70; Rossabi 2005: 1–29). So when, in 1990–1991, the one-party system and the planned economy were replaced by liberal democracy and market-economic reforms, there was no future left for someone like Kolya's father, for time paradoxically stopped with the advent of "transition." His life had come to a standstill.

Small wonder. As representatives of Mongolia's baby-boomer generation, Kolya's parents were old enough to recall how tough life had been after the Second World War, and how much their livelihoods had improved when collectivization and industrialization took off in the 1950s. Indeed, their generation was the first (and only) to grow up and establish families during the "golden age" of Mongolian socialism, back when the majority of people still perceived their country to be on the unbreakable path of "progress" and "modernity" set in train by the revolutions of 1921 and 1924 (Humphrey 2005). It must not be forgotten that, until the 1980s, Mongolia had witnessed decades of unprecedented economic growth as much of its increasingly urban and educated population gradually left behind their pastoralist life to work in factories or in semiurbanized state farms. With the postsocialist transition, some people thus not only "lost the futures for which they had been preparing themselves" (Ghodsee 2011: 13) and were left with "a vision of the future . . . that was now past" (Collier 2011: 6); they also lost the prospect of a future as such. This is why, for Kolya's parents, "democracy" and "capitalism" meant not just the end of socialism but of time as such. In a sense, as he himself put it in the earlier citation, Kolya's parents' future disappeared overnight; they were, effectively, socially dead, for they had been more or less divested of agency.

This family forms our ethnographic focus in this chapter. By chronicling the successes and failures of Kolya and his three brothers, Misha, Lyosha and

Andrei, in the years leading up to and just after the collapse of socialism, we show that they represent a Mongolian variety of what Alexei Yurchak has called "the last Soviet generation" (2006): the cohort of people reaching the ages of twenty to forty a decade after the collapse of the socialist system, who, because they were coming of age just as socialism collapsed, internalized the culture of transition more than anyone else. By critically engaging with Yurchak's argument about the "deterritorialized milieus" of late socialism (2003, 2006), we show how our Ulaanbaatar friends, in Kolya's own words, got "lost" in transition—"lost" not in the sense of being mute victims of radical change but of being possessed by transition to such an extent that it almost became their innermost selves. Faced with the near-impossible challenge of holding on to their new subjectivities and belongings without severing their networks or becoming lost in infinite chains of obligations arising from the ruins of an obsolete socialist counterculture, Kolya's brothers and many of their friends either became stuck in cynical apathy or became consumed by the transition by trying to take advantage of any opportunity that suddenly appeared. Only Kolya, as we shall see, skillfully or luckily managed the balancing act of embracing opportunities and exploring networks without drifting too much off course.

Our aim is thus twofold. On the one hand, we wish to provide what might be called a personalized contextualization of what life is like during times of transition by chronicling Mongolia's rupture from state socialism to market economy through the eyes of key representatives of Ulaanbaatar's "lost" generation, like Kolya, who is going to make an appearance, in various roles and respects, in each of the chapters to come. Second, based on fifteen years or so (1995–2010) in which we partook particularly closely in the life of our Ulaanbaatar friends, we wish to argue that one reason many of them were "lost" is that they continued to live their lives *as if* they were still involved in the "parallel worlds" which, according to Yurchak, were so characteristic of urban life in late socialist society, particularly among the youth. Indeed, as we are going to argue, it is to a large degree because Kolya and the others invested so much of their time and energy in subcultural projects and parallel economic practices that, with the collapse of socialism, so many of them ended up being irreversibly lost in transition.

BETWEEN TWO FIRES

The four brothers grew up in Amgalan, a suburb of Ulaanbaatar that had developed around the railway line toward the east of the city center. Kolya used to go to a local day care center run by the railway organization (the one where his mother worked), and he recalls his childhood in Amgalan as a happy and joyous time. True, there was no central heating and much demanding physical work needed to be done on a daily basis, such as chopping firewood and bringing water from the local well, but the kids, he said, had plenty of possibilities to play and often went to the Tuul River to swim or fish. And then they lived near the railway, and Kolya was lucky enough to speak Russian. "Back then," Kolya fondly recalled,

> big trains from Russia would come with lots of fruit. They were supplying Russian military shops in Mongolia. Of course, as a Russian-speaking person I would often get it for free. Sometimes a group of us Mongolians hid under the trains and used "hooks" to steal the fruit when Russian soldiers were unloading the trains. Sometimes they would catch you, but I almost never had a problem because I spoke Russian. I managed to get big pieces.

According to Kolya, Amgalan was defined as a military zone—it accommodated Red Army military storage houses, fuel supplies, coal reserves, antimissile divisions, and so on—and it hosted a significant presence of Soviet soldiers.[1] Speaking Russian and having a father of half-Ukrainian origin, Kolya and his brothers engaged more eagerly with the Russian community than they did with Mongolians. Kolya enjoyed spending time with Soviet soldiers and looking at tanks and other military equipment, and he often managed to enter so-called Russian shops, either alone or with a Russian friend—he was, after all, only a "half" (*erliiz*) or "local" (*mestnye* [Rus.]) Russian and the shops were reserved for Soviet citizens and members of the Mongolian nomenklatura. While the supply of goods in Mongolian shops was not bad, Kolya recalled, it was not as varied and luxurious as in the Russian stores, where "everything" was available. And indeed, Kolya and his brothers fondly remembered this time in Amgalan as a time of prosperity. There were Soviet soldiers everywhere, plentiful fish to be caught in the river (Mongols traditionally do not fish), and supplies coming in from the USSR—and the *mestnye* Russians had specialized in providing homemade vodka to the many soldiers in return for food and luxury goods.

Amgalan was located in Ulaanbaatar's suburbs, some eight kilometers east of the central Sükhbaatar Square and well outside the zone of Soviet-inspired, and sometimes Soviet-designed and Soviet-funded, apartment blocks, which had been constructed in the heyday of state socialism between the postwar years and the late 1980s (Campi 2006; Pedersen 2017a). Yet, because of their ethnicity, the four brothers were allowed into a Russian-language school in the 15th Micro District near the city center, which was otherwise reserved for the privileged offspring of Soviet specialists and the Mongolian elite of the Communist

Party. Indeed, because their father had Ukrainian heritage, and because being "a Russian person" (*oros hün*)—tellingly, people did not distinguish much between Ukrainian and Russian culture and identity—endowed a higher status than being Mongolian during socialist times, Kolya and his brothers saw themselves as more Russian than Mongolian from a very early age, even though their mother only spoke Mongolian to them and their father was himself an *erliiz* ("of mixed blood").

According to Kolya, however, their so-called pure Russian (*tsever oros*) and pure Mongolian (*tsever mongol*) classmates often looked down upon them because of their working class and mixed background, so the four brothers never came to consider themselves as belonging to any privileged socialist nomenklatura. On the contrary, they often ended up finding themselves "caught between two fires" (as Kolya memorably put it to Lars during a long conversation in a bar), for they were often ill-treated and soon gained the reputation of lazy troublemakers. The Mongols sometimes called them "Russian shitheads," and the Russian soldiers often pejoratively referred to them as "Semyons" (descendant of the White Russian Ataman Grigory Semyonov), yet their access to Russian networks also provided them opportunities that few Mongolians could ever enjoy. Indeed, the oldest brother, Misha, insisted that they and the other "half-Russians" were generally treated with respect during the socialist period. After all, Misha pointed out, they had access to both Soviet and Mongolian shops and nightclubs, and were, he recalled, generally popular in Ulaanbaatar's Russian community, not least because they were considered a good defense against aggressive Mongolians turning up at "Russian clubs" to pick a fight. As Kolya once related,

> In socialist times, the half-Russian community was very tough. Even the Mongolians were afraid of half-Russians. Half-Russians would walk the streets, singing and playing guitar. The community was very big. They were fighting, beating up the Mongols. Misha would go to the Bayangol Hotel where they had nice drinks, nice food, and nice chicks. They always ended up there, drinking heavily. Really cool life . . . they would try all sorts of drinks and meet up with rich Russians who were staying in the Bayangol hotel.

Above all, then, the four brothers seemed to live on the fringes of the establishment. Their intermediate position as *erliiz* placed them in a special position vis-à-vis both Mongolians and more recently immigrated Soviet "specialists" (engineers and other professionals brought to Mongolia to assist its "development") and officers. The brothers were perceived (and perceived themselves) as in-between, sometimes facing the hardships of discrimination and occasionally downright racism (especially after 1990), yet also gaining from the opportunities of their in-betweenness. They may have been low-ranking "Semyons," but they could still get hold of exotic fruits and other rare goods; while working-class and "half-Mongol," they also had access to Russian networks like few Mongolians did.

Lyosha, the second-oldest brother, is a case in point. As a child, he had the reputation of being a "hooligan" and left school in 1982 after only two days in the ninth grade. After a short spell shoveling coal, he nevertheless managed—through a female acquaintance of the family—to secure a job at a storehouse that was delivering food supplies not just to the Soviet military base in Amgalan but to all "Russian shops" in the country. He was responsible for registering and unloading goods from trains, and the salary—MNT660 a month[2] (more than USD80)—was exceptionally good. This enabled him to dress well and buy luxury items—such as bicycles, a Walkman, jeans, and so on—for himself and his family and not least—to the great annoyance of his mother—for his Mongolian girlfriend. At some point, his access to cheap green coffee beans also spurred him to begin with a friend a lucrative trade on the side. They would empty twenty packets of coffee beans into an Adidas bag and go to the upmarket Bayangol Hotel, where they would ask their contact, a bartender, whether "he had any buyers." Some Polish guys, for example, would then arrive and they would exchange bags—identical bags—and Lyosha and his friend would receive goods from Poland that were not on sale in Mongolia—jackets, T-shirts, trousers, shoes etc.—in exchange for the coffee.

None of the brothers were members of the socialist youth organization or dedicated participants in political and institutional life, but nor were they in any way opposed to the Communist Party or to the system more generally. Kolya recalls that, in the 1980s, they were not allowed to talk about "reactionary" historical figures like Genghis Khan and were taught exemplary socialist behavior in school, but while some of his classmates would put a lot of effort into adapting to socialist discipline and the ethos of being a hardworking and obedient student, this was not a great concern to Kolya or his brothers. Far from trying to become a member of the Communist Party's youth pioneers, he preferred to hang out with Soviet soldiers or play "American cowboys and Indians" with his friends in Amgalan. Later, as Kolya grew up, he would dress as a punk and go with his older brother, Lyosha, to the Lenin Club—the cultural center located in the heart of Ulaanbaatar—to break-dance. While causing more than a few raised eyebrows among more conformist members of the Lenin Club, the punk outfits and break dancing were not something that the Mongolian authorities really wanted (or knew how) to sanction, even if what took place during these gatherings was hardly in accordance with the ideal youth cadre. As Misha put it,

> We met in separate groups, according to style. We, for example, were Victor Tsoi fans, and there were Metallica fans, punks and break-dancers. It was all divided. The punks, for example, met in the 4th Micro District and on Sundays they had break-dance competitions. Each group would walk on their own, gather in different places and have their own haircut. We walked around like that, and if we met one of the other groups, we would argue with them. Then we fought and the police would arrive and separate us. Sometimes the police took someone, but we didn't break the law, what we did was not forbidden—so we were released again. We didn't kill anybody. We just fought. To be sure, sometimes a nose was broken, but it never turned seriously bad.

Much as in the USSR, "Western rock and roll had a phenomenal appeal" (Yurchak 2006: 207) in Mongolia back then. Many people in the 1980s listened to Viktor Tsoi, the lead singer of the legendary Russian rock band Kino, and various Western rock bands such as Metallica. Cassette tapes (sometimes originals but mostly copies) were brought into Mongolia by "specialists" from the USSR or Eastern Europe or, in the case of Western music, by children from elite families who had traveled abroad with their parents (see also Marsh 2010: 345–346). Like other rare goods associated with the West (such as, for instance, basketball shoes and, after 1990, Zippo lighters), these tapes were cared for with a passion and zeal that resembled that given to holy religious artifacts, sometimes to the point that children would ask their parents to keep them locked away. At the same time, the large number of Mongolian students attending universities abroad (particularly in the USSR and East Germany, but also in Czechoslovakia, Hungary and Cuba) also introduced new musical styles, the latest fashions and the coolest subcultures to Ulaanbaatar's youth.

During Kolya's late childhood and early adolescence, then, the life of he and his brothers was one whose basic and most precious values, practices and ideas largely unfolded within subcultural spaces beyond the reach of the state. Still, while they spent most of their time and energy listening to new kinds of music and experimenting with new urban styles, they never developed a "public feeling" (*nastroy chelovecheskiy v obshchestve* [Rus.]), as Misha put it, of linking these subcultures with "real life" (*real'naya zhizn'* [Rus.]). The party was in control, and youth like them would never take to the streets to shout "down with socialism," he stressed. Indeed, much as was the case with most people in Mongolia

Second Ring Road (1995)

during late socialism (Humphrey 1994; Pedersen 2011: 81–114), Kolya and the others found it impossible not to acknowledge the monolithic presence of the Mongolian communist state. At the same time, both for them and many others from their cohort—Mongolia's last socialist generation, born between 1960 and 1980—the socialist system was not something to really believe—or not believe—in. Instead, it was something that was simply there and would always remain, perhaps not unlike the way in which people expect the sun to rise and set every day.

PARALLEL WORLDS

The above discussion of the four brothers calls to mind Alexei Yurchak's influential study of youth culture in Leningrad (now St. Petersburg) (2006). For if, according to Yurchak, "the identity of the older generations was formed around events such as the revolution, the war, the denunciation of Stalin; [then] . . . the common identity of the last Soviet generation was formed by a shared experience of the normalized, ubiquitous, and immutable authoritative discourse of the Brezhnev years" (2006: 32). Although Yurchak's argument is concerned with Soviet and more specifically Leningrad society, and although his ethnographic material primarily stems from its well-educated and well-connected urban intelligentsia and may not match the whole of the late Soviet experience

(Humphrey 2008a; Oushakine 2009), we find that some of Yurchak's insights apply to Mongolia as well. In Ulaanbaatar, too, the "performative dimension" of state socialist ideology became increasingly important throughout the 1970s and 1980s, as an ever wider gap emerged between official representations (e.g., production plans) and the social, economic and cultural reality that these claimed to refer to (cf. also Verdery 1995a; Humphrey 1994). Moreover, in Ulaanbaatar this state of affairs led to very little opposition to, let alone resistance against, the communist government. Rather, and echoing Yurchak's argument, the response of our friends, as well as many others from their generation—especially those with privileged access to the system in one way or the other (a fact not stressed by Yurchak)—was to "internally emigrate" into various "deterritorialized worlds" that, "although uninterested in the [socialist] system, . . . drew heavily on that system's possibilities, financial subsidies, cultural values, collectivist ethics, forms of prestige, and so on" (2006: 132).

Made up of any group of friends, neighbors or colleagues who considered themselves *svoi* ("us," "our circle"), a given parallel world into which people would "internally migrate" could revolve around virtually any activity (music, literature or drinking), as long as its raison d'être was understood by its participants to be external (but not necessarily in opposition) to the needs and concerns of the socialist state. One term in particular captured the ethos of such groups of *svoi*, namely *obshchenie* ("conversation, hanging out"), which Yurchak describes as

> an intense and intimate commonality and intersubjectivity, not just spending time in the company of others [but] the communal space where everyone's personhood was dialogized to produce a common intersubjective sociality . . . Practices of *obshchenie* during late socialism became particularly ubiquitous and open-ended . . . For many people, belonging to a tight milieu of *svoi*, which involved constant *obshchenie*, was more meaningful and valuable than other forms of interaction, sociality, goals, and achievements, including those of a professional career . . . The "value" produced in such practices went beyond just milieus of friends; it included the production of particular worlds that were spatially, temporally, and meaningfully *vnye* [at once outside and inside] the regime of Soviet authoritative discourse (2006: 148–150)

Loosely demarcated by a constellation of people who shared a common interest, hobby or passion, a given parallel or deterritorialized world could evolve around more or less any activity, even activities promoted by the authorities. Consider again Ulaanbaatar's Lenin Club, one of the countless cultural centers that could be found across Mongolia and the Soviet Union (Grant 1995; Marsh 2006). Here, young Mongolian socialists and Soviet citizens could join various kinds of "societies" devoted to such "healthy" pursuits as fishing, classical music and traditional dance. However, much as in the case of the Leningrad archaeological society and other similar parallel worlds described by Yurchak (2006), the actual activities taking place under the umbrella of the Lenin Club—like Kolya's break dancing, for example—were often rather different from their official purpose, including informal or downright illicit activities that could not even be superficially said to be in the socialist state's interest. In Ulaanbaatar, as in so many other places within the vast and heterogeneous periphery of the Soviet empire (see, e.g., Humphrey 1998; Ssorin-Chaikov 2003), these parallel worlds often involved informal exchange networks circumventing the supply-driven logic of the planned economy. These often illicit activities, however, still occurred within the framework of a strong one-party state and an anticapitalist discourse. Said Misha,

> When I started doing trade and small business, every second person who knew me would avoid me on the streets. "Oh, Misha doesn't work, he speculates," they would think to themselves, while walking away from me, staring at me as if I was a wolf.

Apart from break dancing or joining a local "gang" (*büleg*) involved in petty crime under the leadership of a "strongman" (*ataman*)—indeed, for a few years Misha apparently developed something of an *ataman*-like status and reputation in the Amgalan district—one of the most popular and cherished pastimes of the four brothers was to hang out with soldiers from the Red Army stationed just outside Ulaanbaatar. While there was nothing suspect about spending time with Soviet soldiers as such, what actually took place during these meetings is unlikely to have pleased the authorities. After all, as Kolya fondly remembers it, an elaborate system of barter and favors was established, which involved the exchange of various foods and drinks (including vodka) and activities (like firing off real rounds on a machine gun brought back from the Afghan war) that were not exactly on offer in the average Mongolian "house of culture."

In Ulaanbaatar as in Leningrad, then, the parallel worlds of the last socialist generation were extremely different from one another. And yet all these subcultures also had certain things in common that set them apart from the world outside. Apart from the fact that any mention of "politics" was irrelevant, and the related requirement of people who were participating to "have fun" (as opposed to carrying out "boring work"), all parallel worlds seemed to aspire toward the goal of *obshchenie*, where "the lives of participants became tightly intertwined through togetherness that was a central value in itself" (Yurchak 2006: 151). This late socialist celebration of intimate togetherness, friendship and fun—detached from official society, state planning and work—echoes that of other marginalized peoples from around the world who, as we discussed in the Introduction, also elevate the present "into a transcendent escape from time itself" where momentary "joy and satisfaction" are more important than past history and future plans (Day et al. 1999: 2). Crucially, however, all this took place within a monolithic and hegemonic socialist state.

While these parallel worlds were often cast in idioms of fun, commensality and togetherness, they were by no means merely frivolous icings on the state socialist cake. Many of them had important if often rather implicit and unspoken pragmatic dimensions, in the sense that people relied heavily on them for all sort of ends and purposes beyond the celebration of *obshchenie*-like social efflorescence and drunken transcendence. Our own data and the ethnographic record more generally make it abundantly clear that, during the socialist period, people in rural and urban Mongolia took very seriously the "social relations of obligations" (Sneath 1993) pertaining to different nonkinship social networks inside or outside the formal system, sometimes to a point where these would trump all other demands, including those made by close family and kin. For while the parallel worlds described by Yurchak entailed "not simply close friendship, but kinship-like intimacy" (2006: 151), it would seem that these networks of friends and acquaintances took on an even more kinship-like nature in Mongolia than seems to have been the case in urban Russia, including many of the social relations of obligations associated with relations between kin. Indeed, while the parallel worlds of late socialist Leningrad were not purely nonpragmatic in Yurchak's account, there is reason to suspect that he may have overemphasized their idealist, cerebral, and noninstrumental aspects. Certainly, in late socialist Mongolia, the exalted sense of commonality, intersubjectivity and togetherness associated with "deep hanging out between friends" could not be detached from the more hard-nosed economic demands of which such relationships were—and are still today—part and parcel.[3]

With the collapse of the socialist state, we show in what remains of this chapter how the propensity for "fun" and "friendship" characteristic of socialist parallel worlds lingered. What disappeared was the "meaningless" monolithic state, not the multiple satellites of "meaningful" social relationships and interactions orbiting around it. More precisely, what happened was that, as the deterritorialized worlds were no longer contained by a state discourse and apparatus, they transformed or "reterritorialized" into some of the only stable anchors in a radically unpredictable sea of permanent transition. Without any hegemonic form to contain them, habits and values cultivated in formerly parallel worlds—antigoal-orientedness, immediate togetherness, and so on—lived on after the demise of socialism, like a citation severed from its semantic context, with serious and often downright disruptive ramifications for people's lives.

TRANSITIONAL LIVES

During 1991 and 1992, Mongolia experienced a severe economic crisis during which thousands of collective farms and factories were closed down, and people started moving around within the country and across its borders, desperately (but also enthusiastically) trying to find ways of earning money and making a "profit" (*ashig*) in the new age of the market. It was a time when social relations broke down. Many foreign "specialists" were returning to the newly independent states within the former USSR, and the Red Army soldiers abruptly left Mongolia, leaving behind a trail of broken hearts, scattered families and kinsmen, and disrupted socioeconomic networks. Above all, Kolya remembers those years as a deeply melancholic phase when time and again he had to part with old friends and ex-girlfriends at the railway station en route with their families to all corners of the former USSR. However, the period also marked the beginnings of a drastic transformation of previous socioeconomic structures and kinship-property dynamics for his parents as well as for the four brothers. In 1989 the family moved away from Amgalan to an apartment block in Ulaanbaatar's 15th Micro District, home to the Russian school that all the brothers had attended and a sizeable Russian community. He recalled the shock of experiencing the sudden shortage of supplies, and how he was served only boiled flour while staying with a Chechnyan friend who had come to Mongolia after completing Red Army service. People "would have to wear the same pair of shoes one year at a time, winter and summer," he said, and "they were hungry."

Over this period, the four brothers and other "half-Russians" gained the reputation—more than ever before—of being troublemakers who would rather drink, fight and play rock and roll than work for high enough grades to enter university. Almost all "half-Russians" had a tattoo on their knuckles—a dot surrounded by radiating lines—that illustrated how they belonged together, and they would talk spiritedly about how to unite, as in the 1980s, when everybody respected or feared them. Back then they were a small minority, Kolya explained (with more than a tinge of nostalgia), that was more aggressive than the Russians and—unlike Mongolians—knew how to stick together. He recalled how he and his schoolmates would bully and sometimes mug well-dressed Russian kids in the early 1990s, something no one would have dreamed of doing in the 1980s. Yet, at the same time, they faced increasing anti-Russian sentiment among Mongolians, even among former Mongolian friends, some of whom had

City neighborhood (2004)

joined the democratic movement, and also had to deal with the fact that many Soviet citizens were leaving the country. Not only did they have to say good-bye to beloved friends and girlfriends, they also had to cope with the crumbling of a Russian-speaking community that had defined many of their aspirations and values, whether based on socialist ideals or Russian styles of punk rock.

As for Kolya's parents, they naturally wanted to advise their children to the best of their ability; they were horrified to see what was happening around them, and yet they felt powerless and simply did not understand the new system. As Kolya once explained to an elderly woman,

> People around your age know traditions and know what is good to do and what is not. But our generation [laughing] . . . We were small during socialist times. We were small when democracy started. It seems that our parents were confused. When the new era started our parents were shocked and were wondering how to raise their children. Since 1990, we have just been doing things in our ways. We took care of ourselves.

Like many other worried and frustrated parents in Mongolia at the time, Kolya's parents were faced with children who—when taking care of themselves—either found it difficult to adjust to the transition or, as we shall see, had in a sense adapted *too well* to it by becoming involved in various forms of "speculation" and potentially illicit activities. Fortunately, their oldest son, Misha, a dedicated participant in the parallel cultures of the 1980s, seemed to be adapting well to the transition. He had many friends and was a very active person (*hödölgööntei hün*, lit. "moving person"). He knew no barriers, it seemed: he understood what money was all about, and he enjoyed the booming Ulaanbaatar nightlife and its many new opportunities for drinking. Eventually, as we shall see, he crossed one barrier too many.

Misha had done well during late socialism. After finishing military service in the early 1980s, he fixed water pipes and water circulation systems for a socialist organization located near the Peace Bridge in Ulaanbaatar until, like his father, he got a job as a welder, which involved extensive traveling in the countryside to install and repair machinery in the many small factories that could be found in all regions of Mongolia back then. In 1985 he met his wife and in 1986 he had his first son. While thus living a relatively ordinary and exemplary socialist life, and being quite happy with the system as it was (if it ever crossed his mind that this was only one possible political system, among others), he was also deeply engaged in the burgeoning parallel worlds in 1980s Ulaanbaatar. Apart from listening to rock music and taking part in the city's nightlife, Misha and his cousin, an artist, for example, would go to the central post office to sell beautifully painted copies of Buddhist masks to the few foreigners around, and later, in 1989, to Erdenet, the second-largest city in Mongolia, where they managed to sell one thousand pairs of Chinese socks to Russians.

At some point around the collapse of the state socialist order, however, Misha ran into trouble and spent a couple of years in prison; however, when he came out in 1993, he seemed to be adapting well to the new transitional economy. He got a job in his father's railway organization for a short spell but then, eventually, became the manager of a Russian company and "was always dressed well," as Kolya remembers it. Maybe he was simply unlucky again or perhaps, to paraphrase Ghodsee, he accepted that "those most willing to test the boundaries were the ones who found themselves on top" (2011: 13), but he soon ran into difficulties once more. The Russian company he was working as a manager for imported German goods from Russia and had taken a huge loan from the bank—MNT250 million!—when his Russian business partners suddenly disappeared to Russia with all of the money, including MNT250 million of the company's own capital. A total of MNT500 million was missing, and Misha was faced with serious charges of fraud (and perhaps some other problems with the law at the time), so he decided to take matters in his own hands and go to Russia to track down his former business partners. This was, however, easier said than done.

At Novosibirsk, on his way to Moscow by train, Misha met a group of Mongolian (ex-)criminal friends and got involved in a drinking party and a fight with a group of Russians who—unfortunately—turned out to be policemen. He was immediately handcuffed and kept in their custody all the way to Moscow and back to Novosibirsk, a trip that lasted at least four to five days. He was regularly beaten up on this trip, and the policemen took his money and confiscated his passport. All this time, Misha was desperately looking for a way to get out of his predicament. Approaching Novosibirsk, he managed to convince the policemen to stop the beating, remove his handcuffs and let him go to the toilet on his own. This was an opportunity that was unlikely to be repeated, and Misha immediately opened the toilet window and jumped from the running train. While not unhurt from the fall, he managed to walk all the way to Novosibirsk where he spent a week recovering, and then moved on to Moscow in renewed search of his fraudulent business partners. His search, however, was to no avail. He was lucky to track down a relative of one of the culprits—she worked in a bank—only to realize that these men were also wanted in connection with a major bank fraud in Moscow. Misha was told to forget about the money, and he now had no choice but to spend a few months in Moscow, where he met a group of traders and worked as a market vendor until he decided to go to Ukraine to pay his brother Lyosha a visit. Lyosha, the second-oldest brother, had left for Ukraine in 1987. He had only intended to visit his grandmother in Ukraine following a failed relationship with a Mongolian girl in Ulaanbaatar. Watching the Soviet television series *Sluzhu Sovetskomu Soyuzu* (I am serving the Soviet Union) in Mongolia, however, had also made him dream of entering the Russian Army, and in the end he ended up settling in Ukraine and doing his military service there.

Life was not easy in Ukraine in the early 1990s, and Misha found his brother working as a trolleybus driver, earning only a meager income on which he could just get by. This needed to change, Misha thought, and after having spent six months in a ramshackle house in a remote Ukrainian village, plowing the fields for old women (and being paid only in kind), Misha managed to get a job at a local market and, before long, had established a small business in which the two of them worked as carriers morning and evening while delivering bread and sausages to hot dog sellers at the market during the day. Eventually the two brothers began selling clothes at the market and soon became known as "the two Mongols." This went on for a year until Misha and Lyosha (who had found a wife and had a daughter in Ukraine) suddenly moved to Irkutsk. They claimed that they wanted to visit a childhood friend but, explained Kolya once, they were really escaping "certain death" in the form of a group of racketeers

En route to Russia (1996)

to whom they had refused to pay protection money at the market. Be that as it may, and to cut a long story short, their trip to the east was no less dramatic than the rest of Misha's travels. They managed to set up a business trading Chinese goods but had lost all their papers before arriving in Ulaanbaatar in the late 1990s.

The stolen money and the unpaid debt were only the beginning of a wrecked and fluctuating trajectory that was constantly propelling Misha into new but failed ventures. He was wanted in Mongolia but managed to hide from the authorities for two years while trading marmot skins with China, before being arrested in 2000. When he was released from prison in 2005, his life seemed for a time to have become more stable. He even succeeded in establishing a plumbing company with a partner using an investment obtained from a sizeable mortgage on his father's flat. Tragically, however, Misha died far too young from natural causes without having managed to pay back his father—and in the meantime his new business partner had disappeared off the face of the earth. He thus left behind a family immersed in both grief and debt.

Of the four brothers, Lyosha was perhaps the one who most lost his bearings during the transition. Sometime after returning to Mongolia from the Ukraine adventure with his older brother, he managed to get his wife and daughter to join him in his home country, at least for a while (they later separated and the wife and daughter settled permanently in Ukraine). He returned to an entirely different world from the one he remembered, and one in which he had few networks left. Indeed, perhaps due to the fact that he had left Mongolia before capitalism took root and the dramatic political changes of the early 1990s, Lyosha expected everything to be just like before. He failed to settle and find permanent employment, and generally seemed unable or indeed unwilling to adapt to the new economic constraints and possibilities. In a sense, his case resembled that of his parents. For him, too, life had "stopped," and he never came or wished to understand the "new rules" of capitalism (Ghodsee 2011: 185). With a striking resemblance to the "shocked subjectivity" identified in postsocialist Romania by Jack Friedman (2007), Kolya explained in 2006,

> The transition was very bad to people who were twenty-five to thirty years old. In the early 1990s, there was no employment, nothing. They didn't know what money was, or how to make money. Maybe they had a proper job in socialist times, but then the factories closed down. Maybe their parents didn't know what to do. They didn't know what the hell was happening to their children. I would hang around and drink, showing that I wasn't spending time properly . . . I'm now twenty-nine, and a lot of people my age are still only just managing to reach an OK level. Usually, it is all about background. Some families figured out what democracy was and started doing business. They knew what business was; maybe they used to be accountants in socialist times. If my parents or I had had some understanding of money issues—democracy and land—I could have done a lot of things in the early 1990s. We didn't know what property was . . . that you can privatize land . . . we never thought that a particular thing could be yours, that you would be owner. I don't know why, but I just didn't have this idea . . . Lyosha has no clue about how things are working, for he is still living in socialist times. He doesn't know how to be sneaky and lively—how to try to do everything to get money—because he is lost. He doesn't know what to choose. Of course, there are not a lot of ways for him to choose.

Both among the Mongolian and the Russian friends of the four brothers, stories of getting lost in transition were abundant. One Mongolian guy, for example, had been a fashion model during socialist times but—in the words of Kolya—at some point in the early 1990s, "He got lost and didn't know what to do" and became an alcoholic. The same thing—"suddenly becoming an alcoholic"— happened to two well-educated, English-speaking Mongolians Kolya used to hang out with on many mornings in a beer club in the early 1990s, while he was still supposedly attending school. Another friend had a law degree from National University of Mongolia but spent all his time drinking with friends, while yet another turned to the bottle despite having secured a good job. Among the minority who did have more or less permanent jobs, we detected a profound sense of dissatisfaction. We constantly overheard discussions about this or that person who "got by" by cleaning furniture or repairing computers but, it was then quickly added, "lives a boring life." Once Lars asked one of Kolya's friends why they did not just find a paid job, and he replied, "We can't work with our hands and legs. Our friends are all like that. All of them work with their heads. We don't want to be under someone." The only way to succeed for these and many other (especially male) members of the lost generation, it seemed, was to do "business" and hopefully make some quick and easy money on your own, as opposed to earning a regular salary from labor and "hard work" in a company or a state institution. Once Kolya convinced a friend that Chinese traders were buying up spiders for medical purposes, and the poor guy, eager to make the most of this opportunity, spent a whole day collecting spiders in his father's garage only to realize that Kolya had duped him.

WALKING THE TIGHTROPE
OF TRANSITION

According to Yurchak (2006), one of the great paradoxes of "the last Soviet generation" (that is, people born between the 1950s and the early 1970s) was that they turned out to be so good at profiting from the USSR's collapse despite—or perhaps even because of—the fact that they had been convinced that the state socialist order was immutable. Much in line with Yurchak, Misha explained this in the following way:

> Of course, those who used to listen to Western songs, those who liked that, those who understood its essentials, who understood what those films and songs were all about, for them it was much easier to live there [in the West]. They were already in the West. The ones who understood those songs had a difficult time in Mongolia, but they had everything in foreign countries, everything was ready. You do not need to change your life there. You just arrive, there is money, there is work. You just live there. You are the master of your own life. If you want to live there and take care of yourself, then just work and everything is yours. But during socialism, when we worked, we worked for the state . . . Yet, the people who liked those things [songs, fashion] and were into them, they were ready [for democracy/capitalism]. They began trading. They were the first [in Mongolia]. The punks were the pioneers.

However, while some punks may have been among the pioneers of capitalism, many people—Lyosha, for example—belonging to Mongolia's "last socialist generation" became a "lost generation" after 1990, who, far from having successfully managed the transition, became permanently disoriented. Nowhere was this postsocialist predicament clearer than in the case of Kolya's younger brother, Andrei. With very few and always rather unhappy exceptions, Andrei had never had a proper job since he dropped out of school in the mid-1990s. Based on the help of other family members and friends, he has, over the years, worked short spells as a welder, miner and tourist guide but never managed to hold on to a long-lasting job. Again and again, Kolya tried to help Andrei by making him obtain a driver's license or enter a language course, but Andrei never managed to see it through. In fact, Andrei *refused* to work because, as he always explained when a new job opportunity was brought up by us or other well-meaning people around him, "I just cannot take the salary seriously." Instead, he would often disappear from his parents' flat—or while working as a tourist guide—for days, spending all his time drinking with Russian or Mongolian friends. While there is a narrative, if rather a broken one, to tell about the other brothers, the repetitiveness of Andrei's life, or his almost apathetic indifference to making something of it, makes his story a very short one to tell.

Of the four brothers, Kolya was the only one who really "made it" during the difficult times of transition. While he certainly did not carry out much heavy physical labor, he did, at least at times, manage well in the somewhat transient world of postsocialist networking, and he began—for the same reason—to increasingly take on the position of an elder brother (*ah*) in the family. "If I say something, they will listen," Kolya often told us. "What can they say?" he would add rhetorically, implying that his older brothers' (lost) ways of life provided no font of authority. So, while Misha was lost in too much movement (and was finally imprisoned), Lyosha was stuck in too much stability. As for Andrei, his life was frozen into a kind of apathetic state of "hanging out," illustrated by the fact that he sometimes spent entire days in Kolya's car, while his brother went about his business. Kolya, on the other hand, had built up a certain respect and managed to earn a reasonable if highly irregular income. He was involved in the tourist business in the summer season, and did various odd jobs and small-scale trade and barter during the winter. Like his older brother Misha (and to some extent Lyosha, at least during the last years of socialism), Kolya could be described as a successful urban hunter who hopped and jumped with the irregular pulse of transition. He took up sudden opportunities as they emerged, while unconcernedly leaving old prospects and old dreams behind. Unlike Misha, however, Kolya managed to do so without being permanently lost in the new age of the market.

Things were not necessarily meant to turn out this way. The early 1990s had been a rough period for Kolya, too. He was prone to drinking, had lost almost all faith in life and, in his own words, "just wished that God would help him." One of his older brothers was in Ukraine and the other one imprisoned, so he

Best friends (1999)

was the oldest son at home and felt responsible for taking care of the family and, not least, for making his father proud. The father had dreamed of building a house, of the family living happily together, but he now felt that the family's pride was crumbling with the collapse of socialism and life as he had known it. Once he had even tearfully apologized to his children for the poor life he could offer them. Kolya had been torn between his inability to make himself useful and a strong desire to protect the family's honor and show his father that his life work as a welder and the head of the family had not been in vain. In 1993 Kolya's luck turned. He got a job for three months in a hotel and suddenly "felt what money was." He could now dress well and be accepted by the Russians—not least the girls—who had often ignored him. This was just the beginning of a long trajectory of successes—interspersed with several failures. Kolya was and remains today a sociable and charming guy who is better at meeting people and picking up languages than at calculating and planning, and during the 1990s, he began to meet foreigners (we were among the very first when he met us in 1995). Over the next decade or so, he found himself earning his money mainly through ad hoc tour guiding and translating and various odd jobs and dealings, and also for a while as an employee of two different NGOs. Later he would plan tours (although the "planning," as we saw in our Introduction, was often more haphazard than customers were allowed to see) and cooperate with a number of shifting local and international partners, with the help of his partner and her family. He even managed to establish a proper company in the mid-2000s and recently received a medal from the Mongolian state for the central role that he has played in developing the Mongolian tourism industry. While his income has fluctuated highly and his business has always remained somewhat change-able and uncertain, there can be no doubt, then, that Kolya, notwithstanding his many failures, has managed relatively well and built up a certain respect, both within his family and among his friends. In many ways, he has turned out to be the bright spot in the family that made his father proud.

So why did someone like Kolya "make it" and others not? What (if any) were the structures and the dynamics that rendered him the family breadwinner and shielded him from losing his way in transition, as his brothers (and his parents) had done in various ways and degrees? One way of engaging with such ques-tions is to hypothesize that, with the abrupt introduction of liberal democracy and capitalism, the parallel worlds that used to be characteristic of late socialist society were no longer contained by any hegemonic apparatus, and were free to run wild. The result was a sort of radicalized and distorted economy of favors from which some profited but many more did not. One certainly gets the im-pression that while, for some members of the lost generation, their familiarity with the old parallel culture made it easier to adapt to the new conditions (as Yurchak argues and the example of Kolya and other "success stories" also con-firms), then for many others the new postsocialist situation either (1) opened up *too many* possibilities (Misha) or (2) allowed them to keep on acting as the disinterested subjects of a redistributive state that no longer existed (Lyosha and Andrei). Thus understood, all of Kolya's brothers were equally lost in transition: one (Misha) because he had been adapting ("moving") too much, and the two others (Lyosha and Andrei) because they had become stuck in nonresponsive states of apathy. While, for the one brother (Misha), the creative liveliness of the parallel culture of the 1980s subsumed his life *entirely* a decade or so later, for the two other brothers, the same happened with the docile official culture of socialism. As we show in the remainder of the book, along with certain other members of Mongolia's last Communist generation, Kolya turned out to be more proficient than his three brothers when it came to hunting for open-ings in the postsocialist city. Kolya was able to walk the tightrope of transi-tion, on either side of which lurked the ever imminent danger of being pushed too much to one side (too little "movement") or the other (too much reckless "movement"). While subjecting himself to the relentless flow of transition by taking up increasing opportunities and ignoring time constraints, Kolya was at the same time—aided by well-connected partners and friends from West-ern countries—able to cut through its infinite networks of potential relations and carve out a space for himself and his belongings. When unable to perform this balancing act, he faced the risks of losing himself entirely to the disorder of "freedom and democracy" (like Misha), or, alternatively, folding completely in on himself as in the dead-party language of late socialism (like Lyosha and Andrei). This balancing act mostly worked, and he was able to contain the flow of relations via trickster-like translations between the *obshchenie*-based sociality of the former parallel worlds and the individualist logic of the new age of the market. Occasionally, however, the experiences of loss and hardship impinging on him from all sides caught up with him, and he was overwhelmed by a deep sense of uncertainty and crisis.

So, if one pattern emerges from our tale of the four brothers and their friends, it is irreducibly heterodox. While urban hunters like Kolya were apt at walking the tightrope of transition, others lost their bearings completely, for there was far from only one way of being entangled in transition; in fact, it was almost as if each and every individual constituted a transitional singularity of his or her own, whose specific and always unpredictable path was irreducible to anyone else's. (To be sure, comparable observations could be made about any given group of people at any given place and time, but there was still a sense that people's trajectories were especially idiosyncratic during times of radical change.) Indeed, a substantial proportion of men and women from Ulaanbaatar's lost generation seemed to be "jumping" from one area of social life to another in the way described. Crucially, this was occurring not only as a result of deliberate planning on their side but as a more or less incidental effect of events or processes that were beyond their control—notably the fact that *other* people were "jumping" as well.

Among many cases we can mention a young man, Bumochir, from the provincial city of Erdenet, who over a period of a few years worked as a small-scale market trader, used car importer and petty fraudster and conman (see Chapter 6), always moving between different venues in search of new and gullible audiences, a career that was eventually followed by a brief spell in prison. When we last spoke to him, he was working as a fireman but he was seriously thinking about becoming a dentist. Or take the following story, which by virtue of its idiosyncratic nature is quite representative of life during the first decade of transition:

My name is Namjildorj. I graduated university in Russia with a diploma to become an electrician. After I graduated, I got a [permanent] job [as an electrician] back during the socialist period. Then came democracy and people started doing trading. The 1990s were the golden years of trade, and I was moving goods from China to Russia. Then later the trading stopped and our culture and economy became strange for a while. No libraries and movie theaters were open. Things had become very strange. There was no work that I didn't do. I worked as Russian teacher, a store keeper in a publishing company, an electrician, a construction worker, and as a cook. Then I worked as reporter in TV, and now I work for a Chinese construction business as a manager.

More often than not, different and sudden changes in occupation and lifestyle involved engaging with an entirely new group of people; indeed, remarkably few social relations seemed to be "carried over" from one area of activity to the next as people seemed to start their "social networking" practically from scratch for every new rupture they underwent. Needless to say, this had profound repercussions for people's lives, and for how we as social scientists should study them. As we shall now show, nowhere was this more apparent than in the context of what might, for want of a better word, be described as postsocialist Ulaanbaatar's "informal economic" sphere.

TOO MANY FRIENDS?

With the collapse of the centrally planned economy in the early 1990s (which was the culmination of an economic reformation process set in train with the reforms of the late 1980s), both the size and importance of different socioeconomic networks, including informal debt arrangements, started to grow exponentially in Mongolia as in other places around the former Soviet Union and East Central Europe (Sneath 1993; Mandel and Humphrey 2002; Nazpary 2002; Ledeneva 2006; Pedersen and Højer 2008). Things had been different back in the "socialist age," as people called the period before 1990, often with more than a hint of nostalgia (see, e.g., Berdahl 1999; Todorova 2010a, 2010b). Of course, people also incurred debts during socialism (Sneath 2012: 467) and they did not always pay back what they owed. But, we were persistently told, most debts back then were more informal; if indeed these obligations could be described as debts, arising as they did mostly from nonmonetary transfers of favors (*ach*) or kin-like obligations (*üüreg*) among closed circuits of relatives (*hamaatanuud*), friends (*naizuud*) and acquaintances (*taniluud*) outside the official economic sphere. Usually, no tally was kept of such arrangements (Sneath 2012), and the return of such favors was often stretched out over very long periods, even years or decades, due to the chronically limited and irregular supply of commodities and services in the planned economy. If, say, I helped you get a home phone line via my good acquaintance (*tanil*) at the Telephone Authority, then you might return the favor ten years later as you helped me obtain a color television via your friend at the state department store.

After 1990, informal debt networks gained increased importance both because there were many more things to buy than before, sometimes at a cost amounting to several times a monthly or even an annual salary (such as cars or newly privatized apartments and plots of land), and because many people lost their jobs following the neoliberal structural adjustment reforms imposed by agencies such as the International Monetary Fund (IMF) and the Asian Development Bank (ADB), or because they found their salaries increasingly diminished by two-digit inflation as a result of these and more nationally specific deregulation and political-economic reform measures (Bruun and Odgaard 1995; Sneath 2002; Rossabi 2005). Although formal loans became available via banks, savings and credit cooperatives or microcredit schemes, the only possible source of credit for many was to buy on credit from shopkeepers or to obtain loans from relatives, friends and acquaintances or—as a last option—loan sharks, moneylenders and pawnbrokers (Højer 2012: Pedersen 2017).

As we have already indicated, friends were expected to help each other with almost *anything* at virtually any time. To recount a telling story, there were countless occasions when Kolya had to leave his partner (and later also his child) for several days at a time because he "had to" participate in "important celebrations" or other "urgent matters" or "acute crises" pertaining to his "closest friends'" lives, even if it was all too clear to both him and his partner that meeting these social demands and moral obligations would entail significant amounts of drinking. This included situations where Kolya would have preferred not to touch any alcohol, let alone partake for very long in what would sometimes turn into a several-day-long binge (on the obligations surrounding alcohol consumption within the Mongolian cultural zone, see Haas 2014). Indeed, it often felt as if hanging out with and assisting one's (male) friends was more important and morally imperative than being with one's family, a notion that was, by the way, actively promoted by the socialist state in the Soviet Union (Boym 1994) and, it is fair to assume, Mongolia. This made good sense during socialism, when the parallel worlds were not (supposedly) tainted by explicit instrumentality or state- or family-regulated obligation. With the collapse of socialism, however, a new situation arose: one needed one's friends as much as before (if not more) and could still make extensive claims and demands on them. At the same time, significant changes occurred in the composition and stability of kinship groups, friendship circles and social networks because of new job uncertainties, business opportunities and migration patterns.

Compared with the socialist economy of favors and its closed circuits of exchange partners, this new postsocialist informal economy involved much wider chains and networks of mutually indebted people, many of whom hardly knew each other, and occasionally significant sums of money. Indeed, for many people in Ulaanbaatar and other Mongolian urban centers, everyday life in the age of the market has increasingly involved an ongoing negotiation of multiple relations of debt (Højer 2012; Sneath 2012; Empson 2014; Pedersen 2017; Waters 2018). As David Sneath puts it, "Debt has become such a very common condition in rural (and urban) Mongolia that to be free of it is something of a dream" (2012: 466). In a somewhat similar vein, in her anthropological study of debt in Northeast Mongolia, Rebecca Empson writes that "although people are expected to repay their loans, few anticipate that they will pay them off within the time period allocated. Similarly, friends in Mongolia mention that due to the absence of a comprehensive credit-check system people live off multiple kinds of loans and repayment schemes, none of which are ever met" (2014: 190). In a similar fashion, we have also often been perplexed by the way our Ulaanbaatar friends seemed to keep on enchaining themselves in new networks of obligation with the same enthusiasm and trust that were such a characteristic feature of the smug parallel worlds of late socialism. Our ambition here is to explore the nature and effects of this paradox: the fact that Kolya and the others keep on lending others money, including debtors of whom they know only little, if anything at all.

With the transition to capitalism, then, the number of debt obligations and the size of loans both expanded dramatically, while the social expectations associated with debt and credit remained the same. Now these relations involved more people and sometimes much bigger sums of money, just as it became less common for creditors to fulfill the obligation to return the money allocated or the favors bestowed on them. The result was that "no one pays back what they owe," as people complained. In fact, as also noted in this book's Introduction, it seemed to be the exception rather than the rule that loans were paid back, certainly within the agreed time and to their full amount.

Consider the following example. In 1998 the father of one of Kolya's acquaintances was forced to move with his family from their flat in the 15th Micro District because of insurmountable debt. The man, who was originally educated as a teacher, had been employed in this capacity at a local school for several years and had borrowed a large sum of money from several sources with which to open a café. The business venture had failed to generate the expected profit, however, and he was soon defaulting on multiple loans. Eventually, one of his creditors—a private moneylender with connections to *atamans* and other strongmen—forced the man to sell his flat at an artificially low price, leaving just enough money for the bankrupt family to settle in a *ger* (the circular nomadic dwelling also sometimes known as "yurt" in English) in the compound of

At home in the 15th Micro District (1997)

the wife's relatives. While relatives and close friends were informed of the family's relocation to Ulaanbaatar's ger-suburbs, some of the man's acquaintances and patrons did not learn about it, at least not at first.[4] Perhaps not surprisingly, many of these happened to be creditors of the bankrupt businessman as well. Eventually, as the weeks and months passed, everyone managed to get in touch with their lost *tanil*, either because they were able to track his new whereabouts down via common friends or because he had made contact with them himself. Still, the relocation provided him with a useful respite from the claims made on him, which enabled him to pay off the remaining debts at a more manageable speed.

This story was far from unique (see, e.g., Chapter 5). In Ulaanbaatar, around the turn of the millennium, many debtors, as the pressure to pay back their loans gradually built up, left their premises—either for a few days or for weeks, months and even years—to take up new residence with relatives or friends somewhere in the sprawling ger townships that surround Ulaanbaatar's Soviet-style city center. While such relocations seldom enabled people to disappear permanently from their creditors' radar—after all, with a population of less than 3 million, one is seldom more than a handful of nodes in a social network away from a given person in Mongolia—they provided a breathing space that gave debtors the necessary time to obtain new loans and, let us not forget, trace down other debtors who owed money to them. Indeed, it was thus quite common for young or unmarried men especially, as well as women, to suddenly pack a bag of clothes and move to another place, sometimes with the intention of taking up new residence there, and sometimes in the hope that the new place could be used as a stepping-stone toward the next move, including, in not a few cases, back to where they had come from in the first place. Alongside credits and debts, such urban relocations often revolved around new and broken relationships in which former partners were left behind at the former place of residence and new ones were waiting at the receiving end—partners who might themselves move to and from somewhere and someone, be that a violent husband or threatening creditor.

In summary, debt and unstable relationships compelled people to move around the transitional city in certain ways, either because they were chasing debtors or escaping creditors, or (as was often the case) both at the same time (see also Pederson 2017a). In some senses, the circulation of loans, debts and collateral was more akin to the exchange of gifts in so-called gift economies than the flow of money in so-called commodity economies (Gregory 1982). As such, it could be described as a sort of *generalized debt*, to paraphrase Levi-Strauss' famous definition of the asymmetric circulation of prestations between more than two social units (1969).

We are, then, faced with another example of what we earlier called apparently irrational optimism (see the Introduction). The case of the four brothers and their equally "lost" friends and peers once again raises the question of how to account anthropologically for the fact that our friends and other members of Mongolia's last Communist generation kept on lending others money, despite mounting evidence that such loans were seldom paid back and never on time, and the fact that debtors were often hard to track down, because they had traveled abroad to work or had gone into hiding in the sprawling shantytowns of the postsocialist city. One possible explanation could be that, during socialism, people spent much of their energy circulating goods and favors within tight networks of friends. When the transition came, many members of this cohort continued treating commodities and money in a quasi-"gift-like" way, for this was how they used to exchange things and favors back in the socialist period, when it made little sense to keep a tally. Thus understood, what we have here tentatively referred to as "generalized debt" emerges as a reverberation of the *obshchenie*-infused habit of deep hanging out.

CONCLUSION

We have now shown how, in Ulaanbaatar in the 1990s, as the children and adolescents who used to belong to "the last Communist generation" turned into the first postsocialist generation, many of them became lost in transition. Some people did not want, and perhaps to some degree were not fully able, to take the "laws" of the capitalist market seriously and instead continued to exchange assets, money, things and favors as if they were still living in the parallel worlds of the past. Representing, as it were, a stronger and less intended version of common "ostalgia" (nostalgia for the socialist past), such people were living their lives within an anachronistic time bubble or, better put, a postsocialist heterotopia (Fehérváry 2002). This explains why Kolya and the others kept on behaving in a gift-economy-like way in contexts that were blatantly profit-oriented and in networks that were obviously not bounded, stubbornly putting valuables into circulation, incurring debts or making others indebted, as if the insulated friendship circles of late socialism's parallel worlds were still in place.

This may appear a strange way to end the first chapter of this book. Did we not just spend so much energy criticizing anthropology's penchant for "continuity thinking" (Robbins 2007) in the book's Introduction? And are we not precisely succumbing to this general fetishization of continuity within this and other disciplines when suggesting that socialism's finite parallel cultures sowed the seeds for the infinite networks of postsocialist urban hunting? In fact, in tracing certain habits of Kolya and his brothers back to the late socialist parallel culture that was such a key feature of life during the late 1980s, our intention has neither been to suggest these features of "socialist culture" somehow or another *led* to a culture of transition, nor are we saying that the two "logics" resemble one another. Rather, as we have tried to show, the big leap between the before and after of the advent of the transition is that the former subcultures of late socialism "jumped," in the course of only a few years, from having been contained within cast-iron state structures to becoming an omnipresent condition of life in the chaos of the early 1990s in particular. While previously present, liminality now "ran loose," so to speak, and it completely changed its character, as the previous exception suddenly became the rule after 1990. We also emphasize that, perhaps unlike in Yurchak's account (2006), very little could or can be *predicted* from this interpretation. It is true that a good many Mongolians—such as the punk pioneers—who came of age in the parallel cultures of the 1980s were, like Yurchak's informants, generally at ease with the age of the market and its cultural forms and also did relatively well economically. But a large number of people instead became chronically "lost," to use Kolya's phrase, in the unpredictable maze of permanent transition. Indeed, while Kolya—and, as we shall see in the chapters to come, some other urban hunters—managed to dance in tune with transition, others proved less apt (or lucky) when it came to "balancing" their hustling attitude with other concerns, and were thrown in all directions by the forces of wild capitalism.

Yet there are indications that the period of permanent transition and radical change peaked around 2000, if by this we understand not just the radical political-economic transformations that Mongolia was subjected to in the 1990s but also the social norms and cultural imaginaries of hustling and gathering that evolved alongside them. In particular, as we shall demonstrate in the next chapter, as Ulaanbaatar's markets became increasingly professionalized and monopolized in the years following the turn of the millennium, its different traders and vendors also became increasingly marginalized. Kin- and friendship-based modes of informal cooperation flourished, but at the same time, many traders faced mounting difficulties: they were unable to obtain stalls, the atmosphere in the markets was increasingly tense and violent, and company and state officials harassed them. By discussing this "colonization" of Mongolia's markets by the tacit norms and values of an emerging neoliberal or indeed post-postsocialist order (Buyandelgeriyn 2008), and the new hardships experienced by our friends, we shall see how the life chances of the lost generation only seemed to become narrower still.

Chapter 2 Market Subjects

> A teacher asks his class: What is a market economy? A pupil replies: I know this one! It's when a lot of people crowd into a fenced area, and push each other around, buying and selling stuff![1]

This joke was made by the Mongolian stand-up comedian Batsüh at some point in the mid-1990s during the height of perhaps the most radical structural adjustments and economic deregulations that the world has ever witnessed (Rossabi 2005; Buyandelgeriyn 2008). In many ways, the joke captures the central theme of this chapter, namely the extreme disorder and chaos with which Ulaanbaatar's markets were associated during especially the first decade after socialism, and the new and often transgressive and subversive economic subjectivities that were perceived to emerge in and around these quintessentially postsocialist sites. Based on fieldwork in Ulaanbaatar's two main markets, the Naran Tuul Market and the Harhorin Market, including conversations with vendors, traders and officials, as well as various written accounts (in particular Morris 2001 but also Anderson 1998), this chapter chronicles the gradual institutionalization, monopolization and professionalization of the city's markets from 1990 to 2005. In particular, we trace the transformation from so-called public markets (*ulsyn zah*) found in Ulaanbaatar in the early 1990s to what eventually became known as the city's "private markets" (*huviin zah*) at the turn of the millennium.

In so doing, we not only wish to contribute to ongoing debates about the nature and specificities of capitalism in the former socialist world and beyond (Lampland 1995; Bockman and Eyal 2002; Dunn 2004; Thelen 2011; Dunn and Verdery 2011) but also to problematize widespread assumptions, within the academy and beyond, of what a private market, a public commons, and their mutual relationship are. Much has been written about the new subjectivities created through consumption in the postsocialist world (e.g., Sampson 1994; Humphrey 1995; Patico and Caldwell 2002; Fehérváry 2002; Humphrey and Mandel 2002; Berdahl and Bunzl 2010). Less attention, however, has been paid to what happens on the other side of the counter, among the people selling the goods (but see Konstantinov et al. 1998; Hohnen 2005; Humphrey and Skvirskaya 2009; Chuluunbat and Empson 2018). This "indifference of researchers may mirror the perspectives of traders themselves—that this activity, widespread though it is, is considered unimportant and not a serious economic sphere" (Konstantinov et al. 1998: 731). Perhaps, as Michael Stewart asks, is it because we "think that we know intuitively what a market is, [that] surprisingly little has been written about how [people] actually think about their activities as traders" (1997: 11)? It certainly is telling that, barring some notable exceptions (Carrier 1997; Hertz 1998; Spyer 2000; Zaloom 2006; Miyazaki 2013; Bear et al. 2015), anthropology has not shown much theoretical interest in trade, traders, and the pleasures of trading itself.

It is just this gap in the postsocialist literature that we wish to fill in this chapter as a means of further developing and substantiating this book's argument about the nature of social life and social agency during times of radical transition. In doing so, the ambition is to turn the hitherto dominant focus on different kinds of postsocialist consumer subjects on its head by focusing instead on the new trader subjects in Mongolia's markets at the turn of the millennium. The sprawling markets of Ulaanbaatar, we show, were absolutely vital to the construction of new economic affects in 1990s Mongolia, but the subjectivities forged were not just consumer identities. Instead, we argue that Ulaanbaatar's markets were a sort of capitalist laboratory site that gave rise to the formation of new "economic sentiments" (to use one of Adam Smith's terms; see Rothschild 2001) for the people trading and selling goods. Indeed, as we demonstrate in this chapter, one of the most striking features of life during Mongolia's first decade of transition was that prevailing conventions concerning the nature as

well as the degree of "social embeddedness" of economic practices was fundamentally challenged if not reversed in the sense that haggling and other practices associated with Ulaanbaatar's markets were perceived as *more* (and not, as
conventional economic sociology and anthropology would have it, *less*) social
than all other sites and arenas.

   In addition to seeking to contribute to a classic discussion within anthropology, the chapter also continues our ethnographic thematization and mapping
of urban hunting that began in the previous chapter. Whereas, in Chapter 1, the
primary protagonists of this exploration were Kolya and his brothers as well as
their mostly male friends from the same lost generation, in what follows we turn
to a differently positioned (and differently gendered) subcategory of this cohort,
namely the predominantly female market vendors and stall owners/managers
populating Ulaanbaatar's urban market. Although, as we shall see, this group
of hardworking and industrious vendors and traders could hardly be described
(let alone understood themselves) as hustlers to the degree that Kolya and many
of his friends could, the forms of agency and subjectivity at display in their
economic practices nevertheless represented a specific subspecies of what we call
"urban hunters." Nowhere was this more evident than in the now defunct Black
Market in North Ulaanbaatar, which for many years was not just the biggest
but also the most (in)famous of its kind in Mongolia. Let us therefore begin by
outlining the history of Ulaanbaatar's so-called Old Black Market, partly based
on recollections of various traders who used to work there and partly on our
own memories of the place from visits we made to it together and separately
between 1995 and 1999.

THE "BLACK MARKET," 1990–1999

In 1990 a sprawling and crowded urban market gradually became established
on a hectare of wasteland known as Denjiin Myanga in Ulaanbaatar's northern
outskirts, near or at the former so-called barter central, which the authorities had
grudgingly allowed to exist since the late socialist years.[2] During the first decade
after socialism, the Black Market (or Northern Market or Denjiin Myanga, as
it was also known) was unrivaled in size and popularity in Mongolia. In 1998, a
World Bank team found that "according to estimates provided by the management, by . . . officials, and by the Ulaanbaatar City Administration, between
60,000 and 100,000 people . . . visit the market on its busy days, Saturday and
Sunday, half as many on weekdays . . . On a given day . . . about 150 containers
of imported goods serving as their own storefronts, and about 800 other vendors
occupying official spaces [can be found there], in addition to the hundreds or

Looking for a new deal (1996)

thousands of vendors, inside and outside of the fence, that do not officially pay their fees. Management estimates that the average container sells out in 1–2 weeks. If this estimate is accurate, then between seven and fifteen thousand containers flow through the market in the course of the year" (Anderson 1998: 28).

Especially during the first and most wild and chaotic years of the Black Market's existence in the 1990s, the composition of the vendors who spent their days working—or, as some of them called it, "standing" (*zogsoh*)—at the Black Market was extremely heterogeneous if measured according to standard sociological parameters such as age, gender and class. Based solely on the handful of people we have talked to who used to work there, those early vendors' backgrounds ranged from unemployed workers and newly migrated herders who had lost their livestock to natural disasters, over-pensioned army officers and former university lecturers and professors—one youngish trader even had a PhD from the University of Moscow. However, over the course of the 1990s, female vendors gradually came to dominate Ulaanbaatar's markets, at least in numerical terms (turnover was quite another matter—most of the biggest traders seemed to be men). Figures are hard to come by, but a survey by the International Labor Organization from the late 1990s suggested that more than 70 percent of the people working in Ulaanbaatar's markets were women (Morris 2001: 65). These numbers are supported by our own data from the capital and more rural contexts (Pedersen 2006), and they also seem to apply to the suitcase traders (*ganzagyn naimaachid*) who still fill the trains from Mongolia to Russia and China.[3] To some extent, this over-representation of women in the informal sector may be explained by the fact that trading in many postsocialist contexts especially during the early years of transition was—and in some contexts still is—a low-status activity associated with people in inferior social positions (Humphrey 2002a; Pedersen 2007a). Certainly, this is how a lot of Ulaanbaatar men whom we spoke to about these matters perceived things, including the four brothers whose life and predicament we described in the last chapter.

However, according to some female traders themselves, the high proportion of women in the markets had a different explanation. As Düütsetseg, a woman of around thirty, explained, Mongolian women have stronger willpower (*setgeliin tenhee*) and are more active (*idevhtei*) than the sad (*gunigtai*) and dispirited (*setgeleer unasan*) men, who became shocked (*shokond orson*) by the transition (cf. Friedman 2007; Pusca 2007) and prone to drink. As Saraa, an Ulaanbaatar-born woman in her early thirties who began her long career as a *zahynhan* (marketer) trading vodka at the Black Market in the early 1990s, explained, "Of the people who do business, between 60 and 70 percent are women. It is because the Mongolian men are bad these days. Really bad. All they ever do is search for their own happiness. They need to find someone who can feed them with money, so they can keep on buying vodka and wine. They beat their wives a lot. For this reason Mongolian women work a lot. Many of them divorce and become heads of households. Women think about how to make a living, about how to feed the kids, I think. The men cannot live up to their responsibilities."

The visitors to the market were not just underemployed migrants from Ulaanbaatar's periurban slums, although they were certainly strongly represented. Indeed, it seemed as if everyone frequented the *Har Zah*: nomadic pastoralists came from the countryside, sometimes hundreds of kilometers, to buy ger components, saddles and flour (as well as shoes, clothes and bags of candy); upwardly mobile middle-class people came to buy microwaves, electric kettles and Tupperware for their recently furnished American kitchens as well as stationery for their English-school-attending children; and even members of the upper classes (politicians, sports stars, tycoons, top officials, etc.) could occasionally be encountered in search of mahogany furniture, marble tiles and gold-rimmed spas for their two-story houses with double garages in the city's new gated communities.

Little wonder, then, that practically any Mongolian person of middle age or older can tell a personal, and often amusing, anecdote from the heyday of the Har Zah, which became renowned, among locals and foreigners alike, for its unbelievably crowded, dusty and pickpocket-filled paths, and, above all, its total lack of organization. Possibly due to its periurban location and unclear ownership status (like all land in Mongolia at the time, the hectare constituting the Har Zah was nominally owned by the state, but the latter only seems to have enforced its laws, regulations and rules very sporadically at this particular site), the Har Zah had few permanent stalls or other fixed structures during the first years of its existence. "The place was utterly mad," recalled Saraa, the former vodka trader. As she went on to explain, gesturing excitedly with an unlit cigarette in one hand and a cell phone in the other, "There weren't stalls or anything. We just stood there holding up the labels of the *spirt* [pure distilled alcohol], and sold everything we had. People would surround us on all sides, and buy like crazy." A trader from Erdenet added, "The market was not specialized back then. People simply constructed a little fence and put up a stall, and got together some things to sell."

All this suggests that, during the first years of its existence, the Black Market, or at least significant parts of it, was literally created from scratch every morning, as vendors would scramble to pick the best spots to sell their wares. In that sense, one might see it as a prototype of what a market (and more generally a country in transition) was imagined to be like in the minds of many Mongolians back then, namely a place where all existing social rules and moral codes are suspended, and where people and things are, for this reason, liable to sudden, unpredictable and often violent transformation (see also Pedersen 2011). Because the Black Market was considered public property (*ulsyn*) until 1998, when it was sold to a prominent tycoon, it was in theory accessible for nearly a decade to anyone who wanted to sell something—although, as one might expect, this was far from always the case in practice. Not everyone had to fight every morning for a good place to sell their goods at the Har Zah; in fact, the best trading spots were already assigned to certain people beforehand. On the one hand, there were bosses (*bossuud*), leaders (*lideruüd*) or "strongmen" (*atamans*) who, through various combinations of riches, connections and physical coercion, or at least the threat of it, had secured themselves de facto control over strategic locations in the market. On the other hand, some vendors were fortunate enough to be related to, acquaintances with, or lovers of "big people" (*tomchuul*), and next to whose trading spots they were therefore allowed to line up their wares. Take, for instance, Saraa. This is how she described her way into the Black Market in 1992:

> In 1992 and 1993, people's livelihood seriously deteriorated. Everything became very hard. Most people had no idea of how to do business. But many bosses knew, so

they grabbed money from private companies and state organizations and went abroad to buy containers full of goods, which they started to sell. As they became richer and richer, us normal people became poorer and poorer. Some of the richest *tomchuul* were in the *spirt* business, which was prospering very well. The shops had only just been privatized, so people did not know that vodka was not supplied directly from factories anymore. The *tomchuul* bought big quantities of *spirt* [from contacts at the factories] at a reduced price of around MNT50 per bottle, and then added to the price of the *spirt* when they sold it. And they sold several tons each day—often, it would be gone in one hour. It really was extremely profitable!

It was around this time that I started selling *spirt*. Since the ninth grade I had been working as a secretary for a company during the school holidays. I was paid MNT2,000 [per month] for this, a really big salary in 1992, and I had been saving up money and thinking a lot about what do to with it. Then a friend told me that it was good to sell vodka, and by accident I got into this business. I had never thought about selling things at the market. I was thinking about going to university.[4] My life was very comfortable; I did not know anything about this world, about vodka and business. I was so embarrassed in the beginning! But then I noticed that people made a lot of money. So I continued and became very interested in doing business.

After some time, a young man approached me. "I have been observing you, standing here selling vodka. You are very hard-working, carrying big loads on your narrow shoulders, never taking a break. Are you from a very poor background?" To which I replied, "No, no, I just like doing this more than working," and he was very surprised! [Laughing] He asked, "Why are you doing this kind of business? You are young and beautiful, and yet you want to stand at the market selling *spirt* like the old *damchin* [speculator] ladies do? In the future you may become a bad person, just like those filthy ladies. You'd better give me MNT120,000 and I will take care of this for you." Back then, that was an awful lot of money, so I was afraid of giving it to him, of losing it. But eventually I gave the money to him, for which he bought 20 bottles of *spirt*. Ah no, perhaps it was forty, I don't remember. He now instructed me, "OK, you, now grab the bottles and go [to the market] and sell them. Eventually, the money will come. It will increase, you will see."

He was a big boss. He helped me because I was such an odd sight. No one could tell I was a trader. I had just turned eighteen, and yet I was carrying big sacks, standing all day selling vodka. We never had any relationship and did not become friends. He felt sorry for me. He was a good-hearted man, full of compassion. "You are my *düü* [junior relative]," he said. He became my *ah* [senior relative]. Because people knew this, they respected me. No one put pressure on me. I easily sold one hundred to two hundred and sometimes even one thousand bottles a day. Box after box. And made a lot of money. So I am very grateful to him.

In 1995 the Mongolian government sold the Black Market to the prominent Ulaanbaatar tycoon Saihansambuu, and in 1997 the *spirt* trade was banned following numerous incidents in which poor people had reportedly gone blind or even died from drinking cheap vodka procured at a bootleg market. These developments, in combination with the increasing institutionalization of capitalism in Mongolia as a whole, added a certain sense of organization to the Har Zah. Still more permanent stalls were constructed, and an element of systematization and organization was introduced in terms of the allocation of trading sites and the costs and taxes levied on market vendors. Such was the demand for vendor space at the market that "soon after [its] privatization, a secondary market for . . . counter spaces developed, demonstrating the popularity of this particular hectare of land. The counter spaces were rented for 200 togrogs per day . . . Some renters would stay the night and resell the spaces the next day for ten times as much" (Anderson 1998: 29).[5] Still, during our visits there in the second half of the 1990s, it remained unbelievably crowded, with no room for expansion to accommodate the growing numbers of guests and vendors due to the densely populated ger slums surrounding its walled perimeter. It was, as so many people told us with so many different words but always with same basic message, a wild (*zerleg*) place, where all sorts of people sold all sorts of goods. As Kolya once remarked, "The market is the only place where everyone goes, rich or poor, powerful or lost."

But precisely what was it that made the Har Zah so "wild"? Exactly what were the processes and characteristics that made this and other markets into unique realms, as if governed by their own sets of rules—or perhaps lack thereof? In what follows, we seek to establish a theoretical framework for gauging these and related questions by revisiting certain old debates in economic anthropology and the wider field of political economy about the nature of capitalism and the market.

THE FUN OF TRADING

When Morten asked Saraa to explain what being a trader at the Old Black Market was like, she smilingly recalled that her (educated, middle-class) parents had strongly opposed her trading adventure, which they considered to be a disorderly and even immoral activity, raised as they (and everyone else from their generation) were within a "socialist discourse [where] the marketplace . . . was depicted as the lowliest position, and the [people] who inhabited it were perceived as the diametrical opposites of the 'New Man' and 'New Woman' of the communist future" (Konstantinov et al. 1998: 730). "It is making you careless, scruffy and mindless," Saraa's parents complained, while conjuring up images of their oldest daughter "drinking the vodka she is selling" like the "terrible speculator women" (*muuhai damchin avgai*) who used to hang around outside Mongolia's markets in the early 1990s, slowly depleting their own stocks of "bad vodka." The problem was also the haughty looks and critical remarks she received from visitors to the market, "especially from girls of my age. Women of my background don't like selling at the market, in fact, they really hate it."

And yet, while Saraa had done well at school and had worked in a "real" (*jinhene*) job as a company secretary, trading gave her an experience of excelling at something few are cut out for. As she explained, "Not everyone can do this kind of business. It is hard work talking all day long. People only buy from traders who talk nicely. Doing so is extremely unnerving (*nervnii*). It makes the mind work hard, and the body. Every evening, I come home having carried tons of wares only to return to the market early next morning. No one else in my family can do this. Not even if they received a million MNT. They would just waste the entire amount. Perhaps I was born with this talent. I am very active (*hödölgööntei*), that's why I can do it."

Indeed, if there was one thing that Saraa repeated again and again in her fond recollections of the "crazy" days at the Old Black Market—in addition to how "damn profitable" trading *spirt* had been—it was just how personally rewarding if not pleasurable it had been. As Saraa herself liked to put it, "It was just *so much fun* at the market back then!" After which she said, in explicit (but respectful) defiance of her parents, "Working at the market is good and satisfies me. I like it; it is good fun. And I go for the things I want. I don't do what my father and mother tell me. I do things in my own way. So I started doing business." It is precisely this liberating and joyful dimension of trading we would like to focus on here, for it appears to convey something crucial about the phenomenology of trading as a social and existential practice that has been partly overlooked in the existing anthropological literature on postsocialist and postcolonial markets.

"Fun," "passion," "pleasure" and "addiction"—these are, in fact, among the most prevalent expressions figuring in the anthropological literature on traders and trading. Consider, for instance, Frances Pine's study of female traders in rural Poland (1999), where she compares the new identities that emerged at village markets after socialism with the ambiguous traits of the trickster figure. "It is in the performance of the deal," she writes, and "in the active agency of the dealer, that the liberating individualism . . . is most clearly seen" (1999: 58). In fact, as Pine goes on to suggest, it is almost as if "the performance of 'the deal' takes over the body, words, and space of dealer" (1999: 5). Another good example, this time from outside the postsocialist world, can be found in Rita Astuti's account of a female fish trader from Madagascar's Veso people. As Astuti notes, it is the woman's "alertness—detectable in her brisk movements, her tense posture, her searching eyes, her unfailing concentration even when she pretends she is not paying attention—that makes her such a successful trader" (1999: 91). Alas, the trader's family does not share her own "rarefied aesthetic pleasure from the calculations, the suspense, and the power of her imagination" (1999: 93). In fact, they complain that the market has become like an "addiction" for her, distracting the wife and mother's attention from expected services within the extended household (1999: 92).

Strikingly similar ideas—that trading is dirty, disorderly and subversive but also fun, liberating and rewarding—can be found in many postsocialist settings. At first glance, this flies in the face of a cornerstone of neoclassical economic theory: the assumption of an (ideal) market constituted by rational, instrumental and "perfectly competitive transactions between buyers and sellers sharing complete market information . . . [so that] an efficiency in production is achieved" (Dilley 1992: 347). Indeed, this is the standard anthropological critique of economic paradigms: that they are premised on an abstract and reified model of human economic life that overlooks or ignores the fact that concrete market actors and capitalist practices always form part of specific social, cultural and political contexts (e.g., Gregory 1982; Gudeman 1986; Parry and Bloch 1989; Humphrey and Hugh-Jones 1992; cf. Mauss 1990). Yet, one might ask, does this default anthropological stance always allow for an ethnographically satisfactory account of people's concrete market experiences, such as Saraa's and other Ulaanbaatar traders' cherished sense of individuality, freedom and fun? For despite—or perhaps because of—the fact that scores of anthropologists and sociologists ever since Karl Polanyi (1957) have repeated ad nauseam that the economic is always "embedded" within wider social, political and cultural structures, there still seems to be a tacit assumption that a core of pure economic calculus somehow exists autonomously from whatever society surrounds it. After all, is this not what the concept of "social context" entails—the implicit and in our view unwarranted assumption of a nonsocial kernel of reality that is ontologically encapsulated from its social shell?

In other words, precisely *because* they have been so eager to emphasize that people are always bound up in moral economies, many so-called substantivist economic anthropologists unwittingly appear to have subscribed to the neoclassical premise that, hidden deep down in everyone's soul and often lurking behind a mask of moral and collectivist discourse, there is a core of ice-cold, proto-capitalist instrumentality (for a good example, see Parry and Bloch 1989). Thus we find that many anthropologists writing about economic life—often against their better will—have compartmentalized the personhood of traders and other market personae into an instrumental, disembedded individual (the trader as trader) on the one hand, and a bundle of social roles on the other (the trader as wife, villager, etc.) (for exceptions, see Carrier 1997; Spyer 2000; Zaloom 2006; Miyazaki 2013). Here, in the trader's personhood largely tacit anthropological assumptions about human agency and the nature of the social reach their limit and come close to collapsing. Accordingly, but without wishing to revert to so-called formalist anthropological models of economic life, it therefore seems to us that we may need to look more carefully at what certain liberal political economists are actually saying about the emotive and affective dimensions of trading and other economic practices precisely in order to be able to take more seriously the postsocialist market and its uniquely subversive but also irreducibly social nature.

As Emma Rothschild has convincingly demonstrated (2001), Adam Smith entertained a quite different and much more psychologically subtle, complex and nuanced image of the trader's "mind" from what he is commonly accused of (or celebrated for) today. Thus, in Smith's theory of economic sentiments, "commercial judgements are a combination of reasons and sentiments. Mercantile policy, in the Wealth of Nations, is . . . a matter of 'jealousy' and 'animosity,' inflamed, from time to time, 'with all the passionate confidence of interested falsehood.' The projectors, or entrepreneurs of new ventures, are men of 'imagination' and 'passion' more than of 'sober reason and experience'" (2001: 27). Accordingly, Rothschild explains, Smith's ultimate aim was not to discover the laws of market exchange ("the invisible hand") but to write an "inner history" of economic man, a philosophical project that required "a dizzying sequence of nouns to denote psychological conditions" (2001: 37). All this suggests that Adam Smith may not be the reductionist par excellence that he is often accused of being by critical social scientists who are (rightly) skeptical of neoclassical economic universalizing presumptions about "economic man." Far from corresponding to the stereotype of austere rational human calculators, who in the moment of trading are particularly detached from their surroundings, Smith's market subjects are instead characterized by an *exalted awareness* of the surrounding environment and by rapidly changing emotional and imaginative states (recall here Pine's depiction above of a trader in rural Poland: "the performance of 'the deal' takes over the body, words, and space of dealer" (1999: 5). This hyperalert, almost possessed self gives a more accurate and subtle idea of how trading is experienced in postsocialist contexts than classic substantivist economic anthropology allows for, given its tendency to reify "the economic" as an encapsulated realm of instrumental individual agency by insisting that economic decisions are always "constrained" by wider societal contexts. Certainly,

Smith's concept of economic sentiments as assemblages of affects corresponds much better to Saraa's and other traders' accounts of all the passions and dangers at Ulaanbaatar's markets in the 1990s.

This affective quality of certain "economic sentiments" complements dominant anthropological accounts of market subjectivities in capitalist contexts. For it is not only the widely reported antagonism and sometimes violence against traders in postsocialist contexts that is at issue—a response that often arises from a perception that traders personify the escalating inequality and excessive individualism associated with the collapse of the modernist welfare state (Ferguson 1999; Nazpary 2002; Humphrey and Mandel 2002). As Nancy Ries put it, "Trading, the predominant (and most visible) economic activity of the day, feeds into the image of moneymaking as an activity by which . . . owners make 'piles of money' without working" (2002: 294). Something else also seems to be at issue, namely the fact that certain traders in postsocialist contexts, both in their own ways and from the perspective of others, are imbued with a hypersocial and almost occult ability to break down boundaries between self and other, between the private and the public, and between commodities and persons. Thus understood, instead of adhering to the stereotype of autonomous, introspective, calculative individuality, trading in the early years of postsocialist transition involved an intensified engagement with the surroundings, both in the social sense that skilled traders almost collapsed the boundaries between their own and their clients' selves "to the point of clairvoyance" (Simmel 1995, cited in Astuti 1999: 91), and in the material sense that certain traders, as we shall see in Chapter 6, were perceived to be invested with the capacity to become at one with their goods.

Could it be that, in their capacity as pioneers in the emerging market economy, people like Saraa were feared for being *too* socially embedded, as opposed to, as in the classic substantivist explanation (Polanyi 1957), not socially embedded enough? It certainly is rather telling that many traders would highlight their social skills as one of the main reasons as to why they were succeeding at the market in comparison with others. For example, after explaining how "men always fail in business since they are prone to drinking and fighting and thus always lose their goods," Naraa, a hard-working vegetable trader in her late thirties, for example, bluntly stated that she divorced her "inept" (*ovsgoogüi*) husband because "he was not up to much and couldn't talk to people. He was not able to give and get things from people. He was unsociable [*zojig*]." Could this hypersocial and superembedded nature of postsocialist trade help us to better understand why traders at the Old Black Market were feared and loathed by other people? To address this and related questions we need to continue our

Market vendor (2007)

microhistory of Mongolia's markets and describe the changes they underwent over the second decade of transition. Only then can we fully answer the question of what was so "dangerous" but also "damn fun" about being a market trader in Ulaanbaatar in the early 1990s.

THE NARAN TUUL MARKET

In 1999 the Black Market was relocated to a newly established and so-called professional site in the southeastern corner of central Ulaanbaatar. The Naran Tuul Market, as the new market was called, quickly took over the reputation of the Northern Market (which remained in operation but in a diminished form) as Mongolia's main market. From that point on, if someone said, "I am going to the Black Market on Sunday," it would automatically be assumed that this person was referring to the Naran Tuul Market. In comparison with its predecessor, however, the new Black Market was much more spacious and much better organized. There were numerous security guards and sometimes even police present, plenty of breathing space (at least outside the most crowded trading spots at the intersections between central alleys), every stall was carefully numbered and registered with the administration, and imposing, panoptic watchtowers were positioned at each of the market's corners. Much as with the increasing number of gated communities that have been built in Ulaanbaatar's southern end since around 2000, upon entering Naran Tuul one was given the impression of entering a site of extragovernmental sovereignty—an arena that was politically and economically disjunct from—and yet at the same time embodying an ideal version of—the surrounding world.

Many Ulaanbaatar residents seemed to take a good deal of pride in the Naran Tuul Market in the first years after its opening. As several people explained to Morten, Naran Tuul was much more sophisticated (*bolovsrongui*) and specialized (*töröljsön*) than any market the country had seen so far. In particular, people liked to point out that many "Chinese goods of bad quality" were not considered worthy of being sold at Naran Tuul ("for this you have to go the Harhorin Market" [in the western part of Ulaanbaatar], as one trader smugly noted). Having said that, Ulaanbaatar was even back then home to a tiny elite for whom the Black Market—as indeed any outdoor market—was an embarrassing reminder of the country's economic backwardness: a dirty, dusty and dangerous venue located comfortably out of sight from the main shopping avenues and malls of the city center, where poor and diseased people "are forced to get their shoes muddy to afford the goods they need," as one man complained. Still, this tiny minority of "new Mongolians" (*shine mongol*) notwithstanding, it is clear that, around the turn of the millennium, the Naran Tuul Market was the ultimate trading place in the country. It was the ideal market against which all other markets were compared.

Alas, Naran Tuul's vendors were not as satisfied with the new markets as its guests. While they enjoyed the spaciousness of the new venue, and the fact that increased focus on security (*hamgaalalt*, lit. "protection") made it possible to crack down on the pickpockets and thieves, they also lamented that they were subject to "all sorts of pressure," which had not been there at the old market. "What do you mean by that?" Morten asked in surprise. "Surely, people must have been under a lot of pressure at the old Har Zah, from *atamans* and other strongmen, who were asking them to pay for their 'protection'?" "No," several people insisted, "there was nothing like that at the old market." Unusually for the region, it would thus seem that there were no rackets operating at Ulaanbaatar's black markets in the 1990s, certainly not in the organized "mafia" form known from post-Soviet contexts (Nazpary 2002; Volkov 2002; Ries 2002). To be sure, there was fighting galore at the Har Zah, and thieves, hooligans and other unsavory types aplenty, just as vendors made recourse to whatever means available (cheating, threatening, flirting, etc.) to secure a good spot. But for the traders who moved with the market to Naran Tuul, this only further highlighted the fact that "at the Old Black Market, everyone did what they wanted themselves. No one was 'eating' us from behind."

"But surely," Morten asked people at Naran Tuul, "if you compare the new market to the Old Black Market, don't you prefer this one?" A male flour trader answered,

> When I look around Ulaanbaatar, I can see that many people's lives are getting better. But it is not like that here. A lot of traders have gone bankrupt. It was too difficult. Eventually, the tariff was lowered a little bit. There was no other way for the market. Many containers stood empty. Back then, we used to pay MNT260,000 to 270,000 per month. Now we pay MNT200,000 per month. Sometimes 195,000, sometimes 200,000. And then 10,000 for each container. And then the carriers (*gürüüshig*), who receive MNT60,000 to 100,000. And the rest is ours. It is difficult. We need to make at least 10,000 per day just to cover our costs.

Indeed, a significant shift occurred in the late 1990s with respect to fees and tariffs imposed on the people working in Mongolia's urban markets. Whereas "the fees for the counter spaces at the [Old Black] market were originally [set] by the Ulaanbaatar Price Consensus Commission" (Anderson 1998: 29), this price mechanism was later scrapped due, it is fair to assume, to the continual pressure for deregulation of the Mongolian economy by successive Mongolian governments and various Western donors and international institutions such as the International Monetary Fund and the Asian Development Bank (Rossabi 2005). In addition to the rising fees paid to the market for rent of counter spaces, vendors also had to buy their counter spaces from other vendors through dealings "on the side," and they became subject to growing tax demands from the government during this period. Again, following standard neoliberal policy practice, the responsibility for collecting these taxes was "outsourced" by the state and put in the hands of the managers of each market (Anderson 1998: 30). This in turn further strengthened the hand of such "market officials" (as many people called them, despite the fact that they were simply managers employed by market owners) over market vendors, who found it increasingly hard to distinguish between what they experienced as the growing greed and graft of both private and state agents:

> Before we used to use our own containers, and make up to MNT400,000 per month [in profit]. We used to pay MNT50,000 as a deposit, that was all. Now it is not like that. There are many officials above us. It is Saihansambuu [the then owner of Naran Tuul]. He has sponsors. There is a big conspiracy behind all this. A sort of mafia. There are a lot of people behind Saihansambuu. They took this place by force. It was

not supposed to be used for the purpose of a market. Initially, they did not get permission. But then there was a conspiracy, a lot of things were going on from behind, and the market was built. Many people's property was at stake. They [realized that they] could make big money, and pushed the new venue through.

"Very well," Morten persisted, "but could you not then invest in a new container for around 500,000 and find a new and better place, where you and some of the other flour traders could do business together?" At this point, the man took a long, deep breath (of the sort one makes when struggling to remain patient with a seemingly deliberately ignorant child) and said slowly with a tired voice, "Not possible. Where would that place be? We would never be given the permission. There is no way they would allow that. The market is the market [*zah l bol zah*]." But what does this actually mean, that "the market is the market"? On the face of it, we recognize here a familiar capitalist reification of "the market" as a thing in and of itself imbued with intrinsic forces that cannot, and should not, be tinkered with (Carrier 1997). And yet, at the same time, there is also something unfamiliar about the perception of the market harbored by this trader and his peers. While "the market" as depicted above does come across as an immutable, objectified thing-in-itself with its own nature and logic, it emphatically does not live up to the expectation that many policy makers and ordinary people (in Mongolia as well as elsewhere in the world) have of a capitalist market. On the contrary, Naran Tuul in 2003–2004 stood out as an exemplar of everything that a real market is *not* supposed to be—that is, an arena for the competitive exchange of scarce resources, where free agents who are all subject to the same transparent rules and laws make rational instrumental choices based on equal access to information about supply and demand. Evidently, this was not what the flour trader from Naran Tuul meant when he remarked, "The market is the market." Rather, for him and other Ulaanbaatar vendors, "the market," far from defining an equitable space for fair competition, served as an instrument for continual and increasing exploitation by people of wealth, power and connections over people without any such economic, political or social capital: "The market is stripping us who are working here. This is the big difference [from before]. We pay huge fees and are forced to work extremely hard. Some people sell just enough to buy food. In the old days, the Black Market was not like that. Back then, the market belonged to the public [*ulsyn*]; it had not become private [*huviin*] yet."

What statements like these point to is a peculiar inversion of what is conventionally associated with "public" (state-run) and "private" (capitalist) domains as opposite poles on a sliding scale of freedom, liberty and autonomy

(Wheeler 2004: 216; cf. Dilley 1992); when listening to what the flour traders and other vendors were telling us, it became clear that the old "public" (*ulsyn*, lit. "peoples'") Black Market was remembered as *a freer place* than the new and "privatized" (*huviin*) Naran Tuul Market. While vendors criticized the latter for its excess of rules, restrictions and "pressures" (*daramt*) imposed by state and commercial actors, they remembered the old market as a site of individual self-determination, limited regulations and a general lack of outside interference—that is to say, as a textbook ideal of a capitalist market! Yet it was not just the state and the managers that made the Naran Tuul Market less "free" and "public" than the old market from a vendor perspective. As the 1990s came to a close and with the consolidation of Mongolian capitalism around the turn of the millennium, another development took place at Ulaanbaatar's markets, which was perceived simultaneously as a source of pressure and of protection by the people working there. We are referring to the informal institutionalization of the vendors themselves into various "families," "communities" and "peoples." In order to describe this development, let us now return to the case of Saraa and her long and memorable career on Ulaanbaatar's market scene.

MARKET COMMUNITIES

Saraa stopped selling *spirt* at the Old Black Market in 1997 when the authorities banned this trade. After a couple of years at home "watching TV and taking care of my sister's children," she set up a flour and rice container at Naran Tuul in 2000. As "staples satisfying people's natural needs," flour and rice did not carry the same negative connotations as her former alcohol trade had done, so this time Saraa enjoyed her parents' full blessing as well as moral and economic support. Saraa was doing well, she thought. She was part of the "flour people" (*gurilchinguud*), who enjoyed high status in the market's hierarchy—"we are only surpassed by the electronics guys," she said proudly—and was also making quite good money: "In recent months, between MNT800,000 and 1 million."

However, the first year at Naran Tuul was not easy for Saraa. Not only had she had to deal with demands from market owners and the authorities, she had also experienced sustained "pressure" (*daramt*) from the other flour traders, who had done everything they could to exclude her from their "community" (*hamt olon*) and to ensure that she knew about this exclusion. From the moment she tried to buy her first sacks of flour and rice from the wholesale sellers, having bought a container and secured a trading spot at Naran Tuul by responding to a newspaper advertisement, it became clear to Saraa just how

much of an outsider she was. For one thing, she stood out from the other vendors by working "alone" (*gantsaaraa*). "Practically all the vendors at Naran Tuul
have relatives [*hamaatan*] and family [*ah düü*] at the market," she explained,
and then began recalling how fraught with difficulties her entry into the flour
people had been. For three months, she was subjected to constant verbal abuse
and angry glances—"sometimes, they even threw things at me when I had my
back turned"—while trying to steer a course through a sea of lies. No one at
Naran Tuul—neither the other flour traders nor the wholesale traders or so-
called changers (*chyenjüüd*, sing. *chyenj*) hanging out at the gates—would tell
her anything about how things worked at the market (at what price to buy
flour wholesale, how to arrange for its transport, how to deal with the market
management, etc.). Meanwhile, the other traders teamed up and began selling
their sacks of flour at below the going rate in order to force her into bankruptcy.
Yet she persisted, relying on her self-confidence (*bardam zan*) and gift of the
gab (*amny figürtei*) to strike good deals with influential wholesale changers (or
"leaders," as she called them), while building up a growing group of loyal customers. And, ever so slowly, the hostility from the other flour traders withered
away, as did their "artificial lowering of prices." Still, it was to take a year before
they fully welcomed Saraa into the *gurilchinguud* by "opening a bottle of vodka
and congratulating me on how stubborn I had been."

Saraa's story is by no means unique. With the possible exception of the
poverty-stricken and dispossessed sellers of cigarettes, matches and candles
who occupy the ground around the market entrances, most vendors at the big
markets belonged to "communities" or "peoples," defined by the category of
goods they were selling. While it is hard to generalize about the nature and level
of organization of these groupings, being part of a vendor community clearly
served several purposes from the point of view of the individual vendor, ensuring that, as elsewhere in the postsocialist world, there was a move toward a situation whereby each market stand would "be held by the same people or families
for several years and [be] treated as [a kind of] monopol[y]" (Konstantinov et
al. 1998: 733). For one thing, as the example of Saraa illustrated, each vendor
community performed an excluding function toward potential new vendors
who wanted to have a bite at the trade, and thereby served to hold down the
number of vendors of a given type of commodity within a given market. Another important function of *gurilchinguud* and other "peoples" was to provide
mutual protection from strongmen (*atamans*) and other unsavory types hanging around the markets. As Otgonbaatar, a twenty-three-year-old lad running
a shoe stall at Harhorin Market, said, "We look after each other here." Indeed,

that was what *hamt olon* was all about: belonging to a group of people whom one could trust and have fun with. As Otgonbaatar reflected,

> If I were to write a book about the age of market like you are, it would be about how good a time us marketeers have. It is a lot of fun to spend the day here. It really is a cozy place to be because you make friends with people from the other stalls. We also celebrate things together, like birthdays and the Lunar New Year [*Tsagaan Sar*]. Mongolian people have always had communities [*hamt olon*] like that.

The fact that vendors like Otgonbaatar saw themselves as belonging to a community involved in shared pastime activities (playing cards, etc.) should not lead one to think that there was no competition, antagonism or conflicts between them. Otgonbaatar made it very clear that, were it not for his partnership with his friend who was running a shoe stall at Naran Tuul, he would not have been able to make a proper living from being a marketeer. "The two of us protect each other like brothers," he explained. "We even call each other 'brother,' which gives us less trouble. People won't try to cheat you when they know that you are not alone, and that you have information about the prices at the other markets." Otgonbaatar and his "dry brother" (*huurai ah*—the term widely used for nonkin senior males with whom one engages in long-term relations of obligation and protection)—also helped each other to procure new shoes to sell, taking turns traveling to Beijing or Ereen on the Chinese border in search of new models at a sufficiently low price in the big wholesale markets there.

Such collaborations were by no means restricted to Otgonbaatar and his companion. During the time that Morten spent at Ulaanbaatar's markets in 2003–2004, both Harhorin's "shoe people" to which Otgonbaatar belonged and the "flour people" at Naran Tuul of whom Saraa was a "member" were largely composed of such collaborations, of varying size and organization and which, to some extent, appeared to be modeled on existing social and cultural hierarchies from rural (pastoralist) and urban (workplace) contexts. While each stall tended to be affiliated with a single household (*ail*) headed by a senior man (*ah*) or a senior woman (*egch*) who was responsible for setting prices, procuring goods from China or big changers and directing the activities of the juniors (*düü*)—it was common for vendors from several stalls to team up to perform various tasks and responsibilities. Such informal "vendor corporations" (as we might call them) typically comprised two or three stalls run by relatives or friends who belonged to one "people," and whose stalls were situated next to or close to one another. They would then share different costs (transportation fees, bribes, etc.), pool their labor when needed and generally try to be of mutual assistance by, say, referring customers to each other (see also Chuluunbat and Empson 2018). This calls to mind the organization of Mongolian pastoralists into more or less durable and formal encampments (*hot ail*) comprising single households, called *ail*, in various and fleeting combinations of kin and nonkin (Szynkiewicz 1993; Park 2003; Humphrey and Sneath 1999).

It is important not to convey an overly neat picture. While Naran Tuul Market certainly came across as superorganized, formally as well as informally, in comparison with the Old Black Market, it would be mistaken to simply map what happened there onto social, cultural and economic forms associated with Mongolia's nomadic or socialist past (forms which, in their own right, were hardly as stable and orderly as they have sometimes been described in the literature). The reality on the ground was still fluid and (seen from the outside) pretty chaotic. For example, the person(s) turning up to work at a stall among Naran Tuul's shoe people would often change on a daily basis (one day it would be the wife, the next day it could be the husband, and at the weekend both might well be present at the market, accompanied by children, family or friends), just as it often seemed unclear or unsettled as to which vendor corporation might be indebted to whom in monetary and other ways (S. Gundersen, personal communication).

Nevertheless, while the different vendor groupings varied greatly in size, composition, status and durability, and while some traders also worked on their own and such trader collaborations were malleable to outside influences and internal changes, it is possible to discern a number of patterns in the organization of market vendors and the way in which their mutual liaisons were experienced and talked about. Without in any way wishing to overstate the historical continuities, the patterns called to mind social and cultural forms associated with past Mongolian traditions, both nomadic and socialist. In particular, for each category of goods for sale (shoes, clothes, etc.), one could identify several vendor corporations, typically comprising an *ah* (senior male) or *egch* (senior female), presiding over several junior or newcomer vendors or stalls. Scaling up, each such constellation of vendors was named a certain "people" after the commodity they sold, and each such community would together perform ceremonies (as for the Lunar New Year) and celebrate public holidays (such as Women's Day). At times, these vendor corporations grew so big, formalized and influential that they controlled the price of the commodity sold by the vendor community as a whole, in which case their figurehead would be known as the *boss*. But, more commonly, vendor communities comprised several vendor corporations engaged in fierce competition over customers, influence and profit, while at the same time always being ready to act as a collective in the face of impinging

Clothes people (2007)

external threats, such as when a newcomer like Saraa with no links to the "flour people" tried to set up shop.

THE DARK SIDE OF THE MARKET

A wide assortment of marginal personae could be found at Ulaanbaatar's markets around 2004. It is impossible to provide an exhaustive list of them (after all, extreme margins often tend to harbor extreme multiplicity; Das and Poole 2004). Still, with the enthusiastic aid of Kolya and his friends (who found this an unusually exciting ethnographic exercise, possibly because it reminded them that there were, in fact, many people in the city who were much more impoverished and dispossessed than themselves), Morten put together a list of the more or less officially recognized, and more or less derogatory, terms used for its population of "market outcasts": *chyenjüüd* ("changers"), *atamanuud* ("strongmen"), *hogiin garuud* ("dumpster people"), *taranshaany hüühdüüd* (street kids; lit. "underground pipe children," referring to one of their primary dwelling spaces), *karmany hulgaichid* ("pickpockets"), and, occupying the lowest status of all, *arhichid* ("alcoholics").

While one may have been able to come across some of these very postsocialist personae in all the different parts and neighborhoods of Ulaanbaatar, its markets were one of the few places where one could find all of them together, and in sometimes large numbers. Indeed, as we shall now substantiate, this is in many ways what the postsocialist market has always been: a sort of gathering point for all the multifarious new economic subjectivities that came into being with the advent of permanent transition in 1990. Yet the crucial difference between Ulaanbaatar's market scene after the turn of the millennium and the "crazy" black markets of this and other Mongolian cities in the early 1990s was that the transgressive subjectivities described at the beginning of this chapter had become confined to particular spatial domains. The Harhorin Market was a case in point.

Everyone, including its own traders, seemed to agree that, in comparison with Naran Tuul, the Harhorin Market was the less attractive and less prestigious of the two. As Otgonbaatar admitted, "Generally, people prefer to go to Naran Tuul. It is bigger and better organized." "Still," he continued, "people from the 1st Micro District [a big neighborhood in the westernmost part of Ulaanbaatar dominated by badly maintained concrete apartment blocks from the 1970s] use the Harhorin Market a lot, just as many of the vendors, like myself, are from around here." Another reason it was sustainable to have a second, general-purpose market like Harhorin in Ulaanbaatar was that it could be described as the city's "market wheel" (Gell 1999)—that is, the fact that Ulaanbaatar's different markets attracted more visitors on certain days of the week than on others. According to various seasoned market customers, this was not just because Mongolian markets tend to be most crowded on weekends and those days when the weather is neither too hot nor too cold but also because every market is closed one day per week (in Naran Tuul's case, this was Tuesday, which in turn made that day a particularly busy one at Harhorin).

Morten's first visit to Harhorin Market happened to be Kolya's virgin trip to this market. The experience was to leave a lasting impression on both of them. Situated on the southern side of a derelict socialist-era footbridge across Ulaanbaatar's traffic artery, Peace Avenue, the market was (and still is) confined to a gated compound of a few hectares, surrounded by low-rise office and apartment buildings. This location meant that the market was rather more crowded than the newer and more spacious Naran Tuul, but its narrow and often roofed paths were still organized into neat lines of straight alleys and numbered stalls, affirming that here was another "professionalized" market that had come to revolve around multiple satellites of vendor communities with a central management at the market's core. Nevertheless, they were both left with a clear sense that Harhorin was "tougher" than Naran Tuul, both in the highly visible sense that a higher number and concentration of alcoholics and other "market outcasts" could be found there (see below), and in the more invisible sense that more gray, shady and semi-illicit activities seemed to take place in or around its premises. Outside the gate, for example, Morten and Kolya noticed several groups of people with each individual carrying a sign with the inscription "buying and selling gold" (a highly conspicuous and in many ways ultradangerous business in postsocialist Mongolia, about which more appears in Chapter 5). Another reason why life seemed to be literally teeming around the main entrance to the market was the presence of bands of roaming street children and other groups of beggars (often with physical or mental disabilities), along with ultrapoor vendors with single items for sale (a glass of blueberries or pine nuts gathered in the forest, a worn-out tool, a handful of cigarettes). The general sense of roughness prevailed inside the perimeters of the market. Unlike at Naran Tuul, where "security" (*hamgaalal*) was a priority for vendors and management, several fights took place at the Harhorin Market during Kolya and Morten's first visit, including the severe kicking of a drunken woman by a group of teenagers for what seemed to be no purpose other than perverse entertainment. Still, the relative lack of control in comparison with its competitor also meant that there was more entertainment at Harhorin, including various groups of musicians and singers (many of whom also seemed to suffer from different disabilities) performing and busking in front of the food stalls in the market's midst.

Only after they had spent several hours at Harhorin did Kolya and Morten notice a tiny doorway behind a row of containers with teahouses in the market's southeastern corner, leading to a "secret" compound. Happily unaware as to what they had entered, it took awhile for Kolya and Morten to grasp the sinister reality in front of their eyes. Initially, they thought they had bumped into a large group of drunks who were seated, as such groups often tend to be, along the walls with bottles in their hands. It was only after a while that they realized that everyone inside the compound was a market outcast. Small wonder that everyone seemed to be staring at them, a few with an angry expression in their eyes but most with sheer surprise. Clearly, this was not a place that ordinary people would ever enter if it could at all be avoided. The stench of the place was overwhelming, with its nauseating mixture of human and dog excrement and rotting food products oozing from the bags of waste collected from the main market by its inhabitants. The size of the compound was perhaps half a football field, and it comprised virtually nothing—no stalls, no chairs, and hardly any people—barring its eighty to one hundred market outcasts, who only seemed to be there because they had nowhere elsewhere to go. Some clustered in groups but many were alone and lying down, either because they were unable to stand or because they were asleep. A few were clinging to things they were desperately trying to sell—food items, packets of cigarettes, pieces of clothing—that they had either stolen or otherwise scavenged from market vendors and customers outside. As Kolya later said, "As soon as they manage to get hold of another MNT200, it will immediately be spent on more vodka."

Övgöntiin ("the people of the *övgön*") was the term used for the dispossessed outcasts inhabiting this microcosmos within Harhorin Market. *Övgön* literally means "old man," but in this context, the term referred to a brand of Chinese vodka sold in Mongolia in the 1990s, whose one-hundred-milliliter plastic bottles had been shaped like an old man. As the cheapest alcohol available, *övgön* was very popular among poor people back then but was eventually banned in Mongolia, as its high concentration of ethanol had apparently made several people blind. The name had clearly struck a chord in the postsocialist imagination, though, and *övgöntiin* was sometimes used to denote the most dispossessed, alcoholic and homeless of Ulaanbaatar at the turn of the millennium. "Look," Kolya whispered, unable to hide his disgust and yet also fascination, "you can always recognize the *övgöntiin* by their swollen, purple faces. The vodka is destroying their liver—it is mixed with all sorts of poisonous substances."

Here, in what some people called the Valley of Drunks (*övgöntiin höndii*), outcasts from the bottom of Mongolian society had been banished to a nightmarish netherworld that was no-go territory for all other people, whether traders or customers. Indeed, the vendors seemed to prefer to act as if it were not there. When Kolya and Morten asked some of the shoe sellers about the compound and its people, the curt reply they received was delivered with downcast eyes and a dismissive voice: "Those people are there because they are drinking all the time." Unlike the rest of Harhorin, the Valley of Drunks had few if any permanent material, social or indeed any other structures or frameworks of reference, and no organization or regulation whatsoever. A steady flow of pickpockets and beggars exchanged their latest spoils into directly consumable items from the warring bands of street children and waste scavengers who compete to service the former's needs.

"It is the dark side of the market," a visibly shocked Kolya remarked (his voice literally trembling and his body shaking) as he and Morten departed the Valley of Drunks through the same gate by which they had entered. Kolya later added, after the two had stood in silence on the footbridge observing the market, unable to take their eyes off the corner they now knew to be the Valley of Drunks, "I think I am going to take my younger brother to this place one day soon. It would be good for Andrei to see this with his own eyes. 'Look, this is what is going to happen if you and your friends keep on drinking and drinking the way you are now doing!' I am going to tell him. It really is shocking—did you see their faces and their eyes? It is like a nightmare in there." And so it truly was, at least (or even) from our smug perspective at the elevated bridge. People of both sexes and all ages (but predominantly what appeared to be middle-aged men) were constantly moving around, getting into arguments, fights and scuffles for what seemed to be no other reason than they had accidentally happened to bump into another. Along the walls or in its midst, individuals were squatting to defecate amid what seemed to be sleeping elderly and children, again apparently following no discernible logic, principle or pattern, subject as they seemed to the law of pure contingence, which Hobbes famously defined as the main characteristic of "the state of nature." The sight was almost unbearable to look at, and yet it was at the same time hard to take one's eyes away from the scene, amenable as it was to introspection about the state of one's own life in comparison to the lives of others. "Try to look at that man down there," Kolya whispered to Morten while gesturing at a hunchbacked drunk with a desperate look in his purple face. "Perhaps he came to the city some years ago, full of hope for a new life. Now, he is just lying here, drinking all day."

The Valley of Drunks, we suggest, was Ulaanbaatar's wild capitalist market par excellence at the turn of the millennium.[6] With its population of ultramarginalized and deprived market outcasts, the Valley of Drunks served a crucial purifying purpose for all the less marginalized individuals and "communities" of established traders, spatially and symbolically affirming what people like Saraa and Otgonbaatar felt to be their proximity to Mongolian society as a whole. As a young Mongolian university professor remarked when Morten told him about his visit to Harhorin, "Yes, 'outcast' is an apt term. For these people are outside the law. If, say, the two of us are drunk on the street, the police will put us in detention. But not the *övgöntiin* because they are drunk all the time." No one expected the police or anyone else to come to the assistance of the abject people in the Valley of Drunks in case they needed it: they were left entirely to their own devices. Somewhat paradoxically, the Valley of Drunks thus emerges as one of the most "public" or "free" (in the transgressive sense of this word associated with the "crazy" and "chaotic" Black Market of the early 1990s) marketplaces left in Ulaanbaatar around the turn of the millennium. Comprising a heterodox residue of market outcasts not included in the "private" neoliberal order, the Valley of Drunks affirmed people looking in at it, zoo-like, from the outside about the omnipresence and violence of market capitalism and about their own degree of safe distance from its most extreme excesses. Not unlike the medieval desert border zones to which trading between Mongolia and China was supposedly restricted,[7] the "public market" thus took the form of a liminality in Mongolia after 1990: an "absolute margin" where social and moral norms could be suspended beyond recognition.

A decade or so later, when these markets had been increasingly regulated and monopolized, it had become confined to certain "margins within margins" (or we could say, markets within markets) like the Valley of Drunks—an interpretation substantiated by the fact that the Mongolian term for market (*zah*) also means "border," "edge" and "margin" (Bawden 1997: 171–72; Wheeler 2004).[8] During Mongolia's first decade of wild capitalism, this absolute margin or liminality paradoxically took center stage in the form of the "crazy" affects associated with the Black Market. But as the transition gradually became more of a known fact of life and thus also became imbued with at least a limited degree of predictability, the social and existential limbo of the original "public" markets also was pushed to ever more marginal locations and peripheral concerns of increasingly institutionalized, professionalized and monopolized markets, giving birth to atrocious zones of pure abandonment like the Valley of Drunks, with its clear associations to other anthropological accounts of the late capitalist and neoliberal governmentality and its perverse excretion (Biehl 2005; Povinelli 2011). But again, this is not to say that Mongolia's markets—or markets writ large—are inherently "less social" than less marginalized places in closer proximity to dominant social, political and moral discourses. Rather, as we have tried to show in this chapter, trade constitutes a distinct mode of human relatedness that is *not less social than but rather is social in a different way* from relations between people in domestic or other moral economies. Indeed, as we have tried to demonstrate, it was this intrinsically subversive or asocial—or, more precisely, *extrasocial*—quality that made places like the Old Black Market and the Valley of Drunks so "wild" and "dangerous" but also, in the case of the Old Black Market, so "exciting" and "fun."

In light of everything that we have presented in this chapter, it should now be clear that, at some point around the turn of the millennium, Ulaanbaatar's markets had become so integrated into the wider structures of the still more established Mongolian capitalist economy and the general (neo)liberal order that they ceased to represent a subversive margin posing a threat to the dominant moral economies of the household and nation-state. What had once demarcated a transgressive "public" arena, beyond the reach of any "private" sovereign, had become colonized by the gradually solidifying social, cultural and political structures and asymmetries of postsocialist society as a whole. Thus, as we have seen, even though working as a market vendor was hardly the biggest dream of people like Kolya and his friends, being a *zahyngan* (marketer) did not carry the same negative stigma as it had in the early 1990s, when virtually every person present at the Black Market was automatically perceived as partaking in amoral "speculator" activities. In fact, from 2000 onward, to work as a vendor at a "professional market" like Naran Tuul could be quite a respectable thing to do, at least if one were fortunate enough to belong to a big and powerful "community" such as the "flour people." Yet, in this process, the traders themselves became marginalized from their own invention. Kin-and friendship-based modes of cooperation flourished, and yet many vendors faced difficulties: it was nearly impossible to obtain stalls, and the atmosphere was tense and sometimes threatening and violent, as company and state officials harassed vendors, especially the ones occupying the more unofficial fringes of the official marketplaces. In that sense, the cases of Saraa and Otgonbaatar illustrate an all-too-familiar scenario from postsocialist transitional contexts, namely that people's possibilities begin to narrow as the pace of change gradually starts to slow down and new structures, asymmetries and hierarchies begin to appear.

Hence one could see the developments in Mongolia's markets that we have sketched in this chapter as a sign that the speed of transition had begun to slow down around the turn of the millennium, and it could, as such, be viewed as part of a wider "post-postsocialist" shift in this and neighboring countries (Buyandelgeriyn 2008). There is certainly no doubt that, in comparison with the frantic first decade of transition, the years after 2000 were characterized by a gradual stabilization, sedimentation and institutionalization of social, economic and political forms across Mongolia. This (relative) sense of stability, order and predictability was the result of several factors, including the showdown of economic reform following the resounding victory of the (formerly communist) Mongolian People's Revolutionary Party in the 2000 elections, and a general improvement of Mongolia's economic growth and prospects that was to culminate with the mining boom in the second half of the same decade. Nevertheless, the novel subjectivities and the new economic forms associated with the "wild" markets of the early 1990s did not disappear with the professionalization of Ulaanbaatar's markets: far from it. As we have presented in this chapter and show much more in the ones to follow, the city was still home to a multitude of stigmatized and dispossessed personae around the turn of the millennium. But a purification had taken place, concentrating the transgressive subjectivities once associated with all traders in the early 1990s around groups of market outcasts restricted to particular social and spatial margins.

CONCLUSION

This chapter's history of Ulaanbaatar's markets seems to have left us with the two kinds of market subjects who represent common but opposite "modes of life" in times of transition ("common" because the situation was clearly quite different for the relatively small and extremely privileged category of market "leaders," "bosses" and "managers," who are beyond the scope of this chapter and indeed this book as a whole). On the one hand, we have the market outcasts, who are forced to live from one moment to the next, socially and spatially imprisoned as they are to fight over the sorry spoils left over from the endless movement of the Mongolian market wheel. And, on the other, there are established vendors such as Saraa and Otgonbaatar, who, by virtue of their being embedded within different social networks and wider moral economies, were spending so much of their energy and imaginative capacity in trying to plan ahead, manipulating spatial and temporal horizons, the scale and extension of which seemed to become slightly more truncated with every day that passed.

However, as we also stressed in this book's Introduction, our focus on urban hunting is not meant to restrict itself to a specific group of people in Ulaanbaatar in the year 2000 or indeed elsewhere in the postsocialist world. Rather, the point is to capture a plethora of different kinds of urban hunters and hustler-gatherers—or perhaps more accurately different degrees of urban hunting and hustler-gathering—a continuum of persons and practices that at the time of our fieldwork spent some (for some much, for others much less) of their time dealing and dreaming in Mongolia's age of the market. Of course, there were also other market subjects at the time of our fieldwork. Noteworthy among these were Kolya and his brothers, as well as other members of Ulaanbaatar's lost generation—people, that is, who remained permanently suspended between the subjectivities of market outcasts and market vendors, respectively. We focus our attention on these other urban hunters in the rest of this book.

Chapter 3 Elusive Property

While sitting on the train on their way from Ulaanbaatar to the Mongolian-Chinese border in 2006, Lars was discussing land ownership with his two traveling companions from the city, Hulan and Kolya. Hulan seriously considered buying a plot in Gachurt, a village close to Ulaanbaatar. Land, or more precisely the urban and residential land that makes up only 2 to 3 percent of the total land area of Mongolia, had just been privatized for the first time in Mongolian history, and the buying and selling of land loomed large in the imagination of small "investors" and urban hunters like Hulan and Kolya. The office for the registration of property in Ulaanbaatar was as bustling as its black markets. Land was a serious issue—the latest addition to "the market"—and stakes were high.

Kolya had recently acquired a plot of land himself, and Lars' other traveling companion, Hulan—a single mother and an enterprising, if not particularly successful, businessperson who had already once tried her luck in the land business—was now planning to invest in yet another parcel of land. At some point in the conversation, Kolya and Hulan turned to the problem of how to "secure" (*hamgaalal*) one's property, and they both claimed that it was critical to fence one's land off after buying it. This sounded utterly strange to Lars' ears, and he felt the need to correct his ignorant friends, who were obviously still newcomers to the world of capitalism. "Of course you don't have to fence land off," he said. "They've introduced cadastral surveys to document land ownership, so why would you put up a fence," he continued, "if your ownership is already legalized?" But his two Ulaanbaatar friends insisted: "It *is* necessary to fence off the land," they claimed. The fourth person in the train compartment, a middle-aged Mongolian man, now came to Lars' help. He corrected his younger traveling companions and concluded that land ownership simply had to be legalized. Paperwork and a cadastral map was all that was needed, he said, and Lars was content—if only for now.

The older man, who—like Lars—did not believe (or want to appear to believe) that erecting physical fences had anything to do with exercising proper rights, was talking from a purely legal point of view. He was "speaking law" —and he and Lars were expressing a belief in the possibility of creating strictly defined property relations between distinct land parcels, final documents, cadastral maps and individual owners, a world where fencing was *just the outcome* of what *already* existed as defined by law. Lars soon came to realize, though, that it was he who was the ignorant one, and that his liberal legalistic way of thinking was not in line with the much more complex practices of land ownership in Ulaanbaatar, where fencing was part of a property's elusive and emergent nature, rather than just an expression of what already existed according to legal documents.

Hulan had learned this lesson the hard way. Some time ago, she had managed to obtain a plot of land in one of Ulaanbaatar's suburbs. There was no unused land left to settle on in this particular district, so Hulan had had to buy a piece of land from an elderly couple who had already settled in the area some years ago. The elderly couple did not legally own the land (and were therefore not in possession of any official papers), but this did not pose a major problem to Hulan, who related that "documents are not important. They [the elderly couple] owned that place. They lived there for two years, so I knew it was true that they had that place. I bought a guaranteed place that later would be put on the map. They [the 'authorities'] would give me permission." So, while she used the expression "owned" (*ezleed avchihsan*), what Hulan had actually bought was a not yet fully realized ownership, at least in the legal sense, and when she took the plot over, she—like all other landowners—needed to secure it. She obtained a loan from her brother, managed to get friends to repay some of their debts, and spent several months' salary buying enough timber to build a fence.

Fencing new land (2006)

The timber was stored in the compound of her new plot's neighbors while she waited for the construction of her own compound to begin. She explained:

> I decided to hire somebody and they started to construct the fence. After some time, they wanted their salary. I didn't know better and gave them the entire amount. And then, although they had only done half of the work, they just left. I didn't know them. They were men, alcoholics. They wanted to drink. They just did half the job and left. After a while I asked someone else. I gave them a small amount of money and we did some work, and after a while only the last side of the fence was left to be done. Then my wood was stolen from the neighboring family's enclosure. I asked my friend's younger brothers to help me and gave them some money. I watched them work and even did some of the work myself. I even hit my finger and they made fun of me. Finally we finished. In the end, I needed MNT50,000 [about USD40] to make the entrance. I had the door made, but could not find anyone to install it, so I kept it in the other family's enclosure. Months have passed. Maybe I will lose that place. When winter is coming people will steal the fence and use it for firewood. I have not been able find a family to live there [to look after the plot]. I did find one family but they moved. In front of my land there is a family who sort of looks after it. Still, some wood disappeared . . . it is still empty, there is no family living here.

This passage illustrates how Hulan's piece of land was in permanent danger of falling apart if no active effort was made to keep things and relations together.

In a poor and rapidly fluctuating human environment, people disappeared, wood was stolen and money was wasted. The difficulties of fencing off a plot of land that was not yet completely owned by her, however, was only part of the problem. Sorting out the documents, Hulan explained, also led to new unexpected problems:

> I don't have enough time to pursue documents. I went to get the right documents but I was not given permission. The land is too close to the central heating pipelines [many of which are above ground in Ulaanbaatar]. Then I met some people who know [how to fix] such documents and they said, "Give us some money" . . . Another person said that there is no permission for my land, and the district leader said that the land belongs to some organization. Then I have to give them some money.

Hulan tried to secure and hold on to her piece of potential real estate over a prolonged period of time but it was threatened from all corners of a muddled world—actually several different such worlds (the legal world of documents, unreliable socioeconomic networks, poor neighborhoods where theft was prevalent and land needed to be secured physically, etc.)—that intervened in unpredictable and awkward ways. It is in this respect that it makes sense to speak of Hulan as an urban hunter. Much like Misha and Kolya, she was constantly alert to emerging possibilities and new "things at hand," trying to track profit without getting lost in the ever-changing terrain of Ulaanbaatar and Mongolia as a whole. Yet she was also prone to be distracted by new signs leading in different directions, just as she would often lose her direction altogether in this difficult-to-read landscape—or, at worst, come to a dead end altogether (as we show in the next chapter).

Bearing this all-too-characteristic tale of Hulan and her land business in mind, this chapter aims to take anthropological discussions about property in postsocialist contexts and elsewhere (Hann 1998; Strathern 1999; Verdery 1999, 2003; Verdery and Humphrey 2004; Nielsen 2008, 2011b) in a new direction by exploring how certain urban hunters in Ulaanbaatar around the turn of the millennium struggled to own various kinds of privatized land by "holding" together always fleeting and ever-elusive assemblages of property relations that constantly appeared to be on the verge of breaking up within an overarching context of disjunctively conjoined "transitional worlds" or "environments." As we shall see, in this context of permanent transition, where property was in a never-ending process of being constructed as capricious assemblages (DeLanda 2006) of personal plans and plots of land, urban hunters such as Hulan and Kolya were in their true element. These were persons who were able to gauge the unexpected not by trying to anticipate and neutralize it but by accepting and "surfing" the unpredictability of radically changing "property" and "value" regimes. If Hulan's plot of land—paraphrasing Latour—could be described as a momentary stabilization or a temporary assemblage that "collects different types of forces [the hardness of the wood, the capacity to transform money into timber and labor, the abilities of the workers to build a fence, the enforcement of legal rules, one's ability to create durable social relations, etc.] woven together because they are different" (Latour 2005: 74–75), then people like her could be described as sort of trickster-like assemblage-managers.[1] After all, the primary rule of thumb for such trickster subjects in Ulaanbaatar's world of emerging property assemblages was "always to make do with 'whatever is at hand'" (Lévi-Strauss 1966: 17) without being restrained by a predefined project or plan.

As such, the work of Hulan and other transition-tricksters / urban hunters was much in line with the prevailing property relations and political-economic transformation in Ulaanbaatar around 2000. Apart from comprising the "internal" heterogeneity of forces described above, these property relations were also characterized by an "external" heterogeneity resulting from the disjunctive relation (Appadurai 1990: 8) between broader postsocialist "environments" such as international discourse on private property, actual existing property assemblages, legal systems, state institutions, kinship networks, (poverty-struck) city neighborhoods, etc. The state bureaucracy, for example, was often not geared toward implementing laws on private property, and ideas of private property did not necessarily go well with indigenous modes of production (Sneath 2002) or the distribution of property in kin relations. Property consisted, as in Verdery's example of privatized fields in postsocialist Romania, "of complexly overlapping use and revenue rights lodged in external conditions that give the holders of those rights incomplete powers for exercising them" (1999: 65). An act in the legal system did not produce the desired effect in the suburbs of Ulaanbaatar, and an act in the suburbs itself, such as putting up a fence, did not produce the desired effect over a prolonged period of time. World Bank specialist Robin Mearns seemed right, then, when he wrote that the practical outcome of many policy reforms in Mongolia had precisely the opposite effect of their stated intentions (Mearns 2004: 134). Many different "environments" worked according to different institutionalized parameters, thus producing a fragmented world of highly unpredictable effects (see also Plueckhahn 2017).

As we show in the rest of this chapter, this world of internally and externally heterogeneous elements came into being with Mongolia's democratic revolution in 1990, a revolution that gradually also came to revolutionize—or, rather, constantly revolutionize—property regimes in Ulaanbaatar. Indeed, if the very notion of "private property," born with the democratic revolution, was probably *the* key trope for leaving behind a socialist regime founded on "the abolition of private property" (Verdery 2004: 142), then exploring the real life of "private property" in the postsocialist era is also key to any understanding of urban hunters and the environment—and the "game" (in both senses of the word)— that brought them into being. Unlike a garden or field that can be owned and harvested at predictable intervals, property in Ulaanbaatar around 2000 was akin to the moving target of prey animals. As in many hunting economies, its availability was always contingent upon if not the unpredictable spirits of the landscape (Kristensen 2015) then the vicissitudes of events beyond an individual person's control (see also Willerslev 2007; Pedersen 2011).

THE MONGOLIAN PROPERTY REVOLUTION

Unlike in Europe, where land ownership has played a pivotal role since at least the seventeenth century (Hann 1998: 12–13, 33), the idea of individualized ownership of land was foreign to most Mongols until the early 1990s. In traditional Mongolian pastoral culture, land was mainly held and managed as common property (Fernandez-Gimenez 2006), and access to resources such as land and hunting grounds was typically under the jurisdiction of political authorities, such as ruling nobles and Buddhist monasteries (Sneath 2002: 197; see also Fernandez-Gimenez 1999, 2006; Sneath 2004). While the early twentieth century saw the rise of a new socialist property polity, this regime was based on an even stronger notion of collective property rights. During socialism, most property, including land, was owned by the socialist state, and trading in immovable assets was, with very few exceptions,[2] strictly forbidden.

So when the new Mongolian Constitution was drafted in 1992 and the Mongolian Law on Land, implemented in 1994, shortly after the democratic revolution, they did more than just break with the recent state-organized socialist economy. Actually, one could say that they initiated a radical break with all past property-right regulations in Mongolia (see, e.g., Sneath 2002, 2004)[3] by providing for the potential private ownership of land without, however, introducing any mechanism for actually transferring ownership of land into private hands (Hanstad and Duncan 2001: 10).[4] While time-limited possession and use rights for land were granted at this time and a number of new laws and amendments on, for example, land fee payments and cadastral surveys were imple-

Land plots at the city edge (from Google Earth, 2009)

mented during the 1990s, it was not until 2002[5] with the Law of Mongolia on Land and the Law on Allocation of Land to Citizens of Mongolia for Ownership, and only after years of heated political discussion (Sneath 2004: 164–165), that Mongolians were allowed proper ownership of land. The law entitled families to a plot of land allocated free of charge—0.07 hectares in Ulaanbaatar but more in other regions of the country—and allowed people already living on a plot (like the elderly couple above), or already holding land possession licenses, to gain proper ownership of their land. Leaving aside the thorny issue of how to define a so-called family, a matter not clarified by the law and subsequently much discussed since it excluded, for instance, single people from the entitlement to land allocations (Bauner and Richter 2006: 11), the key point for the moment is that land owners now had the right to own and thus dispose of land by selling it on the market.

In Ulaanbaatar, this new law seriously affected the vast and sprawling ger districts (*ger horoolol*) located around the capital city to the west, north and east.[6] These ger districts, as they are widely known among Mongolians and foreign expats alike, consist of fenced-off parcels of land (*hashaa*) where people have settled in a traditional nomadic dwelling, the ger, or in small wooden or concrete houses. It is estimated that approximately 60 percent of Ulaanbaatar's population, and a minimum of sixty thousand households, live in such districts (Rossabi 2005: 141; Bauner and Richter 2006: 13). With a population growth of 4.9 percent per year in Ulaanbaatar between 1990 and 2003 (Bauner and Richter

2006: 12), mainly caused by migration into Ulaanbaatar's ger districts from poor and marginal rural areas across the country (but particularly the west), these nomadic shantytowns on the fringes of the capital city have grown tremendously since the democratic revolution. The districts experienced tremendous pressure, in particular, when the harsh winters from 1999 to 2002 left many Mongolian herders without livestock and forced them to migrate to Ulaanbaatar (Kamata et al. 2010: 1). Thus, not only are the ger districts home to the poorer segments of the city's population—lacking water supply, basic sanitation, central heating, solid waste management, access to public transport and so on—but they have also seen unplanned growth (Kamata et al. 2010: vii).

This was where Hulan's and Kolya's newly acquired land parcels were located. Indeed, one implication of the unplanned, complex and seemingly fundamentally unmanageable reality of Ulaanbaatar's ger districts was, as Hulan's case has already indicated, that the new legal language of privatization did not easily translate into suburban reality. One could actually describe the postprivatized world of land as out of sync with itself for a number of reasons. First, law does not easily translate into a muddled reality where the exact boundaries between land parcels are undecided, where different claims of being the entitled owner/possessor of a particular parcel of land exist, where informal land occupation is extant, and where people are unable to privatize because they have settled in areas that were meant to serve other purposes than settlement or are simply unfit for human occupation (Bauner and Richter 2006: 11, 23). Although the Asian Development Bank supported the implementation of a digital cadaster program in the early 2000s, the fact that an estimated 20 percent of land parcels became subject to boundary conflicts between neighbors or new owners made it difficult to complete the cadastral maps and thus identify land parcels and legal ownership rights (Bauner and Richter 2006: 17; see also Asian Development Bank 2010). According to Verdery, such conflicting claims of ownership are one of the major reasons for the "fuzziness" of postsocialist property (Verdery 1999; Sturgeon and Sikor 2004: 7–8). Second, the state system itself—law, administrative structures, and so on—does not form a well-integrated whole. Apart from rapidly changing (and often outdated and not entirely clear) laws, a World Bank report points to a number of problems concerning the management of law itself:

> Although there have been numerous initiatives to improve land management—mostly funded by external donors—the cadastral system (surveys of land boundaries) generally suffers from a lack of administrative capacity and the limited availability of adequate databases. This problem is caused mostly by unsatisfactory or insufficient

cadastral surveys and mapping and inadequate registration of land-owners, users, and possessors.

On the legal side, existing cadastral law does not include procedures for property registration. There also is no legal framework for handling disputes arising during cadastral surveys; such disputes are increasingly common in residential areas. Institutional roles and responsibilities at different levels of government are not clearly delineated, and there is a general lack of administrative capacity, especially at the district levels that are mainly responsible for managing land registration. (Kamaka et al. 2010: 16)

Other reports corroborate this finding (Hanstad and Duncan 2001; Bauner and Richter 2006: 19, 22), and one of them bluntly states that the "real estate market is ambiguous and chaotic" (Bauner and Richter 2006: 25). Analyses point out that not only is the state system internally incoherent, the market-state nexus of the real estate market also lacks institutions such as real estate agents and appraisers in order to fully develop into a real market (Bauner and Richter 2006: 22). Here, one may do well to remember that the state, surveying large abstract territories and dividing them unambiguously and objectively through the uniform standards of cadastral maps, and the market, dependent on the possibility of alienating abstracted and well-defined things such as land parcels, are two sides of the same coin (Scott 1998: 44–45, 51)—and that a well-functioning state system and bureaucracy, then, are not only needed for land taxation purposes but are also a precondition for "nonfuzzy" capitalist property notions backed up by a liberal rule of law.

Furthermore, and related to this, people act on knowledge that is often not produced through the framework of law. This may be thought of as a lack of proper understanding of "the advantage of legally guaranteed ownership rights" (Bauner and Richter 2006: 26) but—in line with the story that opened this chapter—one cannot help wondering whether people have failed to understand "legal guarantees" (as the development regime proposes) or whether this purported "rule of law" is really in touch with the heterogeneous reality that people live in (as our ethnography seems to imply). Indeed, as we demonstrate in the next section, urban hunters like Hulan and Kolya could actually be said to be acting much in line with the surrounding unclear terrain in which not only law and reality were out of sync but where the exercise of law was out of sync with itself and "reality" profoundly fragmented (Hulan's endeavors to build a fence, the fence being stolen and used for firewood, alcoholic workers leaving with the money, etc.). In Ulaanbaatar, people operate in what lawyers might call "gray" zones—and Verdery "fuzzy" ones (1999)—where property is best imagined as emerging assemblages of never completely realized entities that need to be held together by fences, deals, documents, caretakers, kin networks, and so on.

KOLYA'S LAND

The land that Kolya acquired in 2005 is a case in point. It was located in one of the ger districts that are relatively close to the center of Ulaanbaatar, and it was, as such, attractive. When we first heard about the purchase, we were merely told that he had "bought a piece of land." Yet, as we were soon to realize, he did not exactly *buy* the land; he just bought *an address*, so to speak. Kolya had managed to register his address on this plot of land with the local subdistrict (*horoo*) authorities by paying the previous family who used to live there, and since he now "lived" on the land, he had the right to gain ownership over it at some point. The problem, however, was that he bought a parcel of land from someone who did not actually formally (legally) own it (see Verdery 1999: 57). Instead of privatizing it following the implementation of the 2003 Law on Allocation of Land to Mongolian Citizens, the family had simply been registered as living on the plot. This meant that what Kolya had, in fact, paid the family for was to get his name registered on the land at the subdistrict office in place of them, with the potential to claim ownership of it at some time in the future. This indefinite and volatile situation in terms of Kolya's right over the land is illustrated in the following exchange of words:

LARS: So, do you own it?

KOLYA: Well, it is in my name.

LARS: What do you mean? Last year, you told me that there were some papers you needed to fix.

KOLYA: Yes, I haven't done that yet, but I still have a number—to the entrance, so to speak.

LARS: Could you please explain?

KOLYA: I don't know, I don't know.

LARS: You don't know?

KOLYA: Of course I need this permission for the land, but how they got this number . . .

LARS: Do you know what it means to get a number?

KOLYA [SLIGHTLY FED UP WITH LARS' QUESTIONS]: Basically it means that I am the owner anyway.

LARS: I just need to understand it.

KOLYA: I don't know, of course I need these documents saying that "this land belongs to Kolya."

Leaving the anthropologist slightly frustrated, it was evident that Kolya was uncertain about the exact legal meaning of being registered and "having a number," but then again, he was less worried about the law; for now, he simply trusted the setup, that is, the deal and its relevant components. While it is true that, officially, you cannot buy a registration, an address or a plot of land that is not yet privatized and owned by someone, this "legal problem" was already taken care of. Kolya had paid the former user of the land—the family who used to live there—and, together they had visited a notary who had certified the change of registration. The address was now in Kolya's name at the local sub-district office where addresses needed to be registered. Since the land was not yet privatized and could not be sold, it remained slightly unclear as to how this transaction was carried out, but the woman who had arranged the deal apparently had connections in the administration, Kolya told us. This, it is important to stress, does not necessarily mean that she bribed someone, but possibly just that she stabilized a certain aspect of a deeply fuzzy arrangement. So, since legal issues could either be ignored or circumvented, legality was only part of the issue when operating in the "not-yet" and indefinite context of Kolya's land, where "objects" simply did not have any precise legal status but were open to a wide range of possibilities and influences. The property regime as a whole was under transition, and in this context, concrete properties were highly unstable if not labile in nature.

A much more pressing issue was the fact that Kolya had still not settled on the land in 2006. Just as in the previous year when he had "bought it," his property consisted of an empty, unfenced plot of land surrounded by other families and other parcels of land in the middle of a ger district. To be precise, he was registered at the address, but he did not live there. Due to this liminal state of the land—Kolya was somehow holding it, but he did not live on it—he felt that it needed to be constantly secured. In particular, the fact that the land was not fenced off posed a considerable problem for Kolya, who was afraid that someone might steal it, that is, settle on it and then perhaps make claims to ownership over it by having certain official files altered and by making some of the neighbors confirm that a person other than Kolya actually lived there.

Like Hulan, Kolya felt that he needed to fence off the land to make sure that it remained his. Now, the law, of course, does not say anything about fencing off land.[7] According to an official from a subdistrict (*horoo*) office in Ulaanbaatar, a person registered on a piece of land retains the right to this land even if someone else settles on it. A few minutes later, however, the same woman explained that—in practice—registration (i.e., getting your name on a numbered piece of land) was not important, for the neighbors and others would know who lived where (not a great comfort for Kolya, who did not live on his land), and that—at the end of the day—it was better to fence it off (because it "proves" that it is your property), just as it was best to obtain official papers of proper ownership. There have been cases, she warned, where people had filed ownership for land already registered in other people's names. "The law is clear," she concluded, "but people make it unclear."

In other words, when possession or ownership of land is in a state of suspense, it is important that you physically settle on or at least fence off the piece of potential property in order to make sure that it remains yours.[8] The significance of fencing was underlined by Kolya's female partner when she once told us that first you had to fence off and protect (*hamgaalah*) a parcel of land and only then should you make an effort to obtain the right papers. It often happens, she said, that people find a piece of land, fence it off and fight for it, and only then get registered and file ownership for the land. Interestingly, other people are then prone to settle next to the newly fenced off parcel of land and, when enough people have settled in the newly formed neighborhood, she continued, the authorities are forced to recognize the new settlements and register the addresses (see Nielsen 2008 and 2011b for comparable cases from Maputo, Mozambique). People were even speculating in fenced-off land without registering it, she explained, and a market for land changers (*chyenjüüd*) had emerged.[9] The woman arranging Kolya's deal was precisely such a land changer, and at some point she even suggested that Kolya and his female partner should themselves start trading or speculating in land plots. Actually, the land in Gachurt village that was mentioned in the opening paragraph of this chapter was supposed to be Hulan's initial venture as a land changer.

Kolya's problems with his newly acquired land did not stop at the fencing, however. Even if his land were to be fenced off without anyone living there, then—as we saw in Hulan's case—other people from the neighborhood would most likely steal the fence. In other words, Kolya found himself in a difficult situation: On the one hand, the land was not "secured" until a fence was in place, but on the other, he needed to live on the land before a fence could be erected. The problem was not only the fact that he did not have the funds to build a fence let alone a house; it was also that he had no intention of ever living there (due to its distance from the city center). His only comfort was that the neighboring woman who arranged the land deal was still "looking after it." After all, as the land changer, it was she who had arranged the deal between Kolya and her former neighbors, and she would therefore be held responsible by Kolya if the land was "stolen" by some stranger who managed to put up a fence and "change some official papers," as he

Waiting together (2010)

put it. It was thus imperative that Kolya should stay in touch with this woman and maintain good relations with her, in order for the land to remain his. Once in a while he would therefore pay her a visit, and occasionally he would touch base with her on his mobile phone. Yet at the same time, she was also the one who was putting the most pressure on Kolya to build a fence—otherwise she could not guarantee anything, she said—and she was clearly expecting him to acknowledge her help, that is, to reward her in some way or another.

DeLanda writes that "the parts of an assemblage do not constitute a seamless whole" (2006: 4), and yet assemblages of heterogeneous elements do nevertheless have properties—in our case quasi-property properties!—"of their own emerging from the interaction of its parts" (2006: 5). Thus understood, the fenced-off plots of land that could be found in the thousands following the Mongolian property revolution were more than the sum of their parts, without—for that very reason—forming a whole. As "territorializations" of the assemblage (DeLanda 2006: 12), the fences *were*—as opposed to just representing—the fuzzy nature of property in Ulaanbaatar around 2000, for, like urban hunters themselves, they constituted volatile and fleeting stabilizations of an inherently emergent reality of permanent transition. Yet, again following DeLanda, any given constituent element may also "deterritorialize" the assemblage that it has hitherto been helping to stabilize. Indeed, in Ulaanbaatar around 2000, the same element often had both stabilizing and destabilizing effects. This was the case for Hulan's workers, whose skills were a precondition for having her fence built in the first place, and thus for stabilizing her ownership of the land, but who at the same time still also served as agents of destabilization by fleeing before fencing of the land was complete. In much the same way, the fence was made of timber with a view to protecting and stabilizing Hulan's ownership of her land, and yet, especially in the poverty-stricken ger suburbs of Ulaanbaatar, wood represented a scarce resource that was prone to being stolen for firewood. And, finally, Hulan's acquaintances themselves also simultaneously performed both a stabilizing and a destabilizing role, respectively, by, on the one hand, looking after her land, but, on the other, being in a position to quit their informal work arrangements at any time without notice, or—as we shall see in the case of Kolya's land—selling the land off to rural migrants behind the owner's back.

All this shows that, in Ulaanbaatar around the turn of the millennium, the relationship between stability and instability had *itself* been rendered fundamentally unstable,[10] as the postsocialist context of permanent transition had rendered emergent assemblages into omnipresent ethnographic facts and turned many people into urban hunters in the specific sense described above. In particular, among our interlocutors, private land ownership was in a never-ending process of being constructed via hard work that constantly needed to be repeated and reinvented as people's properties—and their hustling and gathering activities, if not their selves—were subject to forces of change beyond their control.

THE FAMILY APARTMENT

There was, however, one potential solution to the problem of how to own a plot of land without living on it, and this was where Kolya's three brothers came in. In 2006 the whole household—including the father, the four brothers, the father's new female partner, the brothers' female partners and some of their children[11]—lived in Ulaanbaatar's 15th Micro District in the same one-bedroom apartment that had originally been allocated to the parents by the Railway Organization where the father worked as a welder during the socialist period (see Chapter 1). While almost the entire housing stock of Ulaanbaatar's concrete apartment blocks located in and around the city center had been privatized between 1997 and 2004, progress was slower for the apartments inhabited by workers employed by state institutions such as the Railway Organization (Bauner and Richter 2006: 12). This explained why the family's own apartment was only about to be "privatized" (*huviinh*) in 2006, when Kolya had been involved for more than a year in the struggle to buy and hold onto a piece of land in the ger suburbs. Due to his Ukrainian citizenship, Kolya's father was not allowed to own the flat himself, and since his wife had passed away a couple of years back, his plan was to privatize the flat in Kolya and his younger brother, Andrei's, names. This decision was based on several partly conflicting considerations. For one thing, Kolya's father found it inappropriate that his two eldest sons, Misha and Lyosha, should still be living at home at a time in their lives when one would have expected them to have established their own households. Indeed, Mongolian traditions of ultimogeniture—that the youngest son inherits what is left of the parents' property[12]—suggested that the flat should be registered in Andrei's name, and that the three older brothers should have moved to their own homes when they got married or had children. On the other hand, Kolya's father was also very keen for Kolya to own a stake in the flat, as he considered him the most reliable of his sons in terms of safeguarding the family property.

The situation in the apartment was volatile, and the atmosphere often tense. The father could be heard complaining about Misha and Lyosha all the time, and Kolya and his Mongolian girlfriend found it increasingly difficult to cope with the endless discussions, fighting and drinking, and increasingly preferred to spend the night at her parents' or friends' places when possible. In an attempt to carve out a space "for themselves," Kolya had tried to secure one of the rooms in the apartment, leaving only the other room and the tiny kitchen for the remaining eight to ten inhabitants of the household. Afraid for his belongings (which included a fancy mobile phone), he always locked the door to "his" room. Otherwise, he complained, "my younger brother will take my clothes and perhaps never return them." Indeed, very few personal belongings were safe unless locked up or otherwise placed where no one else could reach them. At one point, Kolya even locked up some of his clothes in the family's steel safe because he did not want other family members to wear them. While the family could hardly be said to be starving, such things came in handy in times of a sudden need of cash for food or vodka (there was a pawnshop just around the corner), and what's more, Kolya's friend, a compulsive gambler, might be tempted to "borrow" some of Kolya's things if he came by. Only the father received the complete trust of Kolya and his female partner.

Again, we see how Kolya and his household were trying to come to terms with emergent property relations in a context in which kinship obligations and a general sense of economic crisis and impermanence of social forms, even in one's immediate environment, were stalling people's plans. But maybe, Kolya now began pondering, his newly acquired land in the ger district could be a way out of this stalemate. Asking the brothers to act as caretakers of this land, it seemed, offered a perfect solution that could keep everyone happy and serve to protect and even expand the family property. This would not only allow Kolya to help his brothers (which he genuinely wanted to do) while getting them out of the flat; it would also solve the problem of how to hold on to his land by having someone settled on it and thus securing it.

For this plan to materialize, however, a whole new set of problems would have to be addressed. If the brothers were to settle on his land in the suburbs, they could never be asked to leave. The land would, in effect, become theirs, as they would have nowhere else to go, thus leaving Kolya with no possibility of selling or leasing the land to someone else, let alone moving there himself one day. He could, of course, try to convince his brothers to buy the land rather than just allowing them to settle there for free, but whether they would ever pay him was a moot question and most probably very unlikely. Also, if it turned out that the older brothers could not handle living together—a plausible scenario— then one of them might return to the flat one day. If, on the other hand, Kolya settled there himself, his brothers might come to "feel too much at home" in the flat, as he put it. The best he could therefore hope for, he explained, was that the brothers would return from their newly found jobs in Mongolia's bourgeoning gold mining industry with enough money to buy their own land. Kolya (and Andrei) could then inherit the father's flat, leaving only the problem of how to find reliable tenants for his plot of land. A more likely scenario, however, was that the brothers would not be able to save up anything, or would be fired without receiving any salary. This was how many Russian mining companies in Mongolia worked, he explained.

A number of intertwined but also conflicting strategies are at stake in the case study presented above. First of all, Kolya would clearly like to help his family. They all had a strong sense of belonging together—albeit increasingly tested by what Kolya considered to be the excessive drinking and general irresponsibility of his father and his brothers (see Chapter 7). As the de facto older brother of the household—the family provider from whom funds for buying food and other necessities often flowed—Kolya could not ignore the needs of those who expected his help. On the other hand, Kolya would also like to benefit from the situation himself. He bought the land in 2005 for USD250 and it was worth around USD1,300 in 2006, although this still paled in comparison to the flat, the value of which was around USD9,500. Then again, Kolya would do anything not to lose the flat, which he considered to be the family's only future. It could, of course, be sold immediately after its imminent privatization, and the profit shared between the father and the four brothers, leaving all of them with some sort of economic foundation on which to establish their own households, but this would amount to wasting the family fortune; Kolya was certain of that. The money obtained from selling the flat, he worried, would flow out of his brothers' hands within a short span of time (a scenario that was not entirely foreign to Kolya himself). If that were to happen, the family as a whole would be "lost," as they would have missed the opportunity of making something of their one big chance. As we saw in Chapter 1, this was partly what happened when Misha tragically passed away after having obtained a loan on the flat for his new plumbing company.

PROPERTY IN TRANSITION

It should now be clear that property in Ulaanbaatar in the 2000s had not assumed the liberal-juridical character imagined by Western advocates of market reforms and the new Mongolian law, but rather had—from a liberal point of view—a "fuzzy" (Verdery 1999) quality that "lacks the clear edges of an ideologized notion of exclusive private owning" (Verdery 1999: 75), and that makes it difficult to hold on to and contain. Property, at least in the present context of transition, is in a constant process of being formed by the disjunctive relation between moral codes, traditional values, kinship obligations, liberal notions of ownership, theft and insecurity. Kolya had to keep together his relations and himself (who were in danger of being lost in fluid social/kin networks), the land (which was only semi-owned) and his future plans (which were threatened by ever-changing conditions), while "he," "his relations," "the land" and "his plans" constantly underwent changes and were influenced by an environment largely beyond his control. Having the unconcerned and cool attitude of an urban hunter, he was trying to manage unfinished movements that were out of sync with each other but that nevertheless converged to make up ephemeral assemblages such as "Kolya's land," and they did so partly owing to his own more or less haphazard interventions, such as phone calls to the woman "looking after" the land plot. The land came into existence, albeit never completely, by stabilizing a certain set of relations for a period of time.

It seemed certain, however, that at some point "Kolya's land" would dissolve again. While we—and Kolya himself and his female partner—were inclined to think that Kolya would end up selling his plot of land at a huge profit, most likely before it was even privatized (as this would involve new expenditure and, hence, less profit), it actually turned out that the land was "taken over" by someone. A female acquaintance of Kolya's father (to whom we shall briefly return in Chapter 7) allowed a family to settle on the land and only informed Kolya about this at a much later point, when they had been settled there for a

Enjoying a Lucky Strike (2006)

while. She then advised Kolya to sell the land, and he ended up letting them buy it cheaply. He was fed up with the land and needed the money, he said. The woman brought the necessary papers and the new owner, a man from the countryside, to see Kolya. Although suspecting that she herself had profited from the deal by acting as an intermediary, and even though he only received some of the payment, he decided to sign the documents. Predictably, the acquaintance then disappeared for some years—her son died and her life was in a mess (see Chapter 7)—and he never received the remaining money. "If I had this land now," Kolya said in 2011, "I could probably sell it for MNT2 million," but then again, he would have needed someone to look after it. "Andrei could have done it," Kolya concluded, "but he was too lazy."

According to Caroline Humphrey and Katherine Verdery, economists understand property as

> a means of regulating access to scarce resources by assigning persons rights in them relative to other persons . . . This economistic view assumes that when resources are scarce, assigning property rights is a good way of figuring out how to get those resources and keep others out. Once we do that, once we create property rights and deliver them to people, the economists' property ideology says that those people will have an incentive to work well and to use assets efficiently, disciplined by the market. (2004: 3)

So, was land ownership in Ulaanbaatar just a matter of obtaining the right documents and securing property in a legal sense for everything to be fine, as Lars originally lectured Kolya and Hulan in the train en route to China?

Does one necessarily achieve the liberal haven of security and the "rule of law" once the paperwork is done? Of course not—as Kolya knew quite well and repeatedly tried to tell us. Over and over again, he stressed that you have to fence off your land, even after securing legal ownership of it, in order to avoid future hassle. Someone might still settle on your land and—who knows?—maybe they would manage to change some papers or simply refuse to move. Paraphrasing Verdery and Humphrey, within a context of permanent transition such as the one discussed in this book, it is difficult to figure out precisely who "has the resources" and exactly what it means to "keep others out," just as rights are not simply "assigned" and "delivered" by a system that exists beyond the practice of keeping land parcels together. Rather, the way property was exercised in Ulaanbaatar points to the existence of an irreducible, transient world in which few things exist for long periods of time.[13] Rather, in this world of radical change and enduring transition, things take the form of assemblages held together via a continuous collective effort, if by "continuous" we mean the time span, often short, in which the "things" in question (land, relations, plans, etc.) form part of an (equally short-lived) project. "Property," then, only exists through the wider effort of "getting relations right" in a fluctuating and fragmented environment in which the duration of any "project" or plan is, by definition, short-lived. In this environment, urban hunters are more at ease than others.

CONCLUSION

While our ethnographic focus in this chapter has been the changing nature of property in Ulaanbaatar following the privatization of land instigated in the early 1990s, we have also wished to make a more general point, namely that transition as a permanent modality of social, cultural and economic life often outlives the more short-lived political revolutions that brought them about. The goal of the shock therapy of transition may have been to be "comprehensive, impacting on all parts of the economy simultaneously—institutional, legal, political, social" (Friedman 2007: 428), but the shock came to have more duration than the notion of simultaneous and comprehensive impact would have us believe. Seen in this light, Mongolia's property transition, like Ulaanbaatar's culture of transition in general, was not just a no-man's-land *between* the two stable conditions of collective property during socialism and private property during the market era. Rather, transition became a unique state—a state of permanent exception—imbued with its own set of features, dynamics and ways of propelling people to act.

The overarching lesson to be drawn from this chapter's case studies of Ulaanbaatar's property revolution, then, is thus not just the often-stated anthropological fact that legal laws and cultural rules are out of sync with political reality and social practice but rather that the privatization of land in Ulaanbaatar around the turn of the millennium was emblematic of a transitory reality that was out of sync *with itself*. Within the culture of transition, multiple and disparate trajectories—laws being implemented, a business on its way to being established, family relations being threatened, a theft being carried out, money flows from labor that are subject to fluctuating mineral prices and global financial markets, etc.—work independently of each other to produce momentary assemblages such as Hulan's and Kolya's properties, which, in this respect, are always already exceptions (Benjamin 1968; Agamben 1998, 2005). Momentary assemblages such as fenced plots "bud out" from within a radically emergent reality, which—while making possible the construction of the fence in the first place—also immediately threatens to tear it apart. Things were dissolved by what brought them into existence, and property, in this sense, was as much a liability as it was an asset (cf. Verdery 2004; see also Buyandelger 2013: 113). When legal documents and the state cannot stabilize relations between defined person and defined things, it simply takes a great deal of *continuous* effort to maintain ownership by, for example, building fences and keeping them intact. Thus we can only agree with Humphrey and Verdery in their plea not to take the thingness of property for granted by asking how it is "made" (Verdery and Humphrey 2004: 8) in concrete ethnographic contexts, but with the caveat that, in the contexts of permanent transition, property is not simply made; it is always in the making.

Thus, to call the culture of transition a "state of exception" is more than simply repeating an often (mis)used political philosophical cliché. What our ethnography shows is that, in a context of radical change, social life and cultural forms become pervasively incongruent. In Ulaanbaatar around the turn of the millennium, permanent transition was the default state of everything—the law was *being implemented*, the land was *being privatized*, the family was *falling apart*, people were *finding out* what to do with their lives and, more generally, what constituted them and others. This is also the reason why, in a culture of transition, particular kinds of people who are able to seize the moment and juggle ever-changing circumstances are in their element. As a charismatic, streetwise and well-connected urban hunter, Kolya excelled in the seemingly distinctly postsocialist art of "giving in to unpredictability." As discussed in the previous chapter and the Introduction, this involved a unique ability to live with uncertainty (Whyte 1997) in an apparently irrational optimistic or, one could say, "radically certain" manner, while also holding together not just oneself (as someone who is always in danger of being lost in social networks) but also one's land (which also needs to be constantly bounded to prove ownership) and one's plans (which are constantly overturned by new futures) as all such momentary stabilizations were subject to forces beyond anyone's control and prediction. Much like imitating an elk is a precondition for successfully tracking down and eventually killing prey among Yukaghir hunters (Willerslev 2004b), so, too, is becoming one with the irregularity, volatility and changeability of the post-socialist environment and its "game"—property, for example—a requirement for successful urban hunting.

Thus, for people like Hulan, Kolya and many other urban hunters in Mongolia around 2000, liberal property laws—along with their subjectivities and many other laws, rules and principles (including, as we shall see in coming chapters, moral and religious ones)—were not detached from the emergent reality of transition but were simply a part of it, on a par with all other temporary assemblages and emergent forms. Accordingly, it was, at the end of day, not particularly ethnographically important to find out what Kolya "really meant" in telling us that he was "holding" his new plot of land. Rather, the much more pertinent and pressing challenge was how to stay faithful to the old anthropological truism of listening carefully to what people tell you in the field, for Kolya's vague, imprecise and fuzzy ideas of property paradoxically turned out to be entirely to the point. After all, as we have shown, vagueness was the only true essence of much property in Ulaanbaatar around the turn of the millennium.

Chapter 4 Hustling and Conversion

Hulan, who was introduced in the preceding chapter as a not entirely successful Ulaanbaatar female land investor in her late twenties, had, like almost all the others we knew from the lost generation, carried out a variety of odd jobs in her relatively short but eventful adult life. Among many other things, she had worked in one of the numerous new upmarket hotels in Ulaanbaatar, washed cars on the street, and— ignoring how infuriated her male partner had become when realizing this—sold eggs, potatoes and bananas at a square during the Naadam celebrations in July while heavily pregnant. Like many of our Ulaanbaatar friends, Hulan had only completed secondary school and since then had never managed to gain a proper foothold in life, at least if measured against dominant conventions of education, permanent employment, marriage and establishing a household. It is true that she had enrolled in the film school in Ulaanbaatar at one point, but she had then become pregnant in her first year, given birth to a son and never returned to formal education. She had also been married but, in 2006—when Lars first met her—she was single again and living with her son in the home of her middle-class parents in an apartment block close to the center of Ulaanbaatar.

Hulan was a highly industrious person who loved to work, yet she—like Kolya and his friends and brothers—felt unable to "do something" when this work took the form of an ordinary paid job. As she explained to Lars, in one of her frequent moments of self-reflection,

> When I have a paid job, I can't leave whenever I want to. I am stuck there. I have to work without resting and can't leave when I am tired and want to . . . I suffer and feel that I am wasting time. I have to do the same work again and again—and nothing else. I suffer because all the work is the same [*heviin*]. It feels as if I am doing nothing.

Working within the predictable frame of routine employment and fixed salaries amounted to doing absolutely "nothing." According to one of her acquaintances, Hulan's lack of ability to slow down and settle may have been related to the fact that she grew up away from her parents and siblings. Until she was eight years old, Hulan had lived with her grandmother in the Gobi desert because her parents had both been busy with their jobs—and also had an older son—around the time she was born. While living away from your biological parents is not at all unusual in Mongolia, where adoption-like arrangements are widespread (see, e.g., Empson 2011: 151–152), it had made Hulan "into a person with her own mind," the acquaintance claimed. Conversely, one of Hulan's sisters maintained that she had simply been spoiled by her grandmother: she did what she wanted, more or less, and it was difficult to get hold of her. She was often away from home, and one could never be sure what she was up to. Be that as it may, the result was that Hulan's entire way of being exuded impatience; she was lively and gesticulating, loved movement, and her eyes were constantly in motion. A self-ascribed restless soul who was "unable to do nothing" (*zügeer baij chaddaggüi*), and who could not stand what she dismissed as the suffocating predictability of regular jobs, Hulan in many ways thus personified what it means to live in permanent transition, constantly exploring new relations and following profit opportunities, albeit in a peculiarly unsystematic and highly erratic manner.

To some observers Hulan might be seen as living proof that the American Dream had finally made its way to Mongolia. After all, was she not the blood and tissue of the "naturally" emerging market economic networks in this and other postsocialist countries? Certainly, Hulan could easily be seen to embody the *ur-capitalist* assumption that a market, including trade-based networks and entrepreneurial subjectivities, will automatically and spontaneously emerge with the collapse of state interference (see Introduction). This argument, however, has at least two serious flaws. First, individual industriousness was also a valued trait during state socialism, even if it did not take the capitalist entrepreneurial form (see, e.g., Ericksen 2014). Several scholars have described how productivity was highly regarded and awarded both during socialism and, more generally, in Mongolian culture (Humphrey 1998; Zimmermann 2011; Ericksen 2014). Ericksen writes,

> Mongolians admire a quality they call "activeness," which suggests the ability to initiate projects. To say that someone is "*idevkhtei*" (active) is one of the highest compliments. The term "*khödölmörch*" (industrious) can also describe someone who exceeds the basic responsibilities of their position. Similarly, one can say that someone "*zugeer suuj chadahgüi*" (can't merely sit), a compliment that implies that they are working on something all of the time. (2014: 43–44)

Second, the generalized characterization of capitalist subjectivity does not, as we shall see, capture Hulan's unique inability "to do nothing." For while Hulan was undoubtedly an extroverted spirit who spent a great deal of time exploring new relations, including opportunities aimed at increasing her profit, she did so in a particular way that is not easily subsumed under a simple, highly generalized and all-inclusive notion of the "capitalist individual." Rather, as we are going to argue in this chapter (and have already partly argued in the previous one), unlike the systematic, planning and "rational" *homo economicus* that has come to be associated with Weber's account of Protestantism (2011), Hulan could be described as a female urban hunter who, much like her male peers described in Chapters 1 and 2, seized opportunities as they emerged. While more energetic and less unconcerned and easygoing than, for example, Kolya—and more law-abiding than Misha—Hulan also moved from enthusiastically exploring one suddenly emerging business prospect to the other. She always gave the impression of someone alert to (or distracted by) the promises of every moment and any relation. Ever ready to move on and change direction when new opportunities arose, she may have been the most impatient and restless, yet also most eager, of the urban hunters we met.

By describing how urban hunters like Hulan were thus constantly "working out" emerging potentials and social relations as opposed to "working in" and systematically "building up" plans and established networks, we once again in this chapter demonstrate how our friend's social relations, selves and "souls" (see in particular Chapter 7) were molded by Ulaanbaatar's precarious socioeconomic landscape around the turn of the millennium. Yet we also examine the contrast between the explorative and "unscheduled" life of urban hunting and a different form of life that was emerging as a rejection of life in transition during this period. We have already described in Chapter 1 how someone like Kolya—who like others from his generation was torn between a need to dance to the tunes of transition and a desire to detach himself from the occasional stress of hustling and gathering—was able to perform a knife-edge balancing act of genuine urban hunting by ceaselessly exploring new potentials while not falling completely prey to drinking, apathy and too much social networking. While some of Kolya's friends fell off this knife edge and were lost in transition, others tipped the other way, so to speak, and "fell" into a new form of radical detachment from transitional life by becoming autonomous "protestant" individuals. Such individuals tended to see transition not as a world of potential but as a world characterized by loans that were never reciprocated, businesses that often failed and people who could not be trusted; for them, locking up belongings, and indeed selves, became a way of life.

In order to explore the outgoing and unconstrained nature of urban hunting through its relation to this other, as it were, the ethnography in this chapter revolves around two female protagonists: Hulan and Ariunaa. Like Hulan, Ariunaa was around thirty and unmarried, and her father had, like Hulan's father, worked for the army during socialism. Aside from the fact that their fathers were thus both firm believers in the old system, however, they had little in common. In fact, as we shall see, their modes of relating to the perpetual ruptures of times of transition were, in many ways, in outright opposition. If Hulan was a quintessential urban hunter in the sense that she immersed herself within the transient social relations of transition at risk of getting forever lost in it, Ariunaa "the antihunter" detached herself from transition and new social networks as much as possible. To fine-tune this argument in relation to existing studies of socioeconomic relations in Mongolia, however, we start by looking into the common use of socioeconomic networks in relation to Mongolia's (back then) relatively new postsocialist economy.

POSTSOCIALIST ECONOMIC NETWORKS

It is a widely recognized fact that the sudden disintegration of the planned economy and the socialist state allowed for a rapid proliferation of nonstate economic networks in postsocialist Mongolia. "From above," multinational corporations showed increasing interest in the natural resources of the country and invested heavily in the exploration of coal, gold, uranium, copper and other minerals, just as Western nations—but also Japan and, more recently China—

along with numerous nongovernmental organizations and international institutions such as the International Monetary Fund, the World Bank and the Asian Development Bank, gradually overtook Russia's former role as primary donor and economic advisor in the aftermath of the democratic revolution (Bulag 1998; Sneath 2004; Rossabi 2005).

At the same time, a new economic space opened up "from below." In the Mongolian countryside, the privatization programs of the 1990s had dissolved nearly all of the hundreds of former pastoral collectives and state farms within a few years (see, e.g., Sneath 1993; Bruun 1995; Buyandelger 2013). Previous collective ownership of most animals was replaced with private ownership, and alongside exchanges of products and assistance within networks of obligation based on kin and friendship (see Sneath 1993; Szynkiewicz 1993; Odgaard 1996; Humphrey and Sneath 1999: 136–178; Pedersen 2006), new market-based networks for the meat trade, for example, took over from previous state procurement and provision systems. The central state ceased to organize the herding and slaughtering of animals and the distribution of animal products, so herding households themselves were suddenly responsible for producing and selling their own produce-turned-commodities. As herders moved closer to administrative centers, which now also became trading hotspots, new distribution channels were invented to facilitate the transfer of meat, skins and hides from the peripheral pastoral economy to slaughterhouses and markets in urban centers and foreign countries (see also Humphrey and Sneath 1999: 62–65).

As a result, a whole range of new and old companies, as well as various kinds of traders and middlemen, emerged between herding families and meat consumers. Such periphery-to-center commodity chains are created in different ways. While major meat companies, inspired by the way things were organized under a planned economy, would still buy up live animals in rural districts and herd them all the way to the major slaughterhouses of the big cities in the summertime, individual herders or local businessmen would also themselves transport meat to the city centers and sell it at markets such as the Huchit Shonhor in Ulaanbaatar—or sell it on to changers (*chyenjüüd*) or market vendors in the city. Alternatively, changers might buy up meat or live animals in the countryside (although this was getting less and less common) or wait at the two main entrance points to the capital city of Ulaanbaatar, beyond which live animals were not allowed to go, in order to buy up meat or live animals to be slaughtered from arriving jeeps or trucks. Changers were associated with informal and sometimes dodgy business *between* "marketplaces," often involving large amounts of money (for more on different kinds of changers and their wider significance on the postsocialist market scene, see Chapter 6 and later in this chapter). In a sense, then, these changers were the dream come true of net-work theorists. Like Hulan, they explored previously unexplored possibilities, and reminiscent of Barth's entrepreneurs, they earned their profit by making value from creating new connections between otherwise separated spheres of exchange (e.g., Barth 1981 [1967]).

The meat trade is, of course, just one example of such new economies from below, but it highlights how the emerging "capitalist" Mongolian market has worked in novel, explorative and less formalized ways—for example, through changers or middlemen (see Højer 2007; Pedersen 2007a)—and it shows that many Mongolians have found new ways of doing business outside the estab-lished (and collapsed) economy. In Ulaanbaatar, this new economy has typically been recognized by social scientists and foreign consultants under the com-mon denominator of the "informal sector" (see, e.g., Anderson 1998; Bikales et al. 2000; Morris 2001). While it is difficult to define this informal sector, let alone estimate its size, it is undoubtedly a lack of employment opportunities in the formal sector after 1990—mainly due to a restructuring of the economy and a "contraction of manufacturing production" (Morris 2001: v)—that gave rise to an extensive informal economy in Ulaanbaatar. This economy would include the retail trade (kiosks, containers, counters), financial services (pawn-shops and money changers), transport (taxis, minibuses, car parking), various other services (shoe repair, etc.) and also the manufacturing of, for example, soft drinks and bread (Bikales et al. 2000); much of the sector would depend on the connections, made by entrepreneurs, changers and traders, that made goods—such as meat, cashmere and vegetables—move around the market and from far beyond the borders of the capital city to the various marketplaces in the city. To give an example, Enhbayar, a man in his late forties who used to be a train mechanic in socialist times, would sell flour and rice from his container near the railway station only after buying it from trains arriving from Russia or China or, at other times, from changers or middlemen at the Bars wholesale market. Similarly, Bayarmaa, a single mother with six children who used to work in the building material industry, had turned to business when the state-owned fac-tory that employed her went bankrupt in 1993. She was selling vegetables that she herself bought from producers—friends and acquaintances in the Orhon province—and brought by train to Ulaanbaatar. Or take Bayar, a man from Uvs province in far western Mongolia whom Lars met at the Huchit Shonhor mar-ket with his truck in April 2006. He would spend four days traveling 1,350 kilo-meters on mostly dirt road all the way from Uvs to Ulaanbaatar once or twice a month in wintertime with frozen meat. The little business niche he had carved out for himself consisted of buying up livestock from local nomads in remote

The car market (2006)

areas (who, like people elsewhere in rural Mongolia, were always looking for ways to obtain cash in order to be able to pay their children's university fees as well as purchase flour and other daily essentials) every late summer/autumn. He then had the animals slaughtered in November and would keep the meat in a storehouse in the provincial capital until the spring, when he would leave for the capital to sell the meat at different markets. In April, animals are lean and only rarely slaughtered and meat is in high demand. In a similar way, car changers, while mostly not present at the car market in northeastern Ulaanbaatar themselves, would make cars appear at markets by buying up used cars from Mongolians or by importing them from Hong Kong and many other places. They would, like other changers or middlemen, operate behind the scene and in-between and were an indispensable part of the new informal—and some-times straightforwardly illegal—sector.

Similar stories about trading networks, commodity chains, self-made traders and other quintessentially capitalist phenomena and personae could be told about almost any other product sold on the Mongolian markets around 2000. In the world of transition, people were creating and exploring new business networks between countryside and city, within cities and between countries, and there was virtually no limit as to who or what could potentially become a part of these networks. Commodity chains or networks materialized, it seemed, everywhere the state was weak and central planning no longer existed, and changers—in the widest sense of the word—became the organizing glue between existing network nodes or chain links.

How best, then, to theorize the nature of the new socioeconomic relationships that emerged with the transition from state socialism to market capitalism? Here, it is important to heed one of the key lessons from actor-network-theory, which is to systemically question the seemingly self-evident focus on social connectivity in much economic sociology and anthropology by not starting "out assuming whatever we wish to explain" (Law 1992: 380) and thereby not fetishizing connectivity as an instrumental or indeed moral end in itself (see also Strathern 1996 [1989]; Højer 2004, 2007; Pedersen 2013). Only by remaining critical and persistently reflective about the concept of "network" and indeed the concept of "the social" itself (Højer 2003, 2004; Holbraad and Pedersen 2017), we thus suggest, will we be able to take the constant fluctuations and seemingly irreducible transience of relations among our informants sufficiently seriously, as opposed to more or less implicitly subsuming such transient relations under the black-boxed rubric of "informal networks."

So while the postsocialist socioeconomic dynamics described above, in principle, could be, and very much have been, described in network terms, it would, we suggest, be ethnographically imprecise and also theoretically inadequate to portray the activities of urban hunters like Hulan in such generic and vague manners. True enough, her activities were relatively autonomous from existing state and other institutions (including the retraditionalized kinship networks explored in the previous chapters). Nevertheless, it would be a difficult claim to make that Hulan was working within, and in this process helping to create and reproduce, relatively stable socioeconomic networks. The problem is that while a given "network" seems to have a more fluid and ever-extending character than the more rigid and old-fashioned notion of "organization," it is nevertheless still presumed to be imbued with a certain continuity and to be composed of an enduring "traffic," whether conceived of in terms of "commodity chains" (for a review of this literature, see, e.g., Bair 2008) or fluid "regulatory arrangements that operate independently of the state" (Meagher 2009: 7). Networks, that is, are assumed to facilitate, establish and secure the future flow of things, words and ideas; they presume and create a world of connections as an end in itself, whether such connections are based on topological links, agency/utility or informal patterned interactions (Meagher 2009: 9–10).

Similarly, in the literature on informal economy in postsocialist Mongolia, we recognize this idea in notions of "social relations of obligation" (Sneath 1993; Humphrey and Sneath 1999), "trust and reliability associated with kinship relations" (Park 2003), "ritualized exchange" (Szynkiewicz 1993), "informal networks" (Dalaibuyan 2012), "social networks" (Kaplonski 2004: 32–35), and "mutual assistance networks" (Odgaard 1996; see also Humphrey and Sneath 1999: 136–178). The problem is that, by a priori conceptualizing and stabilizing relations in this manner, the results and findings of network analysis and commodity chain studies is already, to some extent, built into their epistemological assumptions.[1] After all, as Latour has pointed out, the moment one starts looking for networks, one also tends to find them (2005: 63). So, while a focus on social networks may be used to account for relatively stable obligations between, for example, kin, friends and former classmates in postsocialist Mongolia (as we saw, for instance, in our discussion of Ulaanbaatar's market vendors in Chapter 2 and also touched upon in Chapter 1), this focus tends to overlook and disregard other, less institutionalized and, for the same reason, more transient, ephemeral and volatile social relations and economic forms (including people's attempts to detach themselves from such relations and forms through avoidance [see Højer 2003, 2004, 2007 and 2019a]), which were also such a prominent feature of life in Ulaanbaatar around 2000.

In short, we find that something fundamental is missing in the "social network" concept—and in associated images of individual "social networkers" in pursuit of different forms of capital, whether economic, symbolic or what have you—which is holding back our understanding of Hulan's and other urban hunters' lives and ways of relating to themselves and others. In the rest of this chapter, we substantiate this critique, as well as sketch the contours of a potential conceptual and analytical alternative, by demonstrating how dominant theoretical ideas about "socioeconomic networks" and different agents' attempts to "socially navigate" the transition cannot properly account for the transient nature of social relations and subjectivities witnessed by us in Ulaanbaatar at the turn of the millennium. We begin by returning to the story of Hulan to show in more detail how she was a good example of a female urban hunter. Only then shall we shift our attention to Ariunaa, who, as we are going to see, was in more than one sense Hulan's polar opposite: an urban antihunter, whose selfhood and way of relating to the constant ruptures of permanent transition and the postsocialist market took the form of introspection and detachment.

GATHERING METAL

Hulan loved exploring new business opportunities, even if they rarely turned out successfully. Her attempt to invest in the bourgeoning land business was one example of a venture that, in some ways, seemed to fail, but which, on the other hand, led her to become involved in still more business activities in her search for the financial means and high-level contacts necessary for securing the documents that would, ideally, allow her land to be legalized (see Chapter 3). One such business, and one in which she actually ended up making a profit, was Ulaanbaatar's infamous scrap metal trade, in which Hulan became a minor player at the time of our fieldwork.

Across Ulaanbaatar in the early 2000s, metal traders were buying up and collecting metal from locals at specified container spots. This metal was then bought by middlemen, or metal changers, who "controlled" these spots through different forms of more or less explicit coercion (see Chapter 5) and often profited well from selling it on to Chinese-owned factories in Ulaanbaatar. Since the participants in this traffic between collecting spots and Chinese-owned factories were almost all men, the metal business was considered tough and masculine, and Hulan only managed to gain access through an old male friend. As she herself put it, this allowed her to work "under the changers' wings." Still, her involvement was fraught with difficulties from the outset:

> It was people I knew . . . But not all of them. Only one or two of them were friends . . . I thought that I should use this chance. "Get me into your business," I said, and they agreed. I decided not to work for a long time, because I know "my size" [*ööriin hemjee*] . . . and it is difficult to do this business for a long time. I was a newcomer. *Maybe someone won't like it*, I thought. So I stopped in the end . . . If people stay in this business for a long time, they will make money. However, people's bad thoughts may cause something to happen. I'm not a man; they are not all my friends. They might say that "you are not doing much—you are just getting money." Or maybe they think that "she is getting rich." The changers are conspicuous.[2] There is no living being who doesn't know them. Oh my God. Everyone knows big traders. It's a very bad thing. There are changers who get killed . . . It is difficult to be part of the circle. They thought that I had money—*What if they hit me and make me fall?* I thought. It would be dangerous. They [the other changers] talk about that. [People] might think that you have money. "Take a taxi and go straight home," they told to me, and I was scared.

By amassing wealth and almost monopolizing a particular and potentially profitable trade, it seems, the metal changers were understood to have transcended the small exchanges of everyday life. Yet, in becoming "big," they were also exposing themselves to new and enhanced forms of visibility.[3] They were conspicuous to an extent that, in Hulan's words, there was "no living being who did not know them." Accordingly, the moment one started mingling with the changers (and perhaps in this process even turned into something of a small changer oneself), one would begin to be seen as a changer by other people. And to be perceived as similar to other metal changers would, so to speak, also mean that one would start standing out from others in the same way as the other changers—including, indeed, standing out from the other changers themselves. Like the other changers, one would then have become a prominent agent, a "big man" among other big men in an environment where competition was harsh, even violent, and money hard to find—and, thus desperately fought for.

For all these reasons, as Hulan explained, increasing exposure inevitably made one prone to attacks, and not just physical attacks but also, and perhaps especially, more invisible and sometimes semi-occult forms of violence and harm. Indeed, while Hulan never used this particular expression when talking about Ulaanbaatar's metal business, her general way of phrasing these matters was strikingly similar to widespread Mongolian ways of talking about *hel am* (Højer 2003, 2004, 2019a; Pedersen 2011: 72–73, 88–89; Swancutt 2012: 127–153). *Hel am*, literally meaning "tongue mouth," is a curse-like dispute that is caused by a person's conspicuousness leading to denigration ("black *hel am*") or too much (insincere) praise ("white *hel am*"), and it often works through slander (Højer 2004). Indeed, Hulan made it clear that she had sometimes found it necessary to consult Buddhist lamas and ask them to read sutras for her in order to protect her from *hel am* and other kinds of what could be called "business magic" (see also Chapter 6). "Maybe people will say," she once explained to Lars in a restaurant close to the State Department Store in Ulaanbaatar, "that Hulan is doing business, making money and has a good family. Maybe someone gives me MNT20,000 and then people get jealous, because I am making money in such an easy way." "Such words are white *hel am*," she continued, "and they influence people in a bad way." Thus, while Hulan's investment—money borrowed from her parents—was doubled during her short spell as a metal changer, she felt uncomfortable about pushing her way into this male-dominated (and possibly illicit) business and was also worried about the always lurking risk that arguments could turn violent when her fellow changers were sharing the spoils. Most important, however, was the fact that Hulan knew "her size," as she put it, which made her worried about dangerously sticking out as a conspicuous and well-off changer. This, above all, was the reason she decided to quit after less than two months in the business. After all, she had never wanted to stay a changer and had already made a fair amount of money.

Unlike the so-called big changers, Hulan was an urban hunter who was attracted to exploring new possibilities through recurrent and radical immersion in ever-shifting social relations and commodity chains as an end in itself. For her, the desired endpoint was not to become a conspicuous "big man" who emerged from the network to stand out from others in the form of a prominent individual somehow rising above everyone else. On the contrary, she was in her element when actively exploring new relations and stumbling across novel potentialities, just before these would gel into stable statuses such as "big man" or, for that matter, contracted wage earner. Not unlike the capricious reality of transition itself, then, Hulan's basic way of being a "hunter" did not square well with organized relations and established status hierarchies. Instead, she excelled at and also rather enjoyed the capacity to constantly lose herself to new business ventures (she would often disappear for days), and she was always impatiently on the lookout for new things to do.

HUNTING PORK FAT

For the same reason, Hulan did not stop trading after her voluntary retirement from the profitable but risky metal business. Her parents had been talking for some time about sending her to South Korea to work, a practice that became increasingly popular in the 1990s due to Korea's relative proximity to Mongolia and what seemed fairly easy opportunities for finding decently paid work and sending back remittances. After 2004, measures were even introduced by the South Korean government to make such labor migration much easier, and many young people were now preparing for Korean language tests to increase their chances of moving to South Korea to work. While Hulan was not opposed to her parents' plan, she had a strong desire "to do something" before leaving. So, shortly after her metal venture, she joined the large number of Mongolian "suitcase traders" who regularly shuttled to and from China by train to buy up cheap goods.

> I had never tried to cross the border back then, but had always been interested in doing so. Going to Ereen [a Chinese border town where most Mongolian suitcase traders go] is like going to a foreign country, so rather than having an empty passport— and instead of just sitting [i.e., doing nothing, passively waiting for the Korea plans to work out]—I decided to go there. Experienced traders had told me that they were making pretty good money and that they would go again. There was no stamp in my passport. I never went anywhere . . . If you just try hard and keep on going . . . I never used to think that I would find money by doing trade. I thought that I couldn't do it. If one tries hard, then destiny will help [*ezen hicheevel zaya hicheene*].

On Hulan's first trips, she followed what seems to be the standard procedure for newcomers to the world of suitcase trading. Having taken orders—for shirts, shoes, jackets, and so on—from friends and acquaintances in Ulaanbaatar, she would go to Ereen to buy the goods and then receive payment from her customers upon her return. It was the old profit that Hulan had made from her short stint as a metal changer that was now paying for her new business venture as a suitcase trader. The arrangements, however, did not work out as planned. She never managed to make any money from her first trips to China and only just managed to recoup the money she had used for various expenses. As she laconically put it, "I played with the money and threw it away" (*toglood hayachihlaa*).

> [People would say] "I'm your friend and will pay [when you come back]." It was dif-
> ficult, because [when I came back] they didn't have any money. Some of them had
> left their job. Some of them had gone to the countryside, they had escaped. Then, as
> a very last option, I took the remaining goods and went around the cafés and shops
> selling them . . . I put the goods in a bag and went to all the cafés. There was no one
> who didn't know me. Then I gave the goods to the waitresses. They said, "Sell it on
> credit. I'll pay you 50 percent now. Seven days from now I'll get my salary. Then come
> and get the rest. I'll be here." I said, "OK," took the money and made a note. When
> I came back the next week, they wouldn't be there. They had left their job. There are
> many situations like that. They simply escaped.

While a widely assumed integral aspect of social networks and informal econo-mies is that "[c]oncrete personal relationships . . . produce trust" such that "where economic transactions are embedded in personal relationships the haz-ards of opportunism are diminished" (Bradach and Eccles 1989: 108), it was quite clear that in Hulan's case—as indeed among several other of our Ulaanbaatar friends (see Chapter 1)—there were only a very limited number of situations in which "concrete personal relationships" would safeguard against mistrust and other "hazards." Far from positive social and moral ideals such as trust and sta-bility, issues of "departure," "escape" or, in more abstract terms, transience and capriciousness were at the heart of social relations back then.

But Hulan did not give up. She was not discouraged by what she considered her first attempt as a suitcase trader and had high hopes that future trips to Ereen would bring her the profit that she was looking for. All her hopes (and remaining funds) were now invested in pork fat. Importing pork fat for sausage production in Ulaanbaatar, Hulan had calculated, would be unusually lucra-tive, and she had even called the owner of a small sausage factory in Ulaanbaa-tar, who confirmed that he was willing to take delivery of pork fat from China (there being virtually no pig farming and thus pork production in Mongolia). So, after counting her remaining profit from the scrap metal venture and spend-ing a few days collecting debts from various debtors, Hulan jumped on the train heading for Zamyn Üüd at the Chinese border. This was her fourth trip

Suitcase trading (1999)

to China. She crossed the border in a packed jeep-taxi, which was what traders usually did at this crossing, and managed to buy eight hundred kilos of pork fat—of "the best quality," she was assured—from a Chinese trader before finding a driver who agreed to take her and the boxes of pork fat back across the Ereen–Zamyn Üüd border.

Unaware that it was illegal to import pork fat, Hulan did not even try to hide the nature of her new business in the making when the car was routinely checked at customs. Even as the boxes were opened by the Mongolian customs officials and the bags of fat were revealed in all their greasy and glistening glory, her chief concern still revolved around the seemingly poor quality of the fat. She had not checked the fat properly in China, she now realized, and the fat—wrapped in plastic but now exposed to the desert sun—did appear somewhat "oily." Hulan was soon made to understand, however, that this was the least of her problems. The customs officers were clearly very angry, she noticed, and they were even beginning to talk about calling the police. This made her extremely anxious, and slowly realizing the gravity of the situation she panicked and decided to escape. When the customs officers went into an adjacent building to deal with some administration, Hulan saw her opportunity to discreetly leave the pork fat behind, and therefore also to leave the poor driver who had taken her across the border alone with the customs officers. Amazingly, Hulan actually did manage to get across the border on her own and also hide for a day or so in Zamyn Üüd—the dusty Mongolian border town in the middle of the Gobi desert—but she was eventually caught on the train just as it was about to depart for Ulaanbaatar. She now had to spend time locked up in custody, which was followed by weeks more of waiting for her case to be tried at a court in Zamyn Üüd. When she finally managed to obtain her release and was able to return to Ulaanbaatar to await trial in Zamyn Üüd, she declared that she would never trade again. Even so, when Lars met her a few months later, she tried to sell him a jacket.

In the years that followed, Hulan's propensity to always seek out new business opportunities continued to throw her life in unexpected directions. She went to China once more but with little success. For a while, she also acquired a wireless telephone that allowed her to sell phone calls to passers-by on the busy streets of Ulaanbaatar (a common way of making money in this and other Mongolian cities before cell phone ownership skyrocketed around 2005; see also the Conclusion in this volume). Yet profit was low and being a "phone-person" (*utaschin*) was low-status and certainly not endorsed by her parents, so she soon decided to sell the phone. Instead (and clearly without being too concerned with her parents' reaction.), she then started to manage a night bar near the Naran Tuul market, on the first floor of a concrete building that had otherwise been reserved for a new supermarket. Apart from sharing the first floor with a noisy down-market nightclub, the major attraction of the bar—in addition to the sheer pleasure generated from having been able to find it in the first place—was a snooker table in the middle of a large, dimly lit room. Yet, perhaps unsurprisingly, customers were few, and she barely made enough to run the place. Later, she became caretaker of a "sauna"—the kind that was regularly frequented by prostitutes and, hence, by police authorities—all the while still trying to obtain a visa for South Korea. She still really wanted to go abroad to work, but she was unable to wait for it to happen. She had to do something and felt that she was losing money and wasting her time if inactive.

Over the years, this state of constant exploration, of endlessly tapping into new business potentials while quickly leaving other options and possibilities for making profit behind, came to cause Hulan an increasing amount of stress. "My mind is not stable" (*setgel sanaa togtvorgüi baigaa*), she would sometimes lament, "and I am unable to wait and always get upset" (*tsag hugatsaag huleehgüi, buhimdaltai baidag*). In order to empower and protect herself, she had Buddhist sutras read (*nom unshuulah*) for her by lamas at the Geser temple in Ulaanbaatar. Like many other struggling businesspersons (see Chapter 6), Hulan would ask the lamas to do the so-called wind horse incense offering (*hiimoriin san*) in the hope of increasing her luck (*hiimor'*) and gaining strength (*süld*), just as she would request special sutras and invocations read for business luck (*ajil üils büteeh nom*), for increasing income (*orlogo*) and for diminishing expenditure (*zarlaga*), as well as for her son to stay healthy (*övchin emgegees salgah nom*) and to protect her from hatred and jealousy in the form of *hel am*. After all, this was precisely what people like her needed in their relentless engaging with a post-socialist reality of fluctuating relations and unforeseen circumstances.

As much as Hulan, like the diehard urban hunters that she in many ways was, had always been drawn toward precisely this world of immanent and perpetual change—including the various desires that it both generated and promised to saturate—and like for so many others from her generation, the transition gradually became associated with insecurity and hardship. Eventually, as she was approaching thirty, she found herself wishing for a more stable future. In 2008 she moved to South Korea to work, leaving her son behind (as is common practice in Mongolia) with her parents, and later she returned (with a new Mongolian husband) to Mongolia and once again established a household and seemed to find slightly more steady occupations. Apparently, even the most devoted urban hunter would at some point start looking for, if not craving, radical predictability of the sort that Ariunaa, as we shall now see, had carved out for herself amid the maelstrom of enduring rupture.

TOO MANY RELATIONS

Lars first met Ariunaa in the late 1990s. She was a hard-working and disciplined woman who would keep appointments to an extent almost unheard of in Mongolia at the time. Ariunaa was unmarried, like Hulan, and also lived with her parents, but unlike Hulan she had a permanent job with a steady income. She had come of age in a world as transitional as that of Kolya's brothers but unlike Kolya she had managed to carve out a much more secure and predictable space within the daily unpredictabilities of life.

When Ariunaa graduated as a *magistr* in Mongolian language from the Teacher Training College (*Bagshiin Deed Surguul'*) in 1995, there were only a few, rather badly paid jobs available in the education sector, and the minority of graduates who did find a job at a school often only did so because they or their families were well-connected—or had perhaps been offering "help" and "gifts"—to school masters and other officials. So Ariunaa remained unemployed until her family decided to open a small street kiosk, a so-called *TÜTS*,[4] next to their apartment block in the northeastern part of Ulaanbaatar in the mid-1990s. At first, the family did not like the idea of doing business, not only because they had no experience with trading but also for more deeply held ideological and political reasons. According to Ariunaa, her father was an honest, strict and high-principled man. Much as we saw with the father of both Hulan and the four brothers discussed in Chapter 1, as master of the household (*geriin ezen*) he had always been a devout "red" (*ulaan*) communist who—unlike, for instance, Kolya's second-oldest brother, Lyoshya—had never dreamed of using his former position as a storehouse keeper (*nyarav*) in the Mongolian army to conduct illicit barter within the interstitial economic spaces of the socialist parallel economy. Ariunaa's mother, for her part, was a very active and talkative person who was always looking for new things to do, and so when the Mongolian government began granting permissions to open street kiosks in the mid-1990s, she managed to convince her husband that their family should join what eventually proved to become a veritable *TÜTS* explosion in Ulaanbaatar and other Mongolian towns. Indeed, during the second part of the 1990s, these characteristic constructions, all of them more or less identical in their simple design of square cubicles with windows facing only to the front, located where enough people would pass by, became a conspicuous part of Mongolia's urban landscape, and remained so until supermarkets took over from 2000 onward as providers of cigarettes, candy, soft drinks and basic staples such as rice, sugar, canned vegetables, soap and toilet paper.

For about a year, Ariunaa helped her mother with the new business, including the task of buying goods from the "disordered, unpleasant and dark black market" located in the northwestern periphery of Ulaanbaatar (which we discussed in detail in Chapter 2). The kiosk business turned out to be lucrative, and the family was making quite decent money. However, the household had only moved into the apartment block adjacent to their street kiosk in 1989, having spent most of their life in the countryside and in Ulaanbaatar's ger districts, and the parents never became accustomed to what they considered the "airless" concrete building. So, the following year, the parents and most of the rest of the household moved into one of Eastern Ulaanbaatar's bourgeoning ger districts and opened a proper shop (*delgüür*). However, Ariunaa stayed behind in the apartment with an elder sister and continued to run the *TÜTS* for a year until the family decided to sell both the apartment and the kiosk. The family was not wealthy and had spent a good deal of money on providing loans to various relatives that had never been paid back, but—in addition to finding the funds to open a proper shop in the suburban ger district—they were able to buy a one-bedroom flat for Ariunaa's younger brother, who was now settling down with his girlfriend. Furthermore, they used the profit from selling the kiosk to obtain a visa for South Korea through a middleman and send Ariunaa's older sister to Seoul. They also bought two *hashaa*s (fenced compounds) and eventually a third one for Ariunaa's younger brother. As a result, soon after the *TÜTS* had been sold, Ariunaa also moved to the ger district, at first with her sister in the older brother's compound (he had already left for South Korea) and later in her parents' *hashaa* (as the sister left for South Korea). Over time, from this household alone, six children were to go to South Korea for work.

Besides helping out in the parents' kiosk and later in their shop, Ariunaa also worked in a private language school as a Mongolian language teacher. For a while, she even entered the so-called Casino School to be trained as a professional dealer. A friend had told her about this "unique opportunity to be trained" in the skills of gambling "by teachers from Macau," and a dealer's salary, she had been assured, was exceptionally good. While thus a promising (if also, in Ariunaa's eyes, a slightly dubious) path to follow, this possibility of working as a professional dealer in a casino was foreclosed when gambling, which had only been legalized in 1998, was again prohibited the following year due to a major corruption scandal. As was so often the case in the 1990s, new prospects disappeared almost as soon as they emerged, just as disillusions, for our informants, were rapidly followed by new illusions.

One such new momentary illusion in Ariunaa's life was the meat trade venture that followed. For about two months, she joined a friend who was selling meat at the Tsaiz market in northwestern Ulaanbaatar. Once more, however, her stint as a dealer/trader turned out to be short-lived, for the meat trade "was not [her] kind of work" (*minii hiih ajil bish baisan*). She had to lie to customers (telling them that goat meat was really mutton), the profit was negligible, and animals were being slaughtered right next to her stand. Besides, the meat business—much like the gold and the vodka trade—was (and still is) widely associated with misfortune and death, and was for some reason dangerous in less tangible ways, too (see also Chapter 5). As one middle-aged female meat trader once told Lars, "Even when the prices go up, Mongols won't stop eating meat, and it makes them angry to pay so much for it." In short, the meat trade was an uncertain business "out of my control," as Ariunaa put it, which was especially challenging for a person like her, who preferred "to know what to do and how to do it." After a few months of dealing meat on the Tsaiz market, she decided to give it up.

While Ariunaa was still helping out in her parents' shop, she gradually came to the realization that she had never really liked the world of commerce. Unlike her mother, for instance, the constant interaction and dealing with customers caused her much worry. Quarrels were common, the ger district neighborhood was deprived, and customers often begged for credit (and, when granted, both money and creditors tended to disappear). At the shop, one had to face

Transporting goods (2006)

all sorts of people, including bad-tempered customers, and Ariunaa took even small issues, such as minor quarrels with them, much too seriously. Indeed, she recalled, troubles and adversities in general would continue to haunt her in her dreams. This was not the case with her parents. Her father was stern—too stern actually—even with regular customers, and her mother always managed to respond playfully, even when faced with unreasonable debtors. While her parents, especially Ariunaa's mother, were thus able to smoothly handle the social relations of commerce, Ariunaa never found herself completely at home in the world of the market. She was not a natural-born trader, nor was she much good as a shopkeeper.

Eventually, as teachers' salaries gradually began to climb to a level resembling an income (however meager), Ariunaa decided to concentrate fully on her actual profession of language teacher. She very much appreciated the predictability that followed from having a permanent job in a language school, and the only major change to take place in her life over the coming years was that she changed jobs from one language school in Ulaanbaatar to another one. Over this period, Ariunaa built up a stable, busy career with a steady income that even enabled her to put money in the bank. Due to inflation, saving money would have been next to impossible in the mid-1990s, but it made much more sense from around the turn of the millennium when inflation decreased considerably.[5] Unlike many people from her generation, Ariunaa was punctual and liked to plan things, and she was not prone to taking risks in her life. So, while she sometimes considered the possibility of opening a language school of her own, she found it too much of a gamble and convinced herself that she needed to be more well-connected to do so. "If you have acquaintances, you are like a steppe; if not, you are like a palm" (*taniltai bol talyn chinee, tanilgüi bol algyn chinee* [Mongolian proverb]), she explained, thus implying that she did not know the right influential people.

On the whole, Ariunaa was a careful and guarded person who was cautious about initiating new social relationships because they were often, she believed, the cause of troubles. Not exactly a gregarious networker, Ariunaa would thus describe herself as a person who was reluctant to get too close to people, and even when people tried to befriend her, she would often pass it off and keep them at bay. A female colleague, for example, once told her a secret, and later the same day Ariunaa received a text message on her cell phone from the same colleague saying that "now we are really close friends" (*za, odoo bid hoyor dotno naiz shüü*). Ariunaa would deliberately answer "yes, yes" (*tiim, tiim*) in order to undermine the seriousness of what was really a proposal to become friends. She was reluctant to being drawn into other people's expectations and, not least, disingenuous motives. Apart from suspecting other people's motives—many just befriend someone for profit (*ashig*), she said—the problem was mainly one of expectations. While not including her parents and siblings in these worries, Ariunaa found that when you get too close to people, they start to expect things from you and such expectations may cause problems when they cannot be met. When it comes to relatives, she explained, this is even more pronounced, as you are obliged to help relatives, whose expectations tend to be higher. Since high expectations can only rarely be met, close relationships, especially with relatives, almost always turn out to be problematic. To explain this, Ariunaa stressed the importance of a proverb that Lars had heard on other occasions as well (Højer 2004, 2019a): "Better stay close to mountains and water, better stay far away from kin" (*uul usny oir n' deer, urag törliin hol n' deer*). Subsistence and keeping to yourself, for her, were valued over relationships.

For Ariunaa, the proverb captured a general feature of relationality that she spoke of as the problem of *hariutslaga*. *Hariu* means "response," "answer" or "reply," and *hariutslaga* is an almost exact equivalent to the English term "responsibility," that is, the obligation or duty to respond to something. It was this *hariutslaga*—especially in the context of new relations or the potential for them—that Ariunaa tried to avoid at all costs. Her strategy, then, was to avoid as much social life as possible (Højer 2019a), and she often withdrew from invitations to join in networks of friends and colleagues. Unlike Kolya and Hulan, who immersed themselves in the open-ended potentials of transition, she strove to be insular and independent, one who did not have to partake in the endless traffic of expectation and responsibility, especially not in a transitional context of constant change and, thus, *hariutslaga* potential.

ESCAPING TRANSITION

Alas, Ariunaa's strategy was not working properly. While her parents were doing relatively well compared to most other households in Ulaanbaatar's periurban shantytowns, and while she had herself successfully made the transition from informal economic hustling to a "proper" job with a fixed salary, Ariunaa was still subject to what she perceived to be an ever-escalating number of demands, expectations and pressures. After all, the hardships that she shared with so many others from Mongolia's lost generation did not just involve the nuisance of loans that were never paid back, the difficulty of managing other people's expectations or indeed the trouble of angry customers. It also involved serious domestic and social problems of the sort that became so widespread in Mongolia after socialism (see Benwell 2006, 2009), such as alcoholism, divorce, violence and premature death, within her family also. There may thus have been a sense in which Ariunaa, for a combination of personal reasons and grounds pertaining to the wider socioeconomic situation, literally craved for a rupture from an everyday life infested with chaos and uncertainty (Højer 2018). In any case, the result was that—like many other women of a similar age, education and background—Ariunaa now departed on a spiritual and existential journey that was to culminate in her conversion to Protestant Christianity:

> When I was in my early twenties, I kept thinking about the meaning of life. Life seemed meaningless, full of dark things, and nothing would attract me. One day, when I was a student, I was reading a book by the Tibetan philosopher Nagarjuna. His theory is about emptiness, and it says, "Everything starts from nothing and ends in nothing." . . . I was very sure that it described life. It didn't encourage me, but made me depressed, because it proved that there was no meaning at all in my life. I didn't see even the tiniest hope.

Such was the bleak manner in which Ariunaa remembered her life prior to conversion: as an empty hole devoid of meaning. Ariunaa had first heard about the Bible and Jesus around 1999, when she had just begun to teach Mongolian to foreigners, many of whom turned out to be American or South Korean missionaries posted to Mongolia in need of language training. For a while she did not pay much attention to it, but then in 2002 she began participating in a weekly Bible study group run by an American pastor. Like so many other people, she initially turned to the study group out of curiosity and in the hope of improving her English but then gradually realized that Christianity was right for her:

> I liked the philosophy of how individuals and relationships between people should be. I got answers. *Where do I come from? Where will I go after dying? Why do I always feel empty and miss something? . . . Why did God create people when he had everything?* I believe that he wanted to feel warm relationships and love from people. He could have created people without a heart and without a choice, people who would do whatever he wants, like robots . . . [But] the Bible encourages me to do the right things, to treat all people with love, and to forgive others, even myself. When I try to do those things, I feel that the dark ties that wrapped me are cut one by one . . . I really didn't make a decision to become a Christian. I just realized that this is the only way for me—and I was already on that path. It was not a sudden event.

While Ariunaa, from her own retrospective and intensely introspective gaze, was already—and had always been—a Christian deep inside, she still describes her conversion as a "life-changing" trajectory of ruptures where "dark ties were cut one by one." She was "encouraged" by the Bible, gradually brought to "a realization" and more generally experienced a severing from the emptiness and "dark things." Once, she vividly described, at a meeting of her Bible study group, she suddenly realized how the fall of man explained why she "always felt a lack inside." Indeed, she could even date her conversion to December 2007. She was sitting in a microbus in Ulaanbaatar, on the way home, and found herself ready to give up Christianity. She had "received answers" but still did not consider herself a Christian and was exhausted and torn from a long-lasting internal "spiritual struggle." Staring out of the window, she suddenly realized—with the help of God—that the decision to become a Christian was not in her power. Instead, becoming a Christian involved moving along, and continuing to move along, the very spiritual path she was already on. "When this thought came to me," she said, "I felt so relaxed, so relaxed." The struggle was gone, and she felt absolutely certain. The next day, she told everyone she knew, and she stopped feeling empty inside.

For Ariunaa, then, the experience of this rupture with emptiness was not just caused by a retrospective rationalization of the past from the perspective of a newfound Christian theology. It was not only Christianity that had caused something to happen "to"—and not just "in"—time (Robbins 2007: 12) by introducing a new model of time and of change, based on conversion and rupture as opposed to temporal continuity (see also Robbins 2004). Ariunaa already felt a profound lack or "void" that had spurred a quest for meaning and depth. Rather than the radical temporal break having originated in the newfound Christian cosmology alone, she herself had been craving rupture long before becoming Christian. Ariunaa, and quite possibly other converts, then, had in other words caused something to happen "to" time *by* joining Christianity. Christianity may well have catalyzed and facilitated a radical change, *pace* Robbins, but this potential for rupture had already been present albeit dormant in her life and her ideas about existence. In Ariunaa's case, then, Christianity was just as much a means as it was a cause, for her conversion was part and parcel of a lifelong and increasingly desperate search for ways and techniques that could detach her and catapult her away from the escalating social expectations and economic demands of life in transition.

Christianity enabled radically new opportunities and *allowed her to act* on firmer ground, while Christian theology offered the possibility of jumping from the meaninglessness, hopelessness and disillusion of transition to the meaning, compassion and encouragement of conversion. Love and forgiveness enabled Ariunaa to detach herself from the reality she had been facing and, not least, from the darkness that had filled it, whether caused by "postsocialist" predicaments or—in her own terms—a world devoid of meaning. The Holy Spirit (*ariun süns*, lit. pure spirit), she believed, was fundamental to all people and ensured that virtue and love, in the last instance, were to be found everywhere, even behind meaningless actions and disillusioned lives. For Ariunaa, as the urban antihunter she was, the environment of transition had been a raging sea of malevolent forces, turmoil and tragedy, and she—like many other women in Ulaanbaatar around the turn of the millennium—was certainly longing for a way to cope with this meaninglessness—and maybe the difficulties of contemporary life—and had found confidence in a Protestant world where relations with others are mediated and secured through God and the ability to forgive. From this viewpoint, God's love and proper relations with others are two sides of the same coin. "The relationship with God is a precondition for one's relationship with others," she reflected, "for without God, it is difficult to have good relations with others." "We may trick each other," she continued, "but not in front of God." Relations were stabilized and easier to deal with and come to terms with—and what she considered the ever-recurrent tragedies and the mess of transition expelled—through an emphasis on love, forgiving, working together, stability, punctuality, family values, a strong work ethic and saving money (see also Højer 2007, 2018).

For quite some time after becoming interested in Christianity, Ariunaa continued to live with her now-elderly parents in their modest *hashaa* deep in Ulaanbaatar's eastern suburbs. Here, she would spend every evening helping out in their shop and also preparing lessons for the coming day. Eventually, however, Ariunaa managed to save up enough money to buy a small one-bedroom apartment close to the city center where she opened her own language school. Here, she would teach Mongolian to mainly foreign businessmen, anthropologists and, not least, missionaries. While the apartment-turned-language-school also increasingly became her home, the two rooms were set up in classroom fashion with desks, blackboards, some language books and a few green plants in the windows, and the rooms were always meticulously tidy and clean. In time, she hired a couple of teachers but eventually fell out with one of them and was left with only one employee: her own sister. In a sense, Ariunaa's long and arduous journey was now complete: she had managed to fully convert from transition to stability in a double sense. For her, this double shift to a new religion and a new occupational status was accompanied by a hardened rhetoric in response to some of the claims made on her by different people around her, ranging from potential suitors to recent acquaintances who wanted to become part of her life. Eventually, around 2003 and 2004, when Morten spent a lot of time with her, her life became stabilized—one might even say frozen—in the same pattern: her business was prospering (without making her really rich), and her relations with various relatives, friends and acquaintances were still strained without having been fully severed (for more details, see Holbraad and Pedersen 2017: 253–263). Taken together, these simultaneous transformations—from "heathen" to believer and from trader to teacher—had effectuated a radical and irreversible shift in Ariunaa's entire constitution as a social, moral and spiritual being.

TAMING SPIRITS

Before reaching our conclusion, let us round off the story of Ariunaa with yet another telling example that demonstrates how the rupture—from permanent discontinuity, social excess and existential emptiness—sought from and found in Christianity had implications not just for Ariunaa but also for her relations with the surrounding world of humans and spirits. Ariunaa's brother had, like many other Mongolians, traveled to Korea to work with his wife. Some years ago, one of his wife's relatives, a female shaman from Ulaanbaatar, had paid them a visit. The shaman had urged Ariunaa's brother to become a shaman. "If not," the female shaman had warned, "something bad may happen to you and your family, someone may even die." So, on returning to Ulaanbaatar a few years later, when Ariunaa had already become a Christian, her brother immediately took up his shamanic vocation. He had a shamanic costume made, held ceremonies, was possessed by ancestral spirits—usually six or seven during one ceremony—and would ask family members to participate in ceremonies for whole days on end. After all, he had followed this call partly to save his family from being struck by misfortune, even death. Ariunaa was the only one never to show up. It took up too much time, she said, and she utterly disliked the whole thing. She was not pleased by the fact that he had spent so much money on the shamanic costume and, possibly, also on payments to his shamanic teacher. She strongly disapproved of his violent behavior when possessed and was worried about the dangers of engaging with spirits. Last but not least, she detested the drinking of vodka and eating of incense during ceremonies (among other practices, some of the spirits ingested incense). Yet when her brother called her one day, begging her to attend a ceremony—he had, after all, he made clear in no uncertain terms, become a shaman for the sake of the family—Ariunaa felt sorry for him and agreed to participate in one single ceremony. However, she was deeply worried about the prospect of having to confront her possessed brother. Would the ancestral spirits declare war on her? Would her brother start to misbehave and throw things at people (as he always did during ceremonies)?

On the evening of the ceremony, Ariunaa, keeping close to her soon-to-be possessed shaman brother, began to pray to God—and found that her fear had suddenly vanished. Soon, her brother became possessed by a spirit, and then another one, but when the third spirit demanded vodka and incense, she acted. She resolutely took the incense from her possessed brother's mouth and spoke to the spirits: "If you are our ancestors and love us, don't make my brother suffer. Don't do bad things. Take care of him. If you are real spirits, see the real God and tell my family about him. If you really love my family, tell them." And behold, the spirits fell silent, and when the next one arrived, it merely asked Ariunaa for a massage (while spirits always make a variety of demands when appearing during possessions, this was an unusual request). She rubbed her brother's shoulders and no further spirits were to descend—they were afraid, she mused—and her brother did not, as was usually the case, turn violent. "Just give me a massage," he/the spirit said. Ariunaa's nieces, observing the séance, were surprised at her power and courage, and she herself was further strengthened in her faith in the Holy Spirit. A month or two later, her brother stopped shamanizing completely.

This incident shows that while Ariunaa, even after her conversion to Christianity, continued to accept and also "believe in" the existence of a multitude of disorderly and havoc-wreaking ancestral spirits associated with the non-Christian world (one of transition and a lack of guiding principles), Ariunaa's response was not to give herself away to them—to become "possessed" or otherwise subjected to them—but to expel, dominate or pacify these occult forces. She even tried to convert and tame the spirits by speaking Christian sense to them: "If you love us, don't make us suffer . . . if you are real, tell us about the real God." The spirits could exist for real, it seems, but only if they conformed to the Christian message of love. For the spirits to be truly real to Ariunaa, then, they could not be of the same "labile" and indeterminate nature as transition itself (Pedersen 2011) but had to be stabilized as Christians and ultimately subsumed under the Holy Spirit.

Like so many other young Mongolians from the lost generation (see Chapter 6), Ariunaa had spent much of her adult life trying in vain to establish a safe distance between herself and what she perceived as the omnipresent spirits and troubles impinging on her from all sides—for example, during the many long nights when worries about the well-being of her family, or the accusations made by friends, prevented her from sleeping. Like several other new converts whom Ariunaa eventually befriended after joining the church, she had therefore been searching desperately for ways to suppress a perceived overabundance of occult forces, which were so diffuse and manifold that she would sometimes find her mind and body facing the risk of being overtaken by "darkness." Yet this did not lead her (or other Mongolian converts we spoke to) to begin to doubt the existence of these non-Christian spirits. In fact, as she herself acknowledged, it was almost as if she were now more convinced of their looming presence, and more worried about their sway over other people's lives. Only now, the difference was that, having found God and put all her trust in him, she did not personally fear the shamanic spirits in the same way she had before. Thus, the reason Ariunaa and her peers were so keen on affirming their belief in God was that they took the demonic spirits—and the place of evil in the world—for granted (Ruel 1982; Chua 2009; Robbins et al. 2014). By striving to remain detached from dangerous spirits and obnoxious men, Ariunaa substituted a vulnerability to multiple harmful external influences with an unquestioned love for a single God with whom one could engage via intense introspective self-relating (see Pedersen 2012; Holbraad and Pedersen 2017).

For Ariunaa and possibly other "urban antihunters," then, the dual transformation to a new Christian faith and a new middle-class status was, essentially, a matter of cutting connections. Certainly there is a revealing correspondence between Ariunaa's and other young, upwardly mobile women's wish to absent themselves from the excessive claims made by friends and family, on the one hand, and their attempt to free themselves from multiple spirits' influence by renouncing and avoiding them, on the other. Christianity provides an escape from two negative influences at the same time. Indeed, this is what conversion

essentially appears to be all about for Ariunaa and many other Christian converts in Mongolia: a severing of a heterogeneous manifold of unwanted social
and spiritual relations in order to fully and finally concentrate one's trust and
obligations around a single relationship—namely, the relationship between an
individual human believer and an almighty God.

CONCLUSION

In this chapter we have presented the stories of Hulan and Ariunaa: two women
from Ulaanbaatar's lost generation who exemplified two virtually opposite ways
of responding to and dealing with the postsocialist world of radical transition.
For the quintessential urban hunter, Hulan, the stabilization of social relations
that the concept of networks tends to connote—whether in the form of "egalitarian" commodity chains or hierarchical monopolies of wholesale traders—
does not capture the constant exploration-cum-annihilation of new relations
and possibilities that came to be so characteristic of her "career." As an inherently erratic, or should we say "systematically unsystematic," hunter of quick
profit, Hulan found it equally difficult, if not suffocating, to cope with the
established commodity chains that emerged in Mongolia in the aftermath of
socialism (such as the shoe people or flour people found at Ulaanbaatar's biggest
markets [see Chapter 2]) and the asymmetrical networks of changers and their
clients, where systematic exploitation and mafia-like coercion were the name of
the game. Above all, Hulan was repulsed by ordinary salaried and contracted
jobs in which the almost erotic thrills, excitements and surprises of urban hunting were totally absent. She, like many others from her generation, was steering
a capricious course whereby the whole trick was to know one's "size" in order to
optimally balance the tightrope of transition.

Ariunaa, on the other hand, was fundamentally averse to performing this
balancing act and to the entire life and world that came with it. Accordingly,
for her the only solution was to detach herself from transition altogether—from
changers, hustlers, shamans and troublesome relations more generally—in the
hope of carving out an insular social and existential space that was clinically
detached from, and thus unaffected (and uninfested) by the always changing
realities and potentialities of the postsocialist city. Far from fearlessly taking
a dive into the violently shifting seas of transition like the extrovert Hulan,
Ariunaa opted for a more introverted religiosity capable of keeping impinging
networks of human and nonhuman "evil" at bay through a commitment to a
single God. And, as we have seen, this detached and more "professional" individuality went hand in hand with certain concepts and expectations of com-

munal life and "civil society" based on trust, unity and truthfulness ("we may trick each other but not in front of God"). As such, Ariunaa's sense of self was diametrically opposed to that of the urban hunters discussed in this chapter and this book. Far from the amorphous, incoherent and capricious selfhood of many of Ulaanbaatar's (mostly male) hustlers, whom Ariunaa may have been inclined to dismiss as proud, boastful (*bardam*) and "messy" people, her ideal was to be modest, honest and devoted and to avoid the troubles and transience of transition by belonging to a Christian community based on self-effacing (*hün yuu ch bish*) relations of love and a God-mediated belief in the essential purity of other human beings. And, tellingly, a widespread ramification of these hyper-Protestant ethics of "minding your own business" by relating to others mostly through fixed contracts in both work and other contexts was that unmarried, educated, and lower-middle-class social climbers like Ariunaa would end up working with foreigners in NGOs and, possibly, joining Bible reading groups with their new colleagues.

In sum, we hope in this chapter to have made it clear that the true personifications of Mongolia's predicament of radical transition were found not only in the wheeler-dealing, restless and boundary-transgressing Hulan, but equally in the introverted, cautious and limitation-conscious Ariunaa, who, in that sense, embodies the flipside of urban hunting. After all, as we also made clear in the Introduction to this book, social life in Ulaanbaatar around the turn of the millennium was not only defined by hunter-like explorations of ever more labile flows of money, commodities and people, or by people who had lost their way in drinking and socializing. It was also characterized by strategies for containing the movement of objects in the form of property, subjects in the form of autonomous (e.g., Christian) individuals and social relations in the form of collectivities based on long-term trust. At the peak of transition and radical rupture, then, an introvert like Ariunaa was as much an avatar of things to come as an extroverted urban hunter like Hulan was a paragon of the present.

Chapter 5 The Spirit of Debt

Like many other urban hunters, Kolya's income was periodic, if not simply fleeting and short-lived, and like many of his friends, he was not prone to saving money, not even for the long and meager winter season. He did not own any expensive pieces of property to put up as security for a bank loan, and sometimes he and his female partner found it necessary to visit a pawnshop, where they could, for example, use her earrings as collateral for a small loan. This was the easy and fast way to get cash when your income was unstable, when all nearby friends were out of money, and when you did not have—or want—the possibility of ensuring your financial stability by saving up funds in a bank account. Attesting to the fact that a very large number of people in postsocialist Mongolia lived under such permanently volatile and changing conditions was the fact that pawnshops (*lombard*) could be found all over Ulaanbaatar around the turn of the millennium. These *lombard*, it seemed, thrived on the durability of postsocialist transition and volatility—and not least on an urban hunter's sudden needs and lack of savings. Yet, while they were thus quintessentially postsocialist institutions and a sign of precarious times, pawnshops also created opportunities for "on-the-spot planners" such as Lyosha who were in need of instant cash. They enabled suitcase traders to raise financial means for their trip to the Chinese border, and they made it possible for students to raise money from one moment to the other when craving fun. As straightforward as this may seem, and as straightforward as pawnshop visits indeed often were (such as when a group of students would pawn a mobile phone to get money for a bottle of vodka), the conversion of personal belongings into ready, all-purpose cash through pawning did not just create instant possibilities for business and fun but was as much an activity that could cause serious worries and problems. Take Bulgan, an elderly female pawnbroker, who, in an almost despondent voice, explained how dealings at the pawnshop were also associated with occult and damaging energies:

> People with money problems will come here . . . They extend the duration of the loan again and again. They are too stingy to pay interest. People have black energy [*har enyergi*] and think that we get too much money. They are angry, feel cheated and have arguments . . . I don't feel comfortable talking to those drunken people. They don't want to pay interest. They don't have much, are angry and can't send good energy to people . . . Such persons will influence me. Being a *lombard* is different from other kinds of jobs . . . People's energy influences other people.

The practice of pawning, which often involved strained business relations and the commodification (and loss) of a customer's personal belongings, allowed for the emergence—from within the pawnbroking business itself—of new dangerous affects. These could be caused by angry customers who had lost their personal belongings, by pawned items haunted by owners' desire to get them back, or by redeemed items infected with the bad "energies" of pawnshops. On the one hand, then, the *lombard* institution was an institution much in line with the life of what we have called urban hunters and the ruptures of transition more generally. It facilitated immediate exchanges and served to raise ready cash for use when faced with a sudden opportunity (or with owing someone money). On the other hand, however, pawnshops also embodied the more sinister aspects of transition, whereby exchangeability and momentary opportunities, so characteristic of urban hunting, often went hand in hand with becoming tied up in the curse-like relations described by Bulgan.

In what follows, we use the pawnshop as a prism for exploring the dangers that arise from falling prey to the dangerous "energies" of transition by being carried away by the unlimited exchange—especially debt—possibilities of the market. As such, we are concerned in this chapter with what might be called the dark side of urban hunting, understood as the dangerous affects that life in transition, and the limitless (ex)change of objects, allow for. Situated at the interface between alienable capitalist commodities and inalienable domestic belongings, and acting as important mediators for the conversion of objects and forms of value between these two spheres, the *lombard* emerges as "a condensed metaphor for change itself" (Oushakine 2009: 47) in postsocialist Mongolia and perhaps in times of permanent transition more generally. After all, as we demonstrate, pawning makes possible otherwise impossible conversions between regimes of value (cf. Bohannan 1955). In doing so, it brings about unseen opportunities for pawnbrokers and clients alike, but it also gives rise to new and unstable economic affects emanating from within the acts of conversion. This, in turn, raises concerns about what might be the most proper and safest way of (ex)changing things in a world where change is ubiquitous.

With respect to our wider theme of urban hunting, then, this chapter—unlike other accounts of this theme we have presented so far—does not tell the story of individual urban hunters. Instead, it explores the shaky, complicated and indeterminate socioeconomic terrain in which they operated. It does so by paying particular attention to a certain "market" institution, that of the *lombard*, which epitomizes the possibilities and the dangers pertaining to a world of sudden value conversions and radical (ex)changes of which the urban hunters were both products and coproducers.

MONGOLIA'S NEW ECONOMY OF DEBT

Historically, moneylending has received bad press in Mongolia. In the nineteenth century, when contemporary Mongolia was dominated by the Manchu Qing dynasty, Mongolians are known to have been heavily indebted to Chinese merchants and moneylenders (see Sanjdorj 1980; Bawden 1989; Atwood 2004; Sneath 2012), even to the extent that some *banners* (an administrative unit under the Qing dynasty) had a debt that far exceeded the total capital value of the *banner* in question (Bawden 1989: 203). The twentieth-century Soviet-backed socialist regime obviously did nothing to suppress this perception of moneylending as unscrupulous, nor did it do anything to hinder the association of China with a presocialist feudal, even capitalist, past of usury, exploitation and backwardness (see Billé 2014), especially from the 1950s when Mongolia's relationship with China became highly strained due to the Sino-Soviet split. Yet, while we shall shortly see how this antiusury and anti-Chinese discourse persisted after 1990, it did so in a new context where concrete debt relationships increased dramatically as a result of the dismantling of the socialist state and the general economic turmoil of the transition period.

The collapse of the centrally planned economy in the early 1990s meant that both the size and the importance of different socioeconomic networks, including informal debt arrangements, started to grow exponentially in Mongolia as well as in many places in the former Soviet Union and East Central Europe (Ledeneva 1998; Mandel and Humphrey 2002; Nazpary 2002; see also Chapters 1 and 4 in this volume). People's income was uncertain, if not entirely lacking, and with the neoliberal reforms and the introduction of private ownership, dealing with risks and uncertainties had also become an individual responsibility that led many Mongolian families to obtain loans in times of difficulty (Sneath 2012). Hence, for many people in the Mongolian capital, life in the age of the market came, to a significant extent, to be organized around relations of debt.[1]

As already noted in Chapter 1, it was not unusual for Kolya and the others to dedicate a significant proportion of an average day to tracking down people who owed them money, or looking for potential creditors from whom they could borrow money themselves (sometimes to pay back money they already owed to others). As such, for many of our Ulaanbaatar friends, income was fleeting and unstable, new opportunities always emerged that required sudden investments (and, hence, loans), and economic relations were characterized by fluctuating asymmetries (most people we knew had been both debtors and creditors, and were often so at one and the same time, on a permanent basis). The following story, told by one of Kolya's acquaintances, was by no means exceptional:

I once met a friend of one of my childhood friends. I didn't know him well. His name was Batbold. He was dealing in mobile phones and wanted me to work with him, so I invested USD7,000 in his business and expected to make a profit of MNT1 or 2 million. We bought a hundred phones and Batbold started selling them from his stall. We never made a contract. He was supposed to pay me back in millions but he always gave me small amounts of money only. In the end he had paid me no more than MNT4.5 million and then disappeared like a stone in water. I needed money, but I didn't have any. It was around New Year. So, still believing that he would pay me back, I pawned my car for MNT500,000. Then I met him once, and he told me—looking very sincere and serious—that he would give me the money and that he was sorry about the whole thing. I trusted him and was waiting patiently, but he never gave me the money. I got an additional MNT700,000 from a pawnshop and I now had a debt of MNT1.2 million. I called Batbold and he said, "I can't get the money. I have already taken my dad's salary as a loan. But I will get your car from the pawnshop," he promised. I waited for a couple of months and took an additional loan of MNT500,000 and now had a debt of MNT1.7 million. I lost my car to the pawnshop, and when I finally met Batbold he said, "I have been trying hard but was not able to find the money for you. However, my sister has an apartment in Nalaih [outside Ulaanbaatar]. I will pawn it and get MNT40 million." I knew that this was way too much for this apartment, but I was working as a loan changer [*chyenj*] and decided to take advantage of the situation. I told him that I could help if he paid me 3.5 million. He gave me MNT3.2 million and gave me the apartment papers. I kept the money, but the following day I sent my friend to return the papers and then called him and said that now we were equal and should part ways. He got furious and kidnapped my friend. There were many guys, and they wanted to kill him. I was afraid—you never knew what could happen. We then met in front of the Ard cinema in Ulaanbaatar. They brought a lawyer and my kidnapped friend, and I brought a police guy that I knew. I thought that it was all over when they released my friend, but Batbold's sister, apparently, has reported the case to the police and I still have problems.

Stories like these were plentiful in Ulaanbaatar, and the only unusual thing about this particular narrative, it seems, was that it very nearly came to an end when accounts were settled. In the Mongolian age of the market—or should we say, with a nod to Graeber and other anthropologists working on debt (Peebles 2010, 2012; Graeber 2011; High 2012; Empson 2014; Waters 2018), the Mongolian "era of credit"—debts were typically not redeemed in any such final sense but were rather continually postponed in an endless chain of other debts. This world of credit was typically driven by informal loans from relatives, friends, acquaintances or private moneylenders, but they were also obtained from "loan redeemers" (*zeel chölöölöögch*) or loan changers, such as Kolya's acquaintance above, who specialized in helping/profiting from people who could not pay their apartment loan installments. They would do so by helping people to pay back their loans and obtain a new loan, with a different term, in another bank.

Yet a number of opportunities for obtaining formal loans also became available during the 1990s and just after the turn of the millennium when we conducted most of our fieldwork in Ulaanbaatar. The pawnbroker institution provided one of several such official ways of obtaining loans, the other legal institutions being "savings and credit cooperatives" (*hadgamlaj zeeliin horshoo*) and banks. The banking system offered large and relatively cheap loans, but for ordinary people, a bank loan was often out of reach. One needed to provide a detailed and feasible business plan or have the right connections to be considered worthy of credit—or both. Knowing someone, or knowing someone who knew someone, made it easier to persuade employees at the bank to decrease the interest of a loan and improve one's credit rating but still, for the majority of people, bank loans were not a realistic option.

As membership organizations that "provide savings and credit services to their members" (Bauner and Richter 2006: 23), savings and credit cooperatives operated on a smaller scale than banks in terms of both number of lenders involved and the size of loans. A minimum of twenty people and at least MNT50 million were required to establish a cooperative in 2006. Unlike pawnbrokers, cooperatives were allowed to accept real estate as collateral, and more generally they operated on a bigger scale with larger sums of money involved. To give an example, the security provided for the first two loans—for a truck trailer (MNT10 million) and a vacuum packaging machine to be used for kimchi (MNT5 million)—that were given by a newly opened savings and credit cooperative in Ulaanbaatar in the mid-2000s was a truck and a two-story factory building. Loans were usually much smaller than bank loans, and the conditions for raising them more lenient—and, since people usually had more valuables (apartments, trucks, etc.) than ready cash in the postsocialist era, savings and credit cooperatives (and pawnshops) were much needed in this period. Indeed, in 2006 it was estimated that savings and credit cooperatives alone granted as much as 90 percent of all loans in Mongolia (Bauner and Richter 2006: 23).

Moving one step further down the ladder to the bottom of the official Mongolian credit market, you find the *lombard*. While the word *lombard* originates from Russia and Central Europe, where it was used for moneylenders from Lombardy in Northern Italy, and while pawnbroking itself dates back to at least AD 1000 in Europe and the fifth century in China and thus historically precedes banking (see Schrader 2000: 10–17; Whelan 1979: 1; Caskey 1994: 12–15), pawnshops, like commercial banks and savings and credit cooperatives, only emerged in Mongolia after 1990. The phenomenon, however, grew exponentially during the 1990s, and in 1999 the city of Ulaanbaatar alone was home to 412 pawnshops that issued an estimated MNT12.4 billion in loans (Bikales et al. 2000: 17). In comparison, "the total stock of outstanding commercial bank loans to individuals was under 3.8 billion togrogs [*sic*] as of December 31, 1999" (Bikales et al. 2000: 17). Pawnshops, in other words, were significant players in the Mongolian credit market around the turn of the millennium.[2]

The pawnshops in Ulaanbaatar were legally permitted to accept vehicles as collateral for loans, but most customers, pawnbrokers told us, came with electronic equipment (especially mobile phones), gold rings, carpets or other items of lesser value. The pawnbroker would carefully examine the objects in question (and would write down, for example, the serial number of mobile phones) and, based on their estimations of quality and market price, would offer a loan of 50 or 60 percent of the value of the item pawned, the interest being approximately 8 percent per month depending on the loan term and the interest rates of competing pawnbrokers (by law, the maximum interest was 12 percent per month in 2007). The loan term could be, and often was, extended again and again. If the customer did not manage to reclaim the pawned item, the pawnbroker would, usually after trying to contact the customer several times, resell the item to another person (everyone could "shop" in a pawnshop) or to a "professional" middleman or "changer" working in the interstices of Ulaanbaatar and other cities' marketplaces (see Chapters 4 and 6) and with whom the pawnbrokers collaborated. As one pawnbroker told Lars, "There are changers for everything."

Apart from turning to kin, friends and acquaintances for credit, going to the pawnshop was the easy way to get a small loan for hustler-gatherers such as Lyosha, and it was indeed also one of the only viable options for most ordinary people in need of ready cash.[3] This obviously left the pawnshops in Mongolia— as tends to be the case with pawnshops elsewhere in the world (see, e.g., Caskey 1994; Schrader 2000)—with a certain kind of customer. While not dirt-poor or homeless, the customers were mainly from the lower middle class and the poorer segments of the population—actually the vast majority of the Mongolian population—those who still possessed enough valuable property to place as collateral for a pawnshop loan. They were often students from rural backgrounds whose limited monthly endowment wired from their families back home had again run out, but they could also be traders who had run out of liquidity to buy new stock or were unable pay an outstanding loan to an acquaintance or (worse) a loan shark, or simply anyone in dire need of cash. Frequently, they were people under some pressure, maybe even angry, at first because they were in need of ready cash and, later on, because they needed to get their pawned— and maybe cherished—possessions back. The pawnbrokers, on the other hand, were not from these poorer segments of the population. To set up in business, they needed to have enough money to open a pawnshop, that is, MNT5 million, and they had thus already been fairly successful in business or simply had the right connections. In our experience, and much in line with the conclusions already reached in Chapter 2, pawnbrokers, like traders, in a very general sense tended to be women and customers tended to be men—hence our use of "she" for pawnbrokers and "he" for customers in what follows.

AN INSTITUTION IN TROUBLE

In 2006, pawnshops were ubiquitous in Ulaanbaatar. In some places, such as one of the entrances to the Bayanzürh market in the eastern part of central

Pawnbroker's hatch (2007)

Ulaanbaatar, one would even find clusters of adjacent pawnshops competing for the same customers. While pawnshops were thus found all over the city—at markets and on shopping streets, visible from street level or hidden away in concrete basements—they were most often located in shopping spaces such as at markets and in buildings occupied by small shops and stalls. The pawnshop itself would typically be a small locked room, covering only a few square meters, furnished with at least a table, a chair and a locker. Communication between pawnbrokers and customers—and the transfer of money and things—typically took place through a small hatch just big enough to facilitate the necessary verbal and physical exchanges but not sufficiently big for a person to pass through, not unlike the ones used by ticket vendors and money changers (and, indeed, drug dealers) in many parts of the world. Most of the pawnbroker's time was spent waiting for customers to come by—and customers, some pawnbrokers complained in 2006, were becoming fewer. Also, most customers, it appeared, were either only interested in getting their items assessed (and would then continue to other pawnbrokers in search of a better offer) or were immediately rejected because of the low value of the items they brought.

Despite being found on virtually any street in the city and being one of the most common business activities, pawnshops were not held in high esteem, nor were the pawnbrokers themselves particularly fond of their job. Take Bayarmaa, a female pawnbroker in her thirties who had come to Ulaanbaatar from Western Mongolia in 1999. She had, like most other people we knew, been involved in trading a variety of different products—marmot skin, spirits, cars—through the Chinese and Russian border crossings in the Hovd and Bayan-Ölgii provinces in Western Mongolia, and she had also managed to graduate from teacher training college before realizing that the future in the Mongolian countryside looked bleak. The salary of a teacher was low, and the petty cross-border trade of the 1990s was slowly being taken over by large companies, she explained. Thus, Bayarmaa decided to move to Ulaanbaatar and, inspired by her relatives, chose to use some of the money earned in trade, combined with a loan obtained from relatives, to open a pawnshop. She was, however, not entirely proud of her job. As she told Lars, "I am embarrassed about being a pawnbroker. People don't like lombard. Mongolians consider the lombard to be a place where they are ripped off . . . It is bad work. I don't like this work. But I think that we are doing white [good] work because we give money to people who don't have any and who can't get any from anywhere else."

While she thus tried hard to morally justify pawnbroking as "white work," she later expanded on the difficulties of pawnbroking by adding that "our Mongolian custom tells us that our way will be fine if we sell milk," thereby implying that being a pawnbroker was not a similarly safe and pure occupation. In Ulaanbaatar at the time of our fieldwork, it would seem, lombard activity was often thought of as immoral by the pawnshop clients, and pawnbrokers themselves would at least see it as potentially troublesome. We can distinguish two reasons for this. One concerns the general and widely reported moral ambiguity of creditors. As Bayarmaa explained,

> When people get money they know that they should pay it back but they don't think of the amount. When they come back to repay the money, they realize that they have

to pay a lot of money. Well, really not very much. They might get MNT100,000 and the interest for this large amount of money is MNT1,000. So they need to pay MNT101,000. But when they come back it seems to be too much money for them. There is the following Russian saying: "When people borrow money they get someone else's money but when they pay it back, they give their own money." It works that way.

The saying suggests that, in the time lapse between receiving and repaying a loan, the money at hand changes from being the creditor's money-on-loan to becoming the debtor's own money, and that, from the customer's perspective, this change calls the validity of a clear-cut creditor-debtor relation into doubt. Indeed, Bayarmaa lamented, Ulaanbaatar *lombard* customers often blamed the pawnbrokers for taking what they had now come to see as "their own money," and brokers such as Bayarmaa were acutely aware of this fact and did their best to take it into account in their interactions with clients. Sometimes pawnbrokers tried to rationalize this accusation by referring to people's "lack of understanding" of the new principles for credit within the context of the capitalist market—"it *is* getting better," one pawnbroker assured. Yet, as the above quote and Russian proverb reveal, debt can always be rendered into a moral question of "who really owes what to whom," as Graeber puts it (2011: 8), and in many other settings around the world, pawnshop owners and other vernacular loan brokers are perceived as morally dubious or even evil (see, e.g., Addo and Besnier 2008; Schrader 2000: 10; Graeber 2011: 9–10).

The second reason the *lombard* institution is perceived as morally flawed is that, as we have already hinted, it is entrenched in a specific Mongolian socialist and presocialist history. Consider the story of Bulgan, the elderly pawnbroker from above: She had worked as a geologist during socialism, but as she was forced into retirement in 1993 due to one of the government cutbacks of the early 1990s, she had now become a pawnbroker. After the collapse of socialism, many well-educated people lost their jobs, and after 1990 it was more than common to find geologists, for example, engaged in activities unrelated to their primary profession. Bulgan was, in her own words, "a person from socialist society" (*sots niigmiin hün*) who was used to stability and a good job, and while she did not dislike her job as a pawnbroker—at least "it was better for an elderly woman than working in the market"—she, elaborating on the passage that was cited in the introduction to this chapter and concurring with Bayarmaa, could understand how some people disliked pawnbrokers:

> Some people with a good life might pass here, and if they need money they might give me their things and after three, four or five days they come and get their things

back, they say "thanks" and leave . . . Some people come and curse me [*haraagaad yavah*]. They don't have a good heart because they are in a hurry, depressed and angry . . . Young people do not need to do this work . . . People think that we are just sitting here getting money, rather than helping them.

In other words, the pawnbroker just sat on her butt and did not produce anything, and in Mongolia as in many other previously socialist contexts, it was often understood that trade—including usury—was not proper (read: productive and collective) work but simply selfish speculation (e.g., Humphrey 2002a: 17, 44, 59; Wheeler 2004: 224; see also Chapter 6). An elderly male interlocutor from Tosontsengel, for example, who used to do business (*panz*) in the countryside during socialism, remarked that "people used to hate 'speculative trade' [*damyn panz*] [in socialist times] because they thought we sucked [*soroh*] other people's labor and didn't do physical work." Apart from money-lenders being morally ambiguous in general, then, there may also be a specific socialist bent to this curse-triggering disapproving perception, as the production of value (read: profit) within pawnbroking can no longer be "associated with the labor invested in the object of exchange" (Oushakine 2009: 53) as was the case during socialism, at least in official ideology. At the pawnshop, value or profit was made out of nothing—by literally sitting on your butt—and not by collectively putting effort into producing objects, such as buildings, that were collectively owned by the socialist producers themselves (Verdery 1999: 71–74). The potentially curse-triggering depreciation of *lombard* activity mentioned by Bulgan and other pawnbrokers, may, however, also be related to other historical features. Mongolian scholars as well as ordinary Mongolians often find it important to highlight what they consider to be a traditional contempt for trading and profiteering in Mongolian culture (for two critical reviews of this romanticized and historiographically eclectic idea, see Wheeler 2004 and Pedersen 2007a), and pawnshops might also be associated with the Chinese moneylenders who crippled Mongolia with debt in the nineteenth century (see Sanjdorj 1980).

Thus, from the pawnbroker's perspective, customers and people in general were prone to have bad thoughts about pawnbrokers. According to Bulgan, even her own relatives were envious of the wealth that she was believed to possess. Knowing that bad thoughts abound, and that anger and jealousy are at the root of disputes and curses in Mongolia, pawnbrokers were thus often concerned about how to manipulate the thoughts and feelings of customers, how to avoid evil thoughts in the first place, and how to protect themselves against the always imminent threats facing them. Bulgan made this connection explicit:

People with black energy will influence me. I have to treat people in line with their situation. If I treat them badly, getting MNT1,000 from them for example, it won't benefit me . . . There are people [most likely Buddhist lamas, diviners or shamans] who fix my problems once every three months . . . This work has black and white curses [the white one being caused by jealousy and the black one by anger]. People, including relatives, think that we have millions of MNT.

Bayarmaa had similar thoughts:

Sometimes people don't like the interest rate. If someone is sensitive about it, I make the interest rate lower and solve the problem. I try not to argue with people. If I argue with people, they will curse [haraah] me . . . I think about it and I'm afraid of this kind of thing.

As a rule, pawnbrokers did not try to fight such curses by engaging in an argument with customers, or through explicit counter-curses, as is sometimes the case in certain rural settings in postsocialist Mongolia (Swancutt 2012). Rather, our impression was that they tried to protect themselves by avoiding curses and encounters with dangerous "energies" in the first place. It thus seemed to be a very deliberate strategy on the part of pawnbrokers to try to be nice and friendly when talking to their customers, and they would take the trouble to explain to each customer that it would be his own fault if he did not manage to reclaim his belongings in time. Indeed, a widespread way of preventing or countering curses in contemporary Mongolia is to try to change the thoughts and the mood of the person cursing you, as that person's state of mind is thought to be the agent of the curse (Højer 2003, 2004, 2019a). Tunga, for example, was a woman from Ulaanbaatar in her thirties. While she, like almost everyone else, had been engaged in various businesses on the side, she had also taken a university degree in management in the 1990s, and quite unusually, been working in the office of the same company since 1984 (although reorganized in the 1990s). Now she was in charge of the company's pawnshop and had learned how to deal with customers:

The people who come to the pawnshop have no money. So, when they come, I need to be calm and to carefully explain to them how to get their things back. I tell them when they have to come and how much interest they need to pay to get their things back. I tell them that if they don't come on time, I will wait for five days and then sell their things. I write down their address and phone number. When time has run out, I call them and say: "Time has run out, you were supposed to get your things." If I do it this way, there will be no argument. It's like money for them—money is property. If I don't do it like that, there will be an argument . . . If a customer does not leave a phone number, and if his things have been sold on when he comes back after a long time, this person will be angry. The person will always think about it. He will feel regret and say: "Oh, I gave the ring and earrings inherited from my mother to the *lombard* and couldn't get them back." Maybe the person feels that I have been stingy. So, I feel that pawnbroking is difficult, because people are not happy and they don't bless me when putting their things in my pawnshop.

Apparently incensed by the topic, and undisturbed by the fact that this conversation with Lars was taking place in a wide-open space between concrete blocks in the suburbs of Ulaanbaatar, Tunga continued:

If the pawnbroker is greedy and sells people's things [too quickly], the *lombard* will be cursed. If a *lombard* person sells a golden ring given by a customer, the customer's resentment stays there. I know some people who worked in a *lombard* from 1991 to 2004. I think that they had accumulated black energy [*har enyergi*] from working in a *lombard* for so many years. They saved their profit from the *lombard* business in a savings and credit cooperative and lost it all . . . Also, the things that people had placed in their *lombard* were stolen by thieves. I think that they lost the money they had worked so hard to earn, because they had accumulated too much black energy.

In addition to explaining the conditions for pawning one's property clearly and pedagogically to their customers in the hope of avoiding any future misunderstandings about "whose money" was involved in these credit schemes, pawnbrokers also reverted to various forms of what might, for lack of a better term, be called "business magic" (see also Chapters 6 and 7). Some pawnshop owners with whom we worked would thus burn incense and, after dealing with angry customers who were considered especially likely to have cursed the *lombard*, "spread sand with spells" (*tarnitai els tsatsah*) obtained from Buddhist lamas. Other protective measures included Buddhist deities placed on the inside wall of the pawnshop, protective mantras placed over the entrance, the regular burning of incense to get rid of "all the bad stuff" (*muu yum*), the use of short mantras by the pawnbroker herself (e.g., to avoid theft) and having regular readings performed by a lama against, among other things, black and white curses (*har*, *tsagaan hel am*). On rare occasions, a pawnbroker might even visit a diviner to make sure that a particularly furious customer had not cursed her. Testifying to the fact that dangers were perceived at all levels was also the fact that the pawnbrokers we met often worked in tiny rooms, only communicating with customers through a small hatch. It is better, as one pawnbroker explained, to keep the things—and the money, presumably—out of clients' sight. Often you are alone, she continued, and "bad people abound" (*muu hümüüs ih baina*).

At the Gandan monastery (2009)

THE SPIRIT OF THE COMMODITY

As already indicated, the items pawned at the Ulaanbaatar pawnshops were considered potentially dangerous in several senses. Most straightforwardly, they could be stolen goods. All pawnbrokers claimed that they would make efforts to avoid accepting stolen items—for example, by not accepting things from people who did not show an ID card—but, even so, they recognized that they would sometimes risk accepting goods that could end up being confiscated by the police and thus lose money. Yet the reason pawned items were often described by pawnbrokers as "misfortunate things" (*gaitai yum*) went beyond such mundane matters. Talking about protection, Bulgan pondered:

> People bring dirty [*bohir*] things. We don't know. Maybe the things are stolen from someone, maybe from the client's own parents. The things that are brought here always contain black energy . . . These stolen things influence [*nölöölöh*] us in some way.

Then she turned to the question of persons and misfortunate things:

> People keep bringing things here and in the end they have nothing to bring. They can't take their things back. Even though they know that they can't take their things back, they always feel regret. They think, *I put my thing there and lost it.* If people don't come to get their things back, we call them for a month. After that, we have to sell. But the memory will stay in the customer's head about the things he lost at the

lombard. They don't realize that it is their own fault that they lost them. Mongolian people are like this.

What these and many other reflections from pawnbrokers suggest is that they were blamed for the loss of not just money but of detachable and yet intimate parts of the customer's person as well: "I put *my* thing there and lost it." While one pawnbroker said that she did not know of having received such "misfortunate things" or things filled with regret (*haramsal*), she still felt the need to stress that the items "would not stay for long" with her anyway. The pawned items would, she implied, just pass through her shop, with the deeper implication perhaps that there would be insufficient time for any potentially "bad things" to emanate from these goods and "stay behind," even after the things themselves were returned to the clients or sold to a new owner. Indeed, she explained, a diviner had once warned her against buying an expensive, dangerous item from a tall bearded man, who—prognosticated the diviner—would soon pay her a visit. Such a man did in fact apparently arrive but she chose not to buy from him.

Such ideas and worries were not unique to pawnbrokers and the *lombard* institution. Persons and their belongings are often thought to be intimately related in Mongolia, and there are many ways in which different categories of things are believed to be bound up with people's histories. In an article on Mongolian death rituals, for example, Humphrey (2002b) shows how objects come to be perceived as inseparable from their owner through the owner's continuous use of them. These observations are very much in line with our material. Indeed, we wish to extend Humphrey's and other scholars' (e.g., Empson 2011) focus on the imbrications between persons and things in Mongolian kinship contexts to market arenas. Market exchange occurs outside established social units such as kin groupings, and it may include, as in the *lombard* case, exchanges that are, in normative terms, *not* supposed to take place (Godelier 1999). At the *lombard*, ideally inalienable belongings (Weiner 1992) not meant to be lost or exchanged may be made momentarily, and sometimes permanently, alienable.

The fact that objects are perceived as imbued with souls (*süns*), intentions (*sanaa*) or energy (*enyergi*), as many contemporary Mongolians also like to express it (see also Chapter 7), suggests that objects are agents in the sense of being extensions of persons and past histories (cf. Strathern 1988; Gell 1998; for similar observations from rural Mongolia, see Højer 2003: 45, 2004, 2012, 2019a; Empson 2007: 114, 135; Pedersen 2007b, 2011; High 2013: 681; Holbraad and Pedersen 2017: 227–37). Such "energized objects" affect—in the same way as persons do—what they interact with (see also Bawden 1963: 234). When

Mongolians purchase a new home, for example, they prefer the former own-ers to be an old calm couple who have stayed together throughout their lives because it is widely presumed that this will positively affect their own future life in the new home. In a similar vein, many Mongolians do not like to wear other people's secondhand clothes, but if they have to, the clothes may be puri-fied over a fire before they are worn. Knives that are found may "have blood on them" and are thought to be dangerous to keep (not so with new knives), and cars, for instance, may be "misfortunate things" if they have been involved in previous accidents, since this has rendered them prone to have more accidents in the future (see Højer 2003, 2004, 2019a).

Certain kinds of objects, however, tend to be more "loaded" than others. Bulgan, the geologist-turned-pawnbroker, reflected that "maybe I shouldn't talk like this, being a geologist, but I think that bad things follow gold," and in Mongolia it is not unusual to hear that life—or the soul—follows gold. Indeed, gold is widely associated with all sorts of difficulties, risks and dangers (see High 2008, 2013, 2017). Such dangers, it is sometimes held, may be countered by having the piece of gold in question melted and reshaped (or, alternatively, if one happens to come across a piece of gold, by picking it up only after having urinated on it and covered it with something). For the same reason, dealing in pure gold and golden things like jewelry was a source of particular worry for some pawnbrokers. As Tunga put it,

> Gold contains black energy if a person is too greedy. That is why people who get gold lose it. When people lose it, it affects them very badly. Gold is suitable for some people, not for others. Gold is generous for some but not for others. I have noticed that very few goldsmiths have good lives. Most are alcoholics, because they earn their livings from gold—or so I think. I think that if a person shares their profits with other people, he will be less affected by black energy.

While this example suggests that certain objects are more "bad" than others, any object may be agentive in this way, for all objects—cars, clothes, knives, items of gold—are potential extensions of previous acts and events. If gold is more potent than other things, this may—apart from its origin in a "polluted" mining economy (High 2013, 2017)—be due to the fact that it is simultaneously extremely mutable (it may be converted into almost anything) and extremely desirable (it is imbued with strong emotive affects and, as the quote shows, per-haps not prone to be shared). It thus lends itself to a particular kind of history where strong (inalienable) emotions, such as greed, anger and jealousy, meet extreme alienability; gold, in other words, embodies an extreme(ly dangerous) flow of strong passions.[4]

Examples of the "spirit" of commodities and other things are legion in the Mongolian context, but here we would like to focus on just one aspect of the general imbrication between objects and their users.[5] We are referring to the fact that, especially in awkward, fraught and ambivalent socioeconomic arenas such as the *lombard*, the "energy" of what is being exchanged is inseparable not just from its previous uses and biography more generally and from the nature of the things exchanged, but also from the affects and attitudes entertained by donor and recipient toward this object as well as toward one another during the moment of exchange. As such, what is being exchanged is imprinted with the intentions and desires that emanate from or run through the persons involved, for apart from the qualities of all the exchanges of which the exchanged item has previously been a part, it now comes to carry within itself the thoughts and emotions harbored by the exchanging persons at the moment of exchange. Apart from being full of gift-like personal aspects before they enter the market and thus simply "penetrating" the realm of commodities (Addo and Besnier 2008: 40), the items exchanged might also, then, become full of gift-like aspects and dangerous agency *as* they enter "the market." After all, we were told, when you give away an object, then your mind-feelings (*setgel sanaa*) will stay within it. If, say, you give away some money, then *the mind* with which it is given is important. As Ariunaa (our main protagonist in Chapter 4), who was known to be a kind and calm person, explained,

> Maybe you did not really want to give away an object but, for some reason, you had to. Then your soul will be attached to that object, it goes through that object to the person receiving the object. Maybe the object retains this energy. The intention stays in the object and influences the person . . . It might be a bad influence but it might also be a good one. If I really want to give money to someone, the opposite is the case. Then the money can be used for many things, and even then there might be some money left. A colleague always tells me that she likes to get money from me— even though she can easily get it from other people as well. She always manages to do something useful with my money.

Perhaps we could call this the "spirit of the commodity"—the *hau*-like capacity of objects (including money) to become imbued with the "energy" of their exchange trajectories, that is, both the past transactions in which they have taken part and the "mind-feelings" of the exchanges in which they are now taking part. Crucially, this logic applies to all contexts of exchange and not just ritualized contexts involving ceremonial gift exchange, including pawnshops and other capitalist arenas. At Ulaanbaatar's markets, people often used the expression *avsan ögsöndöö ölziitei* (blessing to both the buyer and the seller), which was done to ensure that the transaction would be good for both parties. In a similar vein, it might be argued that the commoditization taking place at the *lombard* *facilitated* this "flow of spirit" rather than opposing and neutralizing it in the way often suggested by anthropologists when contrasting gifts and commodities, spirit and money (see, e.g., Mauss 1990; Bohannan 1955; Gregory 1982). Perhaps, at the *lombard*, belongings thus entered a money "'environment' that allow[ed] exchange [and 'energy/spirit'] to get going" (Holbraad 2005: 247), rather than leveling and abstracting the value/spirit of what was exchanged (we continue this discussion in the next chapter).

Small wonder, then, that pawnshops had such a tarnished reputation. They were hubs of belongings imprinted with the moods and affects of people who had been forced to pawn their belongings (or had traded their items only reluctantly), and who might well never manage to reclaim what could be among their most cherished possessions. As such, misfortune infuses all aspects of the *Lombard*; it is an institutionalization of the social life of troubled or dangerous things (cf. Appadurai 1986), which, as such, lives on, accumulates and enhances "bad energies." This explains why so many people did not like to leave their belongings at pawnshops or to buy things from there, for their own possessions could become infected with the "soul" or "energy" of the other possessions with which their stuff would unavoidably come into contact. One would fear, for example, to be hit by the "regret" (*haramsal*) of former owners unable to reclaim their belongings.

While the pawnbroking business was thus embedded in wider regimes of value and moral discourses, we should not lose sight of the fact that it was at the same time understood precisely as a capitalist business. As we have seen, to be a pawnbroker in Ulaanbaatar around the turn of the millennium was essentially to work by exchanging alienable objects and profiting from the often steep interest rates imposed on one's customers, and many *lombard* did indeed consider their activities as a straightforward business activity. However, just the same was true for many of their customers, even though quite a few of them, as one pawnbroker observed with thinly veiled reproach, "had not come fully to grips with the logics of credit." This would seem to imply that, while the gift/commodity distinction is of course not irrelevant to deploy analytically in the Mongolian pawnshop case—calculations were being made, the pure business aspect was often emphasized and pawnshop owners as well as customers seemed to operate with similar conceptual contrasts—it is complicated by the fact that pawning was occasionally done with *personal belongings* that had become temporarily (or indeed permanently) alienated from their owners through the hardships of wild capitalism and radical societal transition.

Indeed, our argument is not that pawnbroking in Ulaanbaatar after the turn of the millennium (or anywhere else) amounted to *either* the exchange of alienables *or* inalienables. Rather, our point is that it was precisely the sheer complexity if not downright opaqueness surrounding, as well as the constant effort involved in, the ongoing conversion of inalienables into alienables and sometimes back again during times of transition (and times of conversion) that produced the troubled environment that pawnbrokers, customers, business-people and urban hunters—themselves particularly engaged in acts of conversion—were part of. Let us now substantiate this important point.

PRECARIOUS TRANSACTIONS

A colleague of Ariunaa once pawned a ring that her husband had given to her. She forgot to redeem it on the specified day, and when she arrived at the pawnshop a few days late, the pawnbroker required her to redeem the ring at a much higher price. Ariunaa's friend got angry and did not have sufficient cash, so she left without ever getting the ring back. Now, Ariunaa said, she felt regret, and the friend had explained to Ariunaa that pawnbrokers use people's things in rituals that force customers to repeatedly come back to borrow money from the pawnbroker. Apart from confirming the anger and regret felt by many customers and the pawnbrokers' fear thereof, as discussed earlier in this chapter, examples such as this remind us that customers at Ulaanbaatar's pawnshops would now and then turn up with personal belongings considered too personal to give away for good.

In such cases, the customers arrive with inalienable possessions, one of their personal belongings, which is really *not* presented as a commodity or gift but only to be held in custody, as it were, by the pawnbroker. In fact, the customers just want to reclaim their belongings and terminate their cont(r)act with the pawnbroker as soon as possible. At first glance, this may call to mind certain aspects of the *dana* gift described by Jonathan Parry (1985), which is sometimes given to Brahman priests in India to get rid of sins by removing "bad" parts of the donor's person. In the *dana* gift, like in the *lombard* case, the things transferred have spirit, yet do not entail reciprocal relations of mutuality between exchange partners. While the *dana* gift, however, is rendered supremely alienable by being given away in order never to be returned, in the case of the *lombard*, the pawned "gift" should never have been alienated from its donor. In both cases, we may speak of an "energized object" imbued with some sort of invisible spiritual capacity, but while in the Indian case "the spirit of the *dana*" (as it were) brings about a desired alienation through one-way sacrificial transfers of sins, in the *lombard* case, conversely, people are forced to give away things that they want to keep, to the effect that the "spirit of the pawned item" becomes inappropriately alienated from the donor and possibly revengeful toward the recipient if never returned. In other words, both cases are examples of "the spirit of the gift" without reciprocity: in the *dana* case the "gift" should never return and in the Lombard case, seen from the customer's perspective, it should never have been given away in the first place (nor lead to any lasting reciprocal relation).

From the perspective of the *lombard* customer, or should we say "donor," pawning one's belongings was thus to lose a part of oneself to the flows of the market. As much as pawning was therefore an efficient and easy way for Kolya and the others to raise ready cash and thus instant opportunities, it also increased the risk of losing the properties of which they were composed as persons. Apart from "losing the earrings inherited from one's mother," however, the pawnbrokers could also lure one into a dangerously durable debt relationship—by "using customers' things to make rituals"—from which one could not escape, and where one kept on losing ever more belongings while the pawnbroker kept making ever more profit. Bayarmaa, the pawnbroker from Western Mongolia, explained:

> People say that once a thing has been left at the *lombard*, then it will be given to the *lombard* again and again. It looks as if a road has been opened in people's minds for giving their things to a *lombard* . . . It is their own fault. There is no magic that makes people want to give their things to the *lombard* . . . After a person has put his things at the *lombard* once, that person will know that there is an easy way to get money. When he needs money, he will think of that easy option. People think that we use magic to call them to the *lombard*. Sometimes they think that I call them [in secret invocations]. One comedy sketch on TV was like that. It was funny.

It should now hopefully be clear that, from the *lombard* customer's point of view, the art of pawning was all about how to avoid entering into a reciprocal—in the anthropological sense of a durable but not necessarily equal—relationship with the dangerously addictive, hard-to-escape world of business exchange and debt into which pawnbrokers were constantly trying to lure you. This is what we mean by suggesting that it was as if people were seeing pawnbrokers through a gift optic in Ulaanbaatar around the turn of the millennium. Customers and pawnbrokers, while explaining this in different terms (magical or psychological), both kept on stressing that pawnshop exchanges, on the part of customers, carried with them a dangerous impetus for continual exchange—of being enchained in (debt) obligations—that one should be aware of and keep at bay. On top of this, customers did not necessarily want to bring their belongings into contact with other inalienable belongings at the pawnshop, as these other pawned items could contaminate their own belongings with damaging energy from other customers who—unwillingly—had had to leave their belongings at the pawnshop. Thus, while pawnshops offered a smart and easy way of converting noncommodities into commodities for people without access to bank loans, such as our Ulaanbaatar friends, it also exposed them to the exploitative, addictive and dangerous structures of market exchange. In this sense, what they really longed for—one could perhaps go as far as to speculate—was actually ways of disentangling (or, should we say, alienating) themselves from the dangers of a radical transition in which even very personal belongings, and possibly even their own selves, could be lost forever.

There was thus a tension or even a paradox built into the very edifice of Ulaanbaatar's *lombard* business at the time of our fieldwork. On the one hand, people pawning their belongings continued to be attached to them in the *hau*-like sense discussed above. On the other, however, they tried hard not to have any lasting social relations with the pawnbrokers in the way one might otherwise expect from other contexts associated with the exchange of "energized objects" (à la Mauss 1990 [1923–1924]). In this sense, the challenges faced by the pawnshop customers serve as a powerful demonstration of one of our key points in this book. It once again shows the constant work required from urban hunters like Kolya and Hulan to perform the volatile balancing acts that allow them to straddle the precarious line between too little and too much engagement with permanent transition, which so often takes the form of endless possibilities for debt and confronting unsafe persons, objects and "energies." Urban hustling and urban pawning, then, are as much arenas of desired risk as of dangerous possibility.

The pawnbrokers, on their side, also had to balance tensions and negotiate paradoxes inherent to the *lombard* economy, albeit in sometimes different or even obverse ways. Whereas, as we just explained, customers wanted to remain attached to some of the belongings they pawned, what pawnshop owners really hoped for was to receive "soul-less" objects that no one really cared for or considered theirs, and which would allow them to enter into a straightforward amoral and abstract business relationship with their customers. Yet, as we have also seen, many pawnbrokers simultaneously tended to see things through the gift-like perspective of real or imagined customers, imagining the pawnshop business as a moral economy that they either tried to justify and defend as a way of "doing good" or dismissed as simply another "bad job" while, at the same time, seeking to mitigate the risk presented by such "energized objects."[6]

For pawnbrokers, then, the ideal pawn business is one that is capable of carving out and maintaining a pure (in the sense of alienated and abstract) commodity exchange, whereby all relations to their customer's "gift economy" of inalienable belongings are cut. Yet precisely by making a great and sustained effort to distance herself and her business from the world of energized objects, the pawnbroker acknowledges the existence and power of such inalienable possessions, including the need to separate herself from them via protective measures. And, paradoxically, this foil of pure, untainted business can only be created and maintained by adopting a cool business-like attitude toward one's customers, that is, by *performing* an "objective" relation to them. They have to convince customers that their mutual relationship is just business as usual and does not involve personal, affective, moral and reciprocal aspects; in other words, they have to stay calm and detached.

We may end the present analysis, then, by observing that pawnbrokers and their customers, many of whom qualify as urban hunters as they are in need of instant cash to profit from on-the-spot business opportunities, both do their very best to hem in a messy transitional reality by establishing clear-cut distinctions between commodities and belongings, or between an objective world of money and a subjective world of morals. Yet, they do so in vain, for these very bifurcations, and not least the many transactions that the market flow enables, also cause the proliferation and excess of tricky transactions, energized objects and troubled subjects.

CONCLUSION

In this chapter, we have sought to demonstrate how the new (debt) "market," and hence the life of urban hunters such as Kolya, is fraught with the dangerous possibilities of material (ex)change. We have thus highlighted certain more sinister or darker aspects of transition and urban hunting (see also Chapters 1, 4 and 6) by exploring debt relations more generally and pawnbroking in particular. At an Ulaanbaatar pawnshop, all the value-transformational and thus morally tainted aspects of transition—in the form of conversions between belongings and commodities, and sometimes back again—become an all-too-concrete social fact. Because it serves as a sort of prism of wider processes and dynamics in Ulaanbaatar around the turn of the millennium, the pawnshop speaks to the more general problem of life in times of economic and moral transition: namely, the problem, and challenge, of carrying out market exchange with (semi-)inalienable possessions without entering dangerous (because lasting) gift-like reciprocal exchanges in objects invested with great emotive affect as well as a deep sense of loss and anger. As we have seen, it is precisely the fact that things are so often personal, moral and emotional—as relations of debt always are—that makes it so difficult for pawnbrokers to shun reciprocity with, and alienate themselves from, their customers. Customers, for their part, end up pawning parts of their own selves in alienable relations when selling their possessions to the *lombard*. Speaking the language of gift exchange, they become indebted to and entangled in the market, and all too often end up as victims of it—and not least its debt relations.

So, on a more general note, optimistically seizing (debt and/or investment) opportunities—as should already be clear from the cases of Misha, Hulan, Kolya and other urban hunters—did also pose a number of challenges, such as losing one's way in the "real estate market" of Ulaanbaatar or when pursuing debtors in Russia. And it certainly involved getting caught up in emotionally charged "market" relations of, for example, the scrap metal trade and pawn-broking. The luring opportunities of the market, then, may have been promising to urban hunters at the moment of (dreaming up) sudden possibilities, but in a quite radical sense one would never quite know what such promises would lead to, nor which relations one would be caught up in when engaging with such possibilities.

By giving in to the fun of dealing in and anticipating lucrative investments, our friends and other frequent visitors to Ulaanbaatar's innumerable pawnshops thus faced the risk of falling prey to and being seduced by the pawnbroker's semi-magic "calling" and, in this process, losing themselves yet more. Indeed, Kolya once said that his family was not just "lost" in transition but "cursed" by it. Remarks like these seem to suggest that, in Ulaanbaatar after the turn of the millennium, losing oneself to the forces and the flow of the market was also potentially experienced as a curse that always loomed—at the pawnshop, in debt relations more generally, and in the transitional reality—as a dark side of the transition and its aspirations, dreams and hopes. It is precisely this potent but demonic interface between the economic and the occult that we wish to explore in more detail in the last two chapters.

Chapter 6 Market Tricksters

In our market, we don't have to deal with mafia like people in Russia, but we do have the changers [*chyenjüüd*]. *Chyenjüüd* don't work, they are liars by profession. They trick people by selling our goods too expensively. A changer may hold up a pair of shoes and show it to the crowd, and then make false advertising like this: "Look! I bought these shoes in town yesterday. Alas, they are too small for me. See, it is original skin! Notice this sole and that stitching!" This is how they con people. Changers tell lies behind our backs!

Such were the words of Otgonbaatar, the young and quite successful shoe trader from Ulaanbaatar's Harhorin Market, whose story we heard in Chapter 2. In making the above complaint, Otgonbaatar was referring to a particular category of middlemen (indeed, they were nearly always men) or "changers" who were ubiquitous in Mongolia's markets around 2000. Unlike the "big changers" discussed in previous chapters, who had established themselves as prominent but largely invisible mediators in Ulaanbaatar's profitable meat, cashmere, metal and car businesses, these petty changers, who tended to hang out at Harhorin and other urban markets, were poor, stigmatized and, for this reason, supremely visible. Since they did not have a stock of goods, or a market stall, these petty changers were constantly on the move, always trying to position themselves at strategic locations in and around the market—such as at the intersections between main alleyways, or near the entrances—from where they could best spot their customers, and the customers could spot them. For this was what being a successful *chyenj* was about, apart from making "false advertising" (and performing a particular kind of flirtatious masculinity associated with lower-middle-class men): the ability to put oneself in a position from which one could see, and could be seen, more than anyone else.

Douglas Rogers has coined the term "the politics of liquidity" to denote "historically and culturally embedded struggles associated with relative degrees of exchangeability among multiple transactables" (2008: 64). "Liquidity," Rogers thus suggests, may be conceived of as the very "'grease' that creates the conditions for any sort of exchange: between the transactors of anything that might conceivably change hands there must be some liquidity to make the transaction possible" (2008: 64). In many ways, this captures the gist of the argument that we make in what follows. By focusing on two seemingly marginal types of urban hunters hanging out at Ulaanbaatar's markets around 2000—namely the *chyenjüüd* and the so-called ball shufflers (*shaarigchid*)—we explore how, also in urban Mongolia after socialism, "liquidity [was] unevenly distributed along—and help[ed] to create—[new] lines of social distinction" (Rogers 2008: 64). In that sense, as we are going to argue, apart from being market outcasts (cf. Chapter 2) operating on the fringes of an emerging capitalist order, *chyenjüüd* and *shaarigchid* were in a sense the very "grease" that made Mongolia's markets go around at the turn of the millennium, for more than anyone else they were imbued with the capacity to facilitate connections and flows between otherwise disparate domains of transitional life.

Evidently, changers and ball shufflers both fall squarely within the spectrum of postsocialist subjects and forms of agency of what we have called urban hunting. Recall that, as we argued in the Introduction to this book, far from being simply a nice metaphor, there are real similarities between how certain urban hustlers in Mongolia at the time of our fieldwork did business and made profits in the postsocialist city and the techniques and practices of obtaining and distributing resources among hunters around the world, including rural Mongolia. As we show in this chapter, the changers and other equally labile and transgressive personae ubiquitous to Ulaanbaatar's inherently unstable and potentially dangerous markets are a case in point. Specifically, we argue in the last part of this chapter that the personhood of these particular kinds of urban hunters invites comparisons with postsocialist Mongolia's shamans, whose capacities are perceived as arising from a similarly labile composition of, and distinction between, body and self (Pedersen 2011). In fact, Ulaanbaatar's markets can be conceived of as quasi-shamanic arenas in their own right, where people were made subject to social, existential and bodily metamorphoses analogous to spirit possession rituals in Northern Asia and beyond (e.g., Taussig 1987; Kapferer 1991; Hamayon 1990; Tsing 1993; Humphrey 1996; Swancutt 2012). Indeed, as we argue in the conclusion, this analogy between wheeler-dealing and shamanism is more than a figure of speech. Certain kinds of market subjects, including changers but also other transgressive personae, were seen to have extraordinary capacities that enabled them to transgress not only prevailing moralities of the postsocialist market but ordinary boundaries of human subjects and material objects. In that sense, these "market tricksters" (as we shall call them) were equipped with a labile kind of body and a porous self optimally suited to survive during times of radical change and lasting transition.

"CHYENJÜÜD ARE CHYENJÜÜD"

A substantivized Mongolian appropriation of the English verb "to change"—which, in all likelihood, became part of Mongolian popular discourse with the advent of the capitalist market in 1990 (much like the expression market "boss")—the term "changer" was first used to denote people involved in currency exchange, but around the time of our fieldwork it was used for any person involved in exchange-for-profit or, as many would call it, tapping into derogatory Marxist discourse from the state socialist period, "speculation." Thus, the word "changer" is never, or almost never, used for ordinary traders, shopkeepers and marketers but is specifically associated with informal—and sometimes shady—business between or within marketplaces involving large sums of money:

> To be a changer means exchanging things, right? People who simply sell clothes from a stall at the market are not changers, but sellers. Changers are not sellers. Changers are people who increase and centralize the exchange of things. They buy cheap and sell expensive. They make money by trading raw materials like hides and metal, or they exchange money. Ten years ago [1994] when there were no banks there were many money changers, but not today. Some changers work for bosses. They buy goods cheaply from bosses and sell them expensively, or buy goods cheap and sell to their bosses for higher prices. Real changers know how to buy things wholesale, how to distribute, lead and manage from above. Other changers are different. They just take care of their immediate needs.

As this passage from an interview with a former marker vendor from Mongolia's second-biggest town of Erdenet illustrates, *chyenj* denoted a broad category of persons of varying socioeconomic background and status, ranging from what people sometimes called the "real" changers of cars, gold, cashmere, wool and other valuable and prestigious wholesale and raw material trade items (see Chapter 4) to the petty changers selling other vendors' goods, the sort who used to hang out at Harhorin and other Ulaanbaatar markets around the millennium, and who are the main subject of this chapter. Like the predominantly female money changers who used to run stalls or simply stood at various strategic locations in Ulaanbaatar's city center (an extremely risky business; indeed, many of them were frequently robbed and had to seek protection from various private security firms) during the first half of the 1990s, the "small" and mostly male changers selling vendors' goods at urban markets were petty middlemen who had managed to carve out a niche in the new capitalist economy by identifying gaps in commodity chains that others found too dangerous, immoral or simply not profitable enough to exploit.

But precisely how did *chyenjüüd* obtain the goods that they sold "too expensively," as Otgonbaatar sourly explained? As described in the above interview passage, some changers would "work for" prominent vendors, wholesale traders and other market "bosses" (see also Chapter 2). Other changers obtained their goods from more ordinary and more established marketers such as the "shoe people" described in Chapter 2, who, unlike themselves, had both a permanent stall at the market and an actual stock of goods. At the Harhorin Market, explained Otgonbaatar, this was done in the form of a "loan" (*zeel*). When "borrowing" a certain ware from someone's stall at the market, the changer would promise to pay the vendor back what this particular commodity was "really worth" after having sold it (more on this below, including the rather tricky issue of what the "real value" of a given commodity might be, and how one might go about establishing it). Yet, given the forthright, aggressive and sometimes even threatening attitude of *chyenjüüd*, one might question whether vendors such as Otgonbaatar had much of a choice. Unless one was fortunate enough to be under the protection of influential bosses with access to the higher echelons of formal and informal market leadership, one was not in a position to say no when dodgy characters hanging out all day at the market wanted to "be friends" and "do business."

Consider, as an example, an incident that took place during one of Morten's many visits to Naran Tuul. Kolya and he spoke to a middle-aged shoe repairman who would every morning turn up at the market and put up a tiny ramshackle table with a hand-powered sewing machine located next to the busy rows of "shoe people." Despite the fact that Kolya and Morten spoke to him for no more than ten minutes, several young men with dark sunglasses and black leather jackets managed to pass by, tapping the meek-looking shoe repairman on the shoulder and reminding him that they "would come back later to have a drink together." While all this chatting and patting was done in a friendly enough (in fact, over-friendly) tone, the shoe repairman later made it clear to Kolya and Morten that it was he alone who would have to bear the cost of the vodka and that, for this and several other reasons, he would prefer not to "be friends" with these guys, who happened to come from the same neighborhood (*neg gudamjny*; lit. "of the same street") as he, always "moving in and out of prison."

While the above incident did not involve *chyenjüüd*, it neatly conveys the atmosphere in which deals were made and things were settled between changers and vendors, namely a tense air of fear and thinly disguised threats couched in a veil of friendship. This is not all there is to say about the asymmetrical and forced nature of the social relationship at hand, however. For not only did the *chyenjüüd* at the Naran Tuul and Harhorin Markets themselves decide which wares they wanted to "borrow" and from whom, it often also seemed to be very much up to them to decide what the "real price" of each item for sale was. "Let us say," Otgonbaatar sighed, "that my partner and I have just brought in some Nike trainers from Beijing. If, say, we are selling these at our stall at the Naran Tuul market for MNT30,000, then some *chyenj* will borrow them and manage to sell them for MNT50,000 through false advertising. This is happening a lot here at Ulaanbaatar's markets. They are full of *chyenjüüd*. If they were good businessmen, they would have started doing their own trading long ago. But they are not—and will be *chyenjüüd* all their lives. All they will ever do is sell one thing at a time. In fact, if *chyenjüüd* are in a gang of four and one sells something, they have to share the money. And then they will always go and drink it all away."

From the perspective of ordinary vendors, then, *chyenjüüd* are a bunch of losers who are unable to control themselves ("they drink all their money away") or to act beyond the immediate opportunities available to them at any given moment ("they are always selling one thing at a time" and are only able to "care for their immediate needs"). They lack the purposefulness (*zorigtoi*) and the knowledge (*medleg*) of how to "calculate big numbers," as Otgonbaatar put it (with a self-important look), needed to become real marketers. Instead, they were forever confined to "living for the moment without any thought of the future," as Bourdieu might have concluded were he to have listened to Otgon-baatar's and many other vendors' complaints.

And yet, a rather telling ambivalence could be observed in vendors' attitudes toward *chyenjüüd*. For while changers were evidently considered both morally dubious and inept at planning, they were not simply looked down upon in the manner of ordinary drunks and other "market outcasts" (see Chapter 2). Quite the contrary: Ulaanbaatar's *chyenjüüd* were also perceived as personifying the very idea of good salesmanship, which—in the words of Otgonbaatar—"essentially boils down to telling lies. Wheeling and dealing. The whole point is to trick people."[1] According to a widespread cultural stereotype, the *chyenjüüd* were in that sense akin to Chinese people. Many Mongolians—especially but not only from older generations—like to emphasize that "unlike the Chinese," "Mongolian people don't know how to lie" (cf. Sanjdorj 1980; Bulag 1998; Billé 2014). This is also the reason, Otgonbaatar's cousin said, why there is so little haggling in Mongolian markets. "Mongols are natural-born consumers," mean-ing that they are willing to buy things at whatever price is asked. And yet, he lamented, the majority of Mongolian marketers failed to take advantage of this by raising their prices. Instead, "When customers express interest in their goods, vendors demand the real price from the start."

It is precisely this ambivalence—the fact that changers were, at one and the same time, talked about as essentially similar to and radically different from ordinary vendors—that makes them so interesting for our present purposes. As Otgonbaatar once remarked, "All people working at the markets are changers!" But then a short moment later, in what was almost part of the same sentence, Otgonbaatar emphasized "how bad the changers are!" rolling his eyes in dis-gust. So, while in one sense representing two qualitatively different kinds of persons with opposing skills and values, "sellers" and changers were also part of the same moral domain and economic arena. For at the end of the day, only a fine line separates selling one's goods "expensively" (*ünetei*) by doing "a little advertising" (*jaahan reklamdah*)—which was just what Otgonbaatar and his cousin boasted that they were so good at—on the one hand and, on the other, selling one's goods "too expensively" through "false advertising," as the changers supposedly did.

All this lends support to our observation that, instead of simply being dis-missed as annoying nuisances that do not belong in a professional market, *chy-enjüüd* were perceived as a necessary evil that should not be done away with. After all, as Otgonbaatar sighed, "Well, you know, *chyenjüüd* are *chyenjüüd*. If they weren't here, the bosses could not sell their things." What this and other similarly resigned comments made by market vendors indicated was that the *chyenjüüd* helped boost their profits. This happened both in the concrete sense that *chyenjüüd* increased the sale of goods in their capacity as middlemen and, as we shall now see, in the more intangible sense that the *chyenjüüd* facilitated the flow of the market as such.

"GIVE ME THE MONEY. IT'S YOURS NOW!"

Morten's "first contact" with the shady *chyenjüüd* underworld of Ulaanbaatar markets occurred during a steaming hot day in the summer of 2003. The incident happened a couple of weeks into his research on formal and informal leaders and economic institutions in postsocialist Mongolia, when he was still in the process of mapping the Naran Tuul and Harhorin Markets and their market subjects, ranging from managers and "bosses" through traders to thieves, drunks, hustlers and other "market outcasts" (see Chapter 2).

While the concentration and compression of bodies, dust and noise was significantly less overwhelming and nauseating than used to be the case at the Old Black Market, entering through Naran Tuul's main gate still felt like passing the threshold into another social world. To be sure, the market was crowded and chaotic outside, too, with the characteristic bustle of trucks, cars, minibuses, motorbikes and people carrying bags and boxes of wares, which seems to be ubiquitous in big urban markets in Mongolia and elsewhere in Eurasia (Mandel and Humphrey 2002; Humphrey and Skvirskaya 2009; Marsden 2016). But it was as if, as soon as you handed over the MNT50 to the sunglasses-clad and scarf-covered middle-aged women seeking shelter from the sun and wind beneath the market entrance, a sudden shift in atmosphere took place. It was almost like a commercial gear change that affected the speed, intensity and, above all, the explicitness by which commodity exchanges were allowed and expected to take place.

Once they were inside, Kolya and Morten were summoned by elderly women with downtrodden expressions and dark-tanned skin (a clear mark of poverty among Mongolians, since it is a sign of outdoor work) in worn rags offering cigarettes and bags of cedar nuts from tiny ramshackle makeshift stalls of cardboard and tape. The scene included tough-looking men sporting black leather jackets, shiny Russian officers' leather boots and fake Ray-Bans who were chain smoking L&M cigarettes and playing pool at tables of the sort that can always be found at Mongolia's markets, no matter what the time of year or weather. There were also noisy flocks of teenage girls flashing colorful Samsung clam cell phones imported by suitcase traders from Korea or China, and stout nomads

Naran Tuul Market (2007)

on a visit in town, wearing traditional *deels* (gowns) and, in the case of some of the men, old-style boots with the toe-end tilted upward. And then, of course, there were all the ordinary vendors who were resting stoically behind their stalls, presiding over more or less prestigious goods.

Mongolian marketers can hardly be described as pushy or even insistent, in the way outsiders might find (and certainly expect) at markets and bazaars elsewhere in Asia and the Near East. In fact, one is constantly told that "Mongolians don't know how to sell things," as opposed to the Chinese traders at the markets in Beijing and in the Sino-Mongolian border town of Ereen, who "are so good at advertising their goods to the people passing by." And indeed, it would not be wrong to say that many of the vendors at Ulaanbaatar's market back then did come across as somewhat passive, as if they were not particularly interested in people seeing their wares, let alone purchasing them.

Still, there were plenty of exceptions to this passive trader stereotype, the most obvious of which was the *chyenjüüd*. We have already noted the propensity of changers to make themselves visible in the heart of crowds, but this was not the only way in which the changers were "adding to the velocity of dealing as a whole" (Stewart 1997: 158). Changers would also sometimes seek to physically place goods into the hands of potential buyers against their will, bringing the notion of middleman to new heights (or, depending on one's perspective, low points). Known as *shahah* ("to squeeze, to press"), this was a widespread sight at Ulaanbaatar's markets during the time of our fieldwork. So instead of actually obtaining the goods they sold too cheaply, as indicated in the citation above, changers seemed to excel at "selling too expensively," to the point of pushing their customers to keep the goods they had imposed on them. Consider, as an illustration of this "inverse stealing" (as one might call it), an incident that took place at Naran Tuul on that same summer day in 2004, at a point when Kolya and Morten found themselves more or less stuck in the crowd on the narrow path between the rows of shoe people and clothes people.

Possibly because Morten was so preoccupied with avoiding eye contact (the day before, at the Harhorin Market, he had been verbally assaulted by two pick-pockets who had felt that he was staring at them, making it obvious to everyone what they were doing there), it was Kolya who was approached by two young men dressed according to the code: dark sunglasses, baseball shoes, Adidas trousers and, indicating their status as changers, wearing not just one but several leather jackets. Victim to the element of surprise (as he told Morten afterward, "They caught me totally off-guard"), Kolya suddenly found himself holding a supersized and very scratched bottle of fake Hugo Boss perfume, which one of the *chyenjüüd* had swiftly and ever so slyly put into his hand in a way that calls to mind the sleight of hand and trickery deployed by skilled pickpockets, albeit in a peculiarly obverse sense and also reverse order (rendering it, in effect, into a sort of inverse stealing).

Over the next ten minutes or so, Kolya increasingly desperately tried to give back the bottle of perfume to the changers. But the latter just kept on stepping back from him while rapidly lowering the price, shouting, in a begging voice thick with thinly veiled aggression, "No, it yours now! You must keep it! We know it is a fake, but it still cost us MNT120,000 to get it. You can have it for 1,000. Just give the money, now." Kolya (who always had a knack for getting out of situations like this) kept on insisting, however, in a calm and soft-spoken voice, that, yes, it surely was a real bargain for a product like that but, still, he would have to say no, as his partner did not appreciate receiving gifts from him that were not the real thing (*jinhene orginal*) but fake copies. And, eventually, aided perhaps by the cigarettes that Kolya had continuously been handing out to the changers and other market outcasts with his free hand, he was allowed to return the bottle to the greasy palm of one of the two *chyenj*, whose attention at this point had already largely shifted to a new potential victim in the sea of people, this time a meek-looking young mother.

A similar dynamic could be recognized among wider categories of Ulaanbaatar inhabitants at the time of our fieldwork—notably, the way certain market vendors addressed their customers as if the latter already owned the goods before purchasing them. Instead of asking people to "please buy shoes" (*gutal avaarai*), for instance, Morten sometimes overheard them asking customers to "please buy your shoes" (*gutalaa avaarai*). He took this to be a mere figure of speech until a Mongolian friend from a family of traders insisted that this interpretation missed the central idea. "Here in Mongolia," she explained, "we think everything is owned already. There is an owner [*ezen*] to all the things that the markets vendors sell . . . If I cannot sell something, it is because that thing is meant for someone who is supposed to come and get it but who has not come." The trader is "just transporting that thing, bringing it closer to the owner. Not everyone around here thinks like this, but some people do. It makes sense."

Let us unpack this statement and see why it indeed "makes sense." As Katherine Verdery (1996) argues, resources in the centrally planned socialist economies (ideally) were distributed according to a principle of objective, not relative, scarcity. Given that quotas were "scientifically" calculated to meet the "natural needs" of each subject, we could say that they were "already owned" by the subjects. In this supply-driven centralized system, where access to "necessary" goods was seen as a universal right, entrepreneurship was a matter of accumulating "not profits . . . but distributable resources" (1996: 28).

What happens to this vertical, supply-driven logic when it is challenged by a horizontal, demand-driven market logic? We suggest that, in Mongolia and possibly elsewhere in the postsocialist world (e.g., Holbraad 2005), the once dominant socialist economic cosmology gave way to a peculiar amalgamation of socialist and capitalist imaginaries. In this new hybrid economic cosmology, entrepreneurship became a matter of facilitating a meeting between two separate realms: the social realm of consumers imbued with a "natural" (socialist) right to own goods and the material realm of goods endowed with another but equally "natural" (capitalist) desire to be owned. Perhaps, from the point of view of both parties involved in transactions, goods were somehow already assigned to owners, much the way all commodities during socialism corresponded to the needs of particular citizens. The only, but crucial, difference was that the vertical logic of state socialism had now been replaced by the horizontal logic of the market. On this interpretation, the flow of commodities did not cease to be perceived as predetermined with the collapse of socialism; only the role and the identity of the middlemen changed. Much like the legendary bosses of collective farms in rural Siberia (Humphrey 1998; Ssorin-Chaikov 2003), Ulaan-baatar's market tricksters were able to collapse disparate flows and ideas about goods into a single reality.

With the changers in the Harhorin Market, to which we return, another characteristic feature of *chyenjüüd*—apart from their direct forms of persuasion—was the fact that they were constantly on the move, trying to position themselves at strategic intersections of busy alleyways from where they could best see, and be seen, by their "prey." Indeed, one almost got the sense that changers were not supposed to stand still, as if doing so would extinguish an invisible flame upon which their craft and prominence depended. We are here reminded of Nancy Ries' observations about "mafia" in Russia:

> One of the key colloquialisms in contemporary Russian is "krutit'sia," meaning simultaneously "to turn, spin, revolve, whirl, squirm, circulate, twist, and contort." It is a common piece of local knowledge that only by knowing how to *krutit'sia* can one keep one's head above water in any kind of enterprise. The Russian mafia are, in a sense, the masters of this dance. Their occupation entails a kind of "meta-spinning" among different realms of enterprise, within and between different social fields and different levels of hierarchy. (2002: 290)

This, we suggest, was also very much the case for Mongolia's population of petty market changers, who were also perceived, by themselves as much as by others, as the masters of a particular kind of "dance," namely the constant movement, maneuvering and "meta-spinning" required to stitch together the components of a still disparate market. In that sense, the changers can, once again, be formally compared with the pickpockets, who also never stood still, both for fear of being recognized and thus potentially caught, but also because the nature of their trade led them to seek out those spots at markets where, at a given time, people happened to cluster the most. As Kolya once remarked to Morten when the latter expressed surprise that there were so few *chyenjüüd* to be seen on Naran Tuul market: "Trust me, they are here: it is just that changers prefer to be somewhere around the middle of the market where there are the most people. Precisely like the pickpockets do!" At the same time, however, the changers and the pickpockets also inhabit diametrically opposed positions on a scale defined by degrees of visibility, for while changers try to be seen by as many people as possible, pickpockets do their best not to be seen by anyone at all. Or, as Bumochir, an ex-conman from Mongolia's second-biggest city, Erdenet, poetically summed up the situation in 2003, "Here in our town, the thieves are like daytime stars—they are around, but always remain out of sight."

So, if the most deft of pickpockets resembled daytime stars in their ability to be present and yet invisible, then the petty changers excelled at being superluminescent, like those stars that become visible first in the evening sky and only fade away with the light of daybreak. This did not, however, apply to "real" changers selling cars from the huge market in Ulaanbaatar's Shar Had district (see also Chapter 4). Unlike their petty peers, these big changers were in control from behind an expensive stock of vehicles imported from Hong Kong, for example, or bought wholesale locally. When doing this kind of business, most potential buyers would only find a note on the windshield with the phone number of the *chyenj* selling the car. In short, big changers caused goods to *appear* to others but preferred not to appear themselves. In this sense, we may perhaps even conceive of the big changers as "inverse pickpockets" within the poetics of visibility and invisibility played out on the Ulaanbaatar market scene. After all, what distinguished the pickpockets from other market subjects was precisely the fact that they caused goods to *disappear* by continually being able to not appear and be visible to others.

Indeed, as our story of Hulan's brief career as a metal-changer illustrated (Chapter 4), one of the biggest excitements but also biggest dangers of being a *chyenj* was that one very literally had to expose oneself to the perspective of other people. As Hulan herself put it, "There is no living being who does not know the *chyenjüüd*!" And when mingling with the changers, one might all too soon come to be seen as one, as she herself learned the hard way. For the process of becoming a *chyenj* could easily, as it did for her, lead to the frightening experience of losing control of oneself as one is cut up and distributed into ever more people's perspectives (Højer 2003, 2004, 2019). Yet, paradoxically, only by virtue of being "divided out" among as many other people's attention as possible would the changer's name and fame grow, not unlike the way in which pop or TV stars may be said to be splintered into a potentially lethal manifold of fragments (posters, Facebook friends, etc.) shared among their fans. Once again, then, we see how the changer is a distorted pickpocket figure. If the pickpocket in his actions performs a concrete act of theft, the changer by virtue of his "false advertising" and other forms of trickery and persuasion makes visible the hidden element of theft that arguably lies at the heart of capitalism. We are reminded here about the trickster figure whose "amorphous nature and incongruous characteristics [have] intrigued anthropologists and folklorists" (Apte 1985: 213) and who in many different parts of the world personifies a fluidity and lability for which he is both famous and feared (see also Pedersen 2011). Like a real trickster, the *chyenjüüd* makes something visible that otherwise remains invisible, namely the otherwise hidden nature of the market: the precarious, even dangerous, trickery needed to sustain its flows.

In sum, changers were simultaneously imbued with too much and too little subjectivity: "too much," because, more than anyone else on the Ulaanbaatar market scene around the turn of the millennium, they were the incarnation of the almost transcendental individual freedom associated with trading and other market activities in postsocialist contexts (as discussed in Chapter 2), but also "too little," for as we have also tried to convey, few people were perceived as being so morally tainted and vulnerable to the market's flows of danger, desire and latent destruction as they. As Ulaanbaatar's "meta-spinners" par excellence, the changers personified the possibilities but also the perils of subjecting oneself (and others) unconditionally to the at once centripetal and centrifugal economic forces set in train by the transition from socialism to capitalism.

"IT WAS ALL ABOUT PLAYING ON PEOPLE'S GREED"

It should be clear by now that the changers played a unique role in Mongolia's transition from state socialism to market capitalism. Nevertheless, Ulaanbaatar and other Mongolian cities were also home to other kinds of market tricksters around 2000. Of particular relevance for our purposes are the so-called ball shufflers.

"Small-ball shufflers" (*shaarigchid*, lit. "small ballers")—that is, people making money from others betting on the location of a ball hidden inside one of three cups shuffled around a table—were ubiquitous at Mongolia's urban markets and other public sites with large concentrations of people in the 1990s. In fact, all markets in provincial towns had their share of *shaarigchid* during the first decade of transition, until the phenomenon died out around the turn of the millennium, due probably to a combination of reasons, including the fact that ball shuffling was eventually outlawed by the authorities and that people had by this time grown more cautious of these and other games promulgated via the promise of quick riches.

"We were playing on people's greed" (*ulsuudyn shunal deer ajilladag*; lit. "working in their greed"), recalled Bumochir, a bright and smiling man in his early thirties, while pretending to enjoy the cup of cappuccino that Morten had just bought him. It was the autumn of 2004, and they were sitting in one of the many new European-style cafés that had opened near the central square of Erdenet, a city that was relatively affluent due, in large part, to its rich iron and copper deposits (*erdenet* means "with treasure" in Mongolian). Bumochir is not a new character in this book. He already made an appearance in Chapter 1, in our discussion of the general tendency for many representatives (and men in particular) of Ulaanbaatar's lost generation to frequently and suddenly "jump" between new jobs and friends (it was Bumochir who, after having made a living on Erdenet's market scene for several years, had eventually become a fireman, only to begin considering studying dentistry).

Of the many different jobs and "businesses" Bumochir was involved in from 1994 to 2004, his career as a ball shuffler had been the most profitable, and the most memorable. "You see," he explained,

> I started working at the market in 1994 or 1995 during my final year of school. Back then society was very difficult. People didn't have any jobs. But everyone could get loans—between MNT10,000 or 20,000—from banks. So people had a lot of money on their hands and all they were thinking about was how to make more. People wanted to make money in easy ways but were ignorant about how. That's why I started playing the small-balls game. One could make lot of money, 200,000 or 300,000 a day! *Shaarigchid* worked by making people's greed even stronger. We made people think they could make money from playing it. For four or five years I played small balls. People trusted each other when Mongolia entered the market economy and didn't know anything about how it worked. Now, no one is playing such games anymore.

Much like the changers, Bumochir and his fellow ball shufflers thus personified Mongolia's first decade of postsocialist transition. Far from being engaged in the production of what Marxists would call "real value" by transforming matter to meet so-called basic human needs, the *shaarigchid* tapped into a discourse and an ideology of greed—that is, capitalism—in the hope of making money out of nothing. They accomplished this feat by exploiting the very structure and value of capitalist exploitation itself ("all people were thinking about was how to make more money . . . in an easy way"). In fact, there was even a sense in which the ball shufflers outperformed the changers at their own game and on their own turf. Bumochir thus stressed that "different kinds of changers—money changers, skin changers and people who came from the countryside to shop for *Tsagaan Sar* [Lunar New Year]"—were among his key targets. For "changers didn't use banks and had a lot of ready money in their hands, so their stakes and losses were always high." Ironically, then, it would seem the *shaarigchid* had found a way of giving the *chyenjüüd* a taste of their own medicine in terms of false advertising. But how did Bumochir become a *shaarigchin*? What was his way into the Erdenet market? Here is what he explained:

> There was this guy in our apartment building who was my age. He had just moved up from Ulaanbaatar, and it was him who introduced the three-cup game here in Erdenet. People knew that in one of those three cups, there was a sponge ball. That's why we were not arrested. It was not considered a trick. We were allowed to play it. We used to pay MNT500 in tax to play at the market. The game developed very fast. First, people's stakes were MNT10 or 20, and we would only earn MNT6,000 to 7,000 per day—this was when a bottle of vodka cost MNT450. In 1993 and 1994, it was just starting. But in 1995, people began playing with MNT1,000 as the lowest stake and up to 200,000 or 300,000 as the highest. This was the time when it became a trick [*zalilan*], and *shaarigchid* would now hide the ball in their hands. By this point, so many people would gather around us while we played that they almost couldn't fit.

What Bumochir is conveying here (apart from corroborating that traders' access to markets took place via friendship networks) is that, at some point in the mid-1990s, the profession of small-ball shuffling gradually became corrupted. As the stakes became higher and the audiences bigger, ball shuffling became an illicit "trick"—perhaps not unlike the way it became increasingly clear to people in the course of the 1990s that the skills, techniques and capacities required to become successful in the age of the market were of a quite different nature than they had imagined during and immediately after the socialist period:

> It really was about teaming up with a few others to trick people. A person working with me would [blend in with the crowd and] say, "Okay, so I put my money here," pointing at one cup. While he pretended to look away, I would then very visibly take the ball from there [the cup he picked] and pretend to put it here [in another cup]. Yet I did not really put it there, but hid it inside my hand. My partner would then point at the first cup [pretending that he thought the ball was still there] and I would lift it [to show that it is empty], and say, "Sorry, brother, you need to pay me MNT1,000." At this point another person working with me would say, "What a stupid person this guy is! I know where the ball is!" This was the moment when I would say, "The person who guesses where the ball is wins 2,000," and when I opened the two remaining cups, I put the ball under the cup that [the outside person] played 1,000 on so that he won money. I would then play a new round, again hiding the ball in my hand, asking, "OK, who wants to put MNT1,000 on the middle cup?" after my two partners had bet MNT1,000 on the other cups. I would then place the ball under the middle cup as I opened it, and the outside person would win MNT3,000. And this was the point where I said, "OK, here is how we play: You can win 30,000

by betting 10,000." Again, my two partners would bet 10,000 on two of the cups and this time I would shuffle them round fast for a while until ending by secretly putting the ball in one of my partner's cups, and saying out loud, "Very well. This gentleman has now won 29,500. I will only take MNT500 in fee for service." Since people in the audience were now convinced that I was not making any profit, they all wanted to play—and the next round, I raised the bets to MNT50,000. When people lose 30 or 40,000, they become strange. Maybe they even lose their minds. You can then trick them by saying, "It's OK. You just need to play one more time to get your money back." Ball shufflers were people who played on the trust of others like this.

What set the *shaarigchid* apart from other people? Tellingly (for such were often the reasons that people gave for their own and other people's successes), Bumochir's reply to Morten's question was deeply couched in the moral narrative of Mongolia's lost postsocialist generation (cf. Chapter 1):

All *shaarigchid* were bad people. As people used to say, "One guy plays *shaarig* and another steals." I remember how the thieves would follow us *shaarigchid* to steal from the crowd. The thieves were afraid of the *shaarigchid*—we were like the *atamans* of thieves. *Shaarigchid* were hooligans. They didn't care for any other job, for they made easy money. People who came out of prisons used to do it a lot. *Shaarigchid* spent the money they made in the right way. They just drank vodka.

These days, no one can make money shuffling balls, and so many former *shaarigchid* have become pickpockets and thieves. Also, many are drunks. Some people I know back from those days can now be found in the Valley of Drunks [see Chapter 2]. Every time they see me, they always shout, "Hey hey, old friend, come over here!" only to ask me the moment I reach them: "Do you have a bottle of vodka?" A few people did manage to make money based on the game and made something out of themselves and their lives. But the main thing to remember is this: Stupid people will stay stupid.

Very well, Morten concurred, but successful ball shufflers must have possessed certain talents. After all, he asked, "Hiding the ball is a talent of sorts, isn't it?" To which Bumochir retorted, with a flat smile and sarcastic tone of voice,

No, small-ball shuffling is not really a talent. The palm of the hand can be used to contain and hide many things. Small balls fit really easy—just like this, just like that [Bumochir demonstrates with his right hand how the palm can contain an imaginary ball]. Sometimes one would hide it and put it into one's pocket. Sometimes two balls would come out. Ha ha ha. The Russians use potatoes, which really isn't good. Our way was much better and more sophisticated. The most important thing was to recognize players who had money and how you could make their greediness stronger. Also *shaarigchid* needed to have a clear and cheerful voice. When we spoke cheerfully and entertained people, big crowds gathered.

The wood market (2003)

So being a good ball shuffler did require mastery of certain skills. Only these were not the circus-like techniques that Morten had first and rather naively expected the *shaarigchid* to master, such as superior dexterity. Instead, the talent for ball shuffling—and, it may be surmised, other forms of trickery in times of transition (including, as established earlier, the superior salesmanship of *chyenjüüd*)—was about grooming a certain "sleight of mind," namely the combination of the social skills, psychological insights and moral shortcuts needed to "team up with a few others to trick people" (for a related study of hustlers in provincial Romania, see Korsby 2015).

But this is not all. The basic lesson that Bumochir and, it is our impression, many others from his generation learned was that, for someone to become rich in the wild and crazy market of the 1990s, what one needed to master was not so much concrete skills (such as accounting, marketing or other competencies surrounded by an aura of professionalism in neophyte capitalist societies). Rather, and above all, the primary personal capacity and social skill required to make it in the age of the market was the ability to cheat or, put more politely, trick others. Or, to summarize the point provocatively but, we think, in a way that is in tune with how Bumochir and several others from his generation came to see things, one needed to be good at being bad.

"HER EYES PIERCE RIGHT THROUGH
THE WARES"

Changers, ball shufflers, and other market tricksters, it is now clear, were far from simply marginal and stigmatized figures. On the contrary, they played an important practical and symbolic role in the dissemination and internalization of the moral discourses and bodily affects associated with market capitalism in Mongolia; in fact, we have gone so far as to suggest that such personae were hypertraders who, in their excessive behavior and bodily comportment, carica-tured the very essence of the market. We are here reminded of our key findings from Chapter 2—namely that trading and other (stereo)typical market trans-actions are not more "disembedded" than other arenas of social life, but are rather *more socially embedded*.[2] Evidently, Ulaanbaatar's market tricksters were far from "economic men" who, at the moment of trade, became particularly detached from their surroundings. On the contrary, their economic practices were characterized by an *enhanced engagement* with their surroundings, both in the sociological sense that, as argued so far in this chapter, they could antici-pate customers' desires "to the point of clairvoyance" (Simmel 1995, quoted in Astuti 1999: 91), and, as we shall now show, in the material sense that they had the capacity to momentarily fuse with the commodities that they were trying to sell. In order to make this point, we need to take a closer look at what takes place during the short but intense moments when a *chyenj* picks a new potential victim on the market and tries to make her interested in his goods.

As already alluded to, the interactions between changers and their custom-ers were highly gendered, flirtatious and at times explicitly sexualized. Indeed, while the changers hanging out at Ulaanbaatar's markets were usually male, one got the impression that their "targets" tended to be mostly female, women whom—with varying degrees of luck and success—they were trying to seduce into buying their wares, not entirely unlike certain Siberian hunters are said to seduce the guardian spirits of the wild animals they hunt (cf. Hamayon 1990; Willerslev 2007). As a changer from Naran Tuul told Morten and Kolya on one of their rare chances to speak properly with one of them (as one might expect, changers were not really interested in being interviewed), "You can rec-ognize your customer the moment you first catch her attention. Her eyes pierce right through the wares" (*nüd n' zügeer baraa ruu orchihson*). Now, one can only wonder what the target "sees" in the changer's eyes during these brief mo-ments. Perhaps it is the changer as a vehicle of a general desire for goods, which his commodity-clad body somehow elicits? Certainly, while customers can be either women or men, there was a clear sense, according to the male traders

Morten spoke to, that women were easier targets of "soft words" (*amny figürtei*). As Otgonbaatar put it, "Young women don't know the prices of things. Young guys know where things are sold, and at what price. They will tell you the precise profit rate, so they write the different prices down. Girls' knowledge about trainers is bad. If you just make a bit of advertising, then they will believe it."

Perhaps the changer's body and self, as he flirts with his gullible customer, might almost be said to undergo a shamanic metamorphosis in the sense that his person, for a brief moment in time, is no longer distinguishable from his wares. For how else are we—in an ethnographically more sensitive way than automatically dismissing this claim for being "metaphorical" would seem to allow (cf. Henare et al. 2007)—to account for statements such as "her eyes pierce right through the wares"? By meeting his female victim's eyes, it is as if the changer comes to inhabit a vantage from within his goods by virtue of her attraction not to him, but to the commodities that he wears. On this interpretation, which is admittedly somewhat speculative, the changer momentarily takes on a perspective that is "magically" lodged *inside* the goods that he sells. At this specific conjunction of time and space, the changers undergo the dangerous but also liberating metamorphosis into an exalted state of commercial entrancement, which, as suggested in Chapter 2, might even be associated with the fun and joy of trading on a much more general basis.

To substantiate this interpretation, it is instructive to turn our attention to another ethnographic context characterized by bodies, minds and perspectives in perpetual motion and exchange. We are thinking of Northern Mongolia's shamans, diviners and other occult specialists with whom we have both worked (see Højer 2009; Pedersen 2011). Indeed, it is precisely the ability to move between different human and nonhuman persons by momentarily taking up the perspective of their different bodily vantages that shamanism is all about. Thus, among Northern Asia's shamans and hunters, to engage successfully with the spirits of the forest, one needs to orchestrate oneself (in the sense of molding the configuration of one's mind and especially one's body) in a certain way—for instance, by mimicking the sounds or movements of the wild animals (bears, wolves, deer, etc.) whose bodies these nonhuman souls are understood to inhabit (Pedersen 2001; Willerslev 2004b, 2007).

In the same way, we suggest, *chyenjüüd* at the moment of trading are immersed in a mirror hall of multiple perspectives (Willerslev 2007), where agency is a function of one's capacity to inhabit certain vantages that are particularly good to see—and from which to be seen. For as with the Darhad shaman at the point of contact with her spirits (Pedersen 2007a), or the Yukaghir hunter imitating his prey (Willerslev 2004b), successful action here essentially boils down to making one's body assume those appearances that are particularly good to be seen. This, we argue, is what being a *chyenjüüd* is all about (apart from the ability "to tell lies"): to momentarily assume a transhuman bodily vantage. Such is the "magic" of *chyenjüüd*: they see what objects would see if they could see. By sensing his victim's eyes meeting his, the *chyenj* also senses that her eyes are absorbed into his goods as the intensity of the trading moment and the sensuous proximity between him and the commodities he displays facilitate a momentary extension of his person to encompass the perspective of his wares. In undergoing this momentary bodily extension, the changer is equipped with another kind of body—namely, it is tempting to say, a commodity body.

In sum, the changers emerged as the ultimate commercial actors of post-socialist Ulaanbataar, for more than anyone else they mastered the quasi-occult act of submerging and extending their minds and bodies into the materiality of the goods they sold. Indeed, if Morten had to pick one lasting memory from his fieldwork in Ulaanbaatar's markets in 2003–2004, it would have to be the simultaneously tragic and comic, frightening and hilarious, image of wildly gesticulating changers wearing five or more leather jackets, sweating profusely while overeagerly trying to convince customers. Indeed, a key thing that set apart such petty changers from more ordinary vendors (as well as the "real" changers operating behind closed car or office windows, safely removed from the chaos of the markets) was the fact that they were using their own bodies to display their goods. Not unlike the wheeler-dealers populating some European beaches with their arms fitted with fake golden watches for sale at "a special price for you," it was almost as if the changers' own selves and bodies had been infused by, if not taken over by, the materiality of the commodities for which they were doing their false advertising. Although the *chyenjüüd* represent an extreme case (barring, possibly, the case of fashion models), their proximity to the goods they were selling was not unique. Alaina Lemon, for instance, points out that "non-Russian minorities, long associated with illicit trans-border trade and contraband . . . [were] often depicted with foreign cash clinging onto their bodies, *as if made of like substances*. Ironically, such minorities were nevertheless excluded from the most elite of hard currency exchange fares and networks, both within the country and at its borders" (1998: 25, emphasis added). Indeed, we have already encountered several examples of this "disturbing effect of things coming too close" (Spyer 1998: 9) in previous chapters of this book, including the "speculator women" who spent all day getting drunk from the vodka they were also selling (Chapter 2), and the different kinds of pawned valuables—in particular but not only gold, meat, vodka and belongings imbued with personal histories—that affected pawnbrokers and their customers in detrimental ways (Chapter 5).

So, if *chyenjüüd*, "speculator women" and pawnbrokers all shared one thing, despite otherwise different predicaments, it was the ever-present danger of absorbing the substances of the commodities they were trading in, to a point where the ontological distinction between discrete subjects and discrete objects momentarily blurred or even collapsed.[3] Perhaps one might even go as far as to suggest that, given this fusion between the subject engaged in commodity exchange and the commoditized objects exchanged, this relationship was not, as many anthropologists might expect, one characterized by extreme alienation, but by radical inalienability. Not unlike what the Maussian gift does for its donor, these "inalienable commodities" imbued the trader's person with a transactable, material form that reached beyond his self and body, prompting the notion that changers are especially (disturbingly) intimate with their goods. The changer, then, quite literally *is* what he sells, or is so at least during the short but intense eruptions of commercial entrancements that define his salesmanship. In that sense, we can think of changers as inversions of the *flaneur* figure of mid-nineteenth-century Paris (Benjamin 1997; cf. Baudelaire 1964 [1863]). Instead of his identity being an image of the commodities that he buys, as with the flaneur, the changer's subject is a mirror image of the goods that he sells. For if Benjamin's flaneur is defined by a boundless desire for commodities that he tragically tries to meet, the *chyenj* is defined by an insatiable desire for selling, which blurs the contours between him and his goods.

CONCLUSION

Much as has been found to be the case with other marketplaces in the post-socialist world and beyond (see Chapter 2), Mongolia's black markets around the turn of the millennium were crucial sites for the construction and negotiation of new kinds of social agency, economic forms and moral values. However, as we showed in Chapter 2 and further substantiated both ethnographically and theoretically in this chapter, the nature of these new market subjectivities, discourses and affects could not be reduced to questions of consumer identities and commodity fetishism alone. The visitors to Mongolia's urban markets were not simply forging new identities in a global economy, as some anthropologists and sociologists working on consumption have argued (e.g., Miller 1995). Nor, on the other side of the counter, were the traders merely ciphers of abstract and alienated market forces, as some Marxist economic anthropologists come close to suggesting (e.g., Friedman 1990). On the contrary, certain traders were perceived (and perceived themselves) as being imbued with capacities that allowed them to transgress not only prevailing norms and moralities within and beyond markets but also the ordinary boundaries of human bodies and minds.

The different kinds of market tricksters with whom we have been concerned in this chapter offer a case in point. To some extent, as we have seen, one's degree of success as a changer and a ball shuffler was thus perceived as a function of one's ability and willingness to extend, distribute and sometimes even dissolve one's person into the totality of all the goods and affects circulating on the market. Small wonder, then, that the *chyenjüüd* were called what they were. These people were not just exchanging goods like other traders; they also—it could be argued—to some extent *changed themselves* into what they sold. Not unlike the way religious specialists like shamans become one with their gods, one could argue that market tricksters like *chyenjüüd* are capable of becoming one with their goods.

Chyenjüüd and ball shufflers, it is now clear, were genuine middlemen; rather than simply adding value to a certain stock of goods by moving it from one place to another, they made their profit by "adding to the velocity of dealing as a whole" (Stewart 1997: 158).[4] Thus it would be a mistake to reduce this species of urban hunters to passive victims of a "creeping commoditization" (Comaroff and Comaroff 1998) arising from the transition from state socialism to market capitalism. On the contrary, it was almost as if they had *more* agency and were *more* socially embedded than anyone else. Perhaps this is why they were grudgingly tolerated despite their obscene, threatening and sometimes even violent behavior. Arguably, it was due to the presence of *chyenjüüd* and other morally ambiguous and excessive figures that the invisible forces of the market could be elicited at all.

Within the wider economic cosmos delineated by postsocialist Mongolia's politics of liquidity (Rogers 2008), the minds and the bodies of the changers and ball shufflers emerge as the most supremely "liquid" of all, and it was this hyperlability—a propensity for trickery, flirtatiousness and metamorphoses—that made the flow of commodities possible as such. Small wonder, therefore, that these and other market tricksters operating in the interstices of Ulaanbaatar's markets were perceived, by themselves and others, to be imbued with almost magical abilities. Since changer subjects—for brief but, as we have described, also very intense moments—almost collapsed into the objectness of their goods, they gained access to a semi-occult perspective "from within" these wares, from which they were able to gauge their clients' intentions by experiencing their desire from the point of view of the desired. As Ulaanbaatar's commercial shamans par excellence, these people thus embodied not only the dangers, challenges and opportunities arising from the art of dealing and dreaming in times of enduring transition but also an extreme case of the capacity for the mental and bodily mutability that all urban hunters had to possess.

Chapter 7 The Work of Hope

In the autumn of 2004, Kolya began frequenting a female Buddhist astrologer (*zurhaich*) who was offering her services from a tiny shack in the midst of Ulaanbaatar's oldest ger slums in the vicinity of the country's main Buddhist monastery, the Gandan Hiid. Kolya had first heard about the astrologer from a friend of his father (the same woman who, as described in Chapter 3, was some years later to sell his plot of land). Having recently been widowed and following various ill-fated trading ventures in which she tried to import skin-care products from Irkutsk, the woman had been suffering from both emotional distress and economic problems. But, as she had told Kolya and his father over a cup of salty milk tea, soon after she started to see the astrologer, her feelings and finances had been "centered" (*tövlörsön*). Two days later, Kolya went to visit the astrologer for the first time, and over the next months she became an important spiritual guide for him and his group of friends.

Based on interviews with and participation in divination sessions with this Buddhist astrologer, as well as case studies of Kolya

and other devoted clients of hers, this chapter explores the imbrication between metaphysical concepts of the person and postsocialist economic forms
in Mongolia around the turn of the millennium. The first part of the chapter
describes how, for Ulaanbaatar's religious entrepreneurs as much as for their
clients, concepts of human agency are becoming ever more multiple, destabi-
lized and "fuzzy" with the transition to a liberal market capitalism. We describe
how the astrologer "fixed" (*zassan*) Kolya's "soul" (*süns*) in the aftermath of a
violent assault that he was subjected to in a bar. We argue that, within a postsocialist context in which people are compelled to untangle otherwise "fuzzy"
property relations (Verdery 1995) and other economic arrangements into discrete and transactable components, a similar decomposition takes place *within*
people's selves as their personhood becomes fragmented into disparate existential capacities, such as, for instance, "luck" (*hiimor'*), "life-force" (*süld*) and
"might" (*javhaa*). Only during those rare instances in which people are able
to gain control over the chaotic economic and spiritual flows of radical transition are these fragmented components of their selves momentarily reassembled
into complete social persons and individual subjects. We further explore this
"economy of fortune" (da Col and Humphrey 2012) in the second part of the
chapter, where we return to the case of Hamid and his Cadillac presented at
the opening of this book. Engaging with recent anthropological work on hope
(Crapanzano 2003; Miyazaki 2004, 2006, 2013, 2014; Zigon 2009), we explore
a string of lucky—and not so lucky—events that took place during a summer's
day Morten spent with our friends cruising around Ulaanbaatar in Hamid's
old car.

As we shall argue, practices of "hope" (*naidvar*) allow for a momentary integration of otherwise capricious and fragile chains of creditors and debtors dispersed across the city of Ulaanbaatar as people's multiple spiritual components
(*süld*, etc.) and their equally dispersed economic possessions (property, etc.) are
temporarily brought together. Indeed, we shall show it is during such moments
of hope, and these moments only, that people are perceived, by themselves as
much as by others, as forming fully complete persons. In making this argument,
we return to one of the central concerns in this book: the blurring of boundaries
between dealing and dreaming in times of transition and the challenges this
alternative form of social and economic agency poses for established anthropological and sociological theories of practice. By returning to Kolya and to the
story about Hamid and his Cadillac, we aim to explore a particular attitude to
the future (and to time and to change more generally), as well as a certain social
imaginary, which we call the work of hope.

CALCULATING PEOPLE'S FATE

Following the collapse of state socialism in 1990, Ulaanbaatar witnessed a veritable religious awakening. Over the following decade, thousands of more or less institutionalized occult experts from hundreds of new temples, churches and other places of worship and healing began catering to Mongolians seeking spiritual advice and magical solutions to problems and worries arising from life in transition. Although an increasing number of shamans began practicing in Ulaanbaatar in those years (Merli 2006), and while a range of new religious/spiritual movements (Baha'i, Qi Dong and so forth) established themselves in this and other cities, the bulk of religious activity was centered around two established world religions—first and foremost, Vajrayana Buddhism of the Tibetan-Mongolian variety (in particular, the reformed Gelugpa or so-called Yellow Hat variety) and, to a lesser extent, Christianity as practiced, preached and disseminated by Western and South Korean missionaries representing a variety of mostly Protestant but also Catholic denominations (see also Chapter 4).

Like many Mongolians, Hamid and the others assumed a pragmatic attitude toward this open-ended religious landscape, soliciting help from different occult practitioners depending on the specific nature of the problem they were facing and the often changing reputation and popularity of individual specialists. The so-called private lamas (*huviin lam*) were probably the most popular ("private lama" denotes all religious specialists of a Buddhist inclination who have not been formally educated as monks at one of Mongolia's monastic schools). While rumors of incompetency and suspicions of swindling abounded, clients from all sorts of backgrounds visited private lamas to mitigate problems pertaining to life in the age of the market.

The astrologer whom Kolya went to see was a case in point. Born and raised in Mongolia's Arhangai province, Tsetsegmaa was at this point a rotund and smiling woman in her mid-forties, who, since moving to Ulaanbaatar in 1992, had built up quite a reputation for solving people's financial or marital problems, or both. In particular, as Kolya's neighbor confided to Morten, Tsetsegmaa was known for her ability to help people—women in particular—who had fallen victim to violence due to their own or others' excessive drinking. Tsetsegmaa was typical of Ulaanbaatar's private lamas, who predominantly seemed to be women from poverty-stricken periurban ger towns who had not undergone formal monastic training. As she explained,

> Studying to become a lama at the Gandan [monastic] School was never an option for me. The religious schools are closed to women. Instead, I joined the Community

Astrologer's shack (2007)

of Astrology Researchers when it opened in 1992 to learn the Mongolian astrology there. Eventually, in 2002, I graduated with a doctoral degree from the private Buddhist university. Immediately after graduation, I worked at the Women's Religious Center. There is also a temple [for women] called Tögsbayasgalant, and another one called Narhajid. I could have been a temple monk at any of these, but decided not to. For one thing, I didn't find the salary acceptable. But the main reason was that my views did not fit. Many who perform divination [*üzej hardag*] these days play tricks with people, pretending that they know about these things. A suffering person will think, *OK, maybe if I go there I will be saved?*, and then she turns up and has her emotions played with. I am against that. Religion should not become business. The rules of society have become those of a business society, so religion and business are being mixed: If you don't give money, then you will perish! I am not like that. I accept whatever the people who come to see me are able to give to me. From what did this person become sick? Why are things happening to her? These are the kinds of things that I try to heal.

So, it was Tsetsegmaa's own decision not to become a lama at one of the several women's temples that opened in Ulaanbaatar as part of the popularization and pluralization of religious institutions following the collapse of state socialism (Merli 2006; Bareja-Starzynska and Havnevik 2006; Pedersen and Højer 2008; Balogh 2010; Ellis 2015; Abrahms-Kavunenko 2016). "In any case," as she explained, "at the university we were just reading religious books. What my mother gave to me was much more than that." As she seldom failed to mention to clients when she first met them, Tsetsegmaa was a descendant of learned (*erdemtei*) people imbued with magical abilities. Her grandmother, who like other maternal ancestors had taken vows, could foresee things by closing her eyes, and her forefathers were holy men who cured people with their hands. Tsetsegmaa's own gifts had mostly been passed down from her mother, like the ability to "see into" people by using the senses. But the ability to cure bleeding sores by licking them had surely been passed down from her father's side.

Above all, however, Tsetsegmaa considered herself a *zurhaich* who, by complementing her inherited talents with many years of study and practice, had come to master the "science" (*shinjleh uhaan*) of astrology. Tsetsegmaa would thus always begin a healing session by performing a standardized divinatory algorithm known as "Mongolian astrology" (*Mongol Zurhai*). In her case at least, this first involved asking the clients their age and the size of their households, after which they would be politely requested to "pick a number." Then the actual "seeing" (*üzeh*) could begin. It involved adding up the year (in the zodiac), age, size of household and other numerical information offered by the client, and then "reading backward" (*ergüülj unshih*), as Tsetsegmaa put it, by using an algorithm known as the "nine tables" (*9-iin hürd*), available in most calendars sold on Ulaanbaatar's buoyant market for religious books. The resulting numbers—which would always be 0, 3 or 6—were then used for "calculating people's fates" (*hünii huv' zayag tootsoh*) by scrutinizing their distribution and form (*mayagaar*) across the tables.

While Tsetsegmaa's astrological algorithms and her divinatory knowledge seemed to conform to standard Mongolian Buddhist traditions (for other studies of Mongolian astrology, see, e.g., Bawden 1963; Swancutt 2012), one thing that distinguished her from her peers was the fact that her astrology was always performed on a chunky, solar-powered calculator. Indeed, this piece of technology seemed to be one of the main reasons her clients had come to her in the first place. Consider, for example, how Kolya spread the word about her after visiting her for the first time: "The other day, I went to see a *zurhaich* who uses a calculator to see things. It is so exciting!" Less than a week later, several of his friends had become devoted clients themselves, having heeded Kolya's advice and approached Tsetsegmaa. In all these instances, as well as at other astrology sessions that Morten witnessed at Tsetsegmaa's place, she used the calculator to reach her verdicts. Even when no actual astrology was done, numerical data about clients' position in the zodiac and about the size of their households was meticulously typed into the calculator and then followed by several minutes of concentrated "seeing," which were interrupted only by Tsetsegmaa's sudden and always somewhat aggressive hammering on its battered keyboard.

Once, as Kolya and Morten had just left Tsetsegmaa's shed following another afternoon of Mongolian *Zurhai*, Erdenebold, one of Kolya's Mongolian friends who ran a small bar with his wife, exclaimed, "This astrologer is unusually detailed [*nariin*] in her approach. What she does has nothing to do with magic. It is a form of science." Several other clients of Tsetsegmaa, including Kolya, shared this conviction that her verdicts were scientific, and that her unusual degree of accuracy resulted from using a calculator as an astrological tool. And yet, as Erdenebold often emphasized, "No diviner can be 100 percent accurate." Thus, as he went on to say in the manner of a seasoned expert, "Over the years, I have tested many diviners. Usually, a good one is about 60 percent right. Some are really bad—they will only tell you the truth one out of two times, perhaps even less. This one [Tsetsegmaa], however, is exceptional: I would say that her verdicts are right 80 percent of the time. She is by far the most precise astrologer that I have come across!"

It was, we believe, no coincidence that Erdenebold's assessment of Ulaanbaatar's astrologers and the quality of their divinatory verdicts took a quantified form. The intense atmosphere surrounding Tsetsegmaa's "seeing by numbers" often called to mind the "excitement" and "danger" experienced by Saraa and other traders working in Ulaanbaatar's markets (Chapters 2 and 6), which was another site where chunky solar-powered calculators were ubiquitous. Indeed, in much the same way that Erdenebold and the others thought that the esoteric truths of the *Zurhai* were accurately elicited by Tsetsegmaa's calculator, many of Ulaanbaatar's market and shop vendors (as well as their customers) seemed to believe that the use of electronic calculators—even for the simplest of operations, such as "1,000 plus 500"—which most Mongolians could easily perform in their heads—produced a more accurate result. Within the crammed confines of Tsetsegmaa's shed, as in the equally claustrophobic alleys of Ulaanbaatar's black markets, an infinite number of existential and economic possibilities (fates, prices) were narrowed down to a much smaller

Calculating fate (2004)

number of probabilities that, however, could *never* be reduced to a single truth that was 100 percent accurate—for such a degree of precision (*nariin*) simply does not exist in a world subject to permanent transition and unpredictability. Like elsewhere in the world (Whyte 1997), all Mongolian diviners are known to be mistaken in their verdicts sometimes, even if the logic of divination itself may at the same time be imagined to be indisputably true (Holbraad 2012). But perhaps Tsetsegmaa and other diviners' inability to be 100 percent accurate was also perceived as pertaining to an irreducible uncertainty inherent to the reality of transition itself. Possibly, for Kolya, indeterminacy was an unavoidable aspect of life in transition that no calculation, divine or not, could fully reduce.[1]

FUZZY SOULS

Having "calculated a client's fate," Tsetsegmaa would turn to the question of how to heal (*zasal hiih*, lit. "to fix") his or her specific problems and worries. While clients visited Tsetsegmaa for all sorts of reasons, judging from the sessions Morten attended, a large proportion of them were working in Ulaanbaatar's markets or in other forms of trade; economic entrepreneurs involved in the informal economy seemed to be flocking to Ulaanbaatar's private lamas in particularly great numbers at the time of our fieldwork. As she explained,

> Clients' problems depend on the nature of their business. For example, a car trader may complain, "I am not selling anything these days. I have been working with German cars for some time, but this business has turned bad. Are Japanese cars better? Or Korean? Which one is right?" Then I look whether it should be Japanese, Korean or Singaporean cars, and tell him. I see that he must start bringing cars from Japan for these will sell really fast. Also, when people bring cars from abroad they need to pass through border customs, where different kinds of leaders try to block things [i.e., ask for bribes]. So, to ensure that things go smoothly at the border, a car trader will instruct me, "There is a person with this face at the customs. Can you think about him please?" Or someone might say, "I have a lot of cars, but the owners are not there. Please, can you tell me, who will come to buy and from which direction will they come? Today, three people came and looked. Will they return and buy?"
>
> Or a market vendor might lament, "The people from the stall next to me have been spreading rice onto their goods for luck [*budaa tarniduulj*]. We are arguing a lot, and their envy has harmed my business. We have always sold similar goods, but now [the customers] only buy from them. Please, give me some of your rice!" Soon after he had spread my rice on his goods, his business will start running again. Look [Tsetsegmaa holds a small transparent plastic bag in her palm]: In here, there is rice of five different colors. Rice is manifold, it multiplies; it grows when planted. I whisper a spell [*tarni*] before I give [the rice] to people in order to help their *setgel* [feeling-minds], and they then go and spread it. It eases the selling. Also big traders doing specialized trade come to me, including secret and harmful business like importing and selling *spirt*, or people who smuggle traditional medicine from Tibet via Mongolia to Poland. They come to get my flour in order to avoid the customers catching them. But people who are smuggling and selling terrible drugs don't come to me.

As a rule, the more serious the problem identified by Tsetsegmaa in the astrology, the more elaborate the occult interventions required to fix it. For example, if a market vendor were found to have been inflicted with harm (*horlol*) via malicious gossip (*hel am*) emanating from people around him (see Chapter 4), then Tsetsegmaa would deem it sufficient to ask a lama at a local temple to have a purification sutra read during the weekly prayer ritual there. Often, however, more elaborate and therefore much more costly magical procedures were necessary to make clients' "luck rise" (*hiimor' sergeh*), culminating in the ritual of calling back the *süld* (life-force), which Tsetsegmaa's clients underwent if they had been unfortunate enough to "lose their *süld*" following drunken fighting or a violent assault. Here the stakes were colossal: if the *süld* was not restored to the victim soon, he could die.

This is what happened to Kolya following an assault in a bar by two Mongolian guys who were out celebrating their recent return from Seoul with fat wads of dollars earned by working illegally in the Korean car industry. The moment Kolya returned home from the trauma hospital, where he had spent several days in intensive care due to severe blood loss, his father's friend insisted that he be taken to Tsetsegmaa to have his *süld* checked, "because, my child, you really look so awfully pale." By applying the Mongolian *Zurhai*, Tsetsegmaa quickly determined that Kolya's *süld* had indeed been kicked off course in the attack. With a somber expression, she now turned to Kolya and explained that his *süld* had been transformed and diminished from the shock that his *setgel sanaa* (state of feeling-mind) had experienced in the attack, and that it was therefore of the utmost importance to summon it back as quickly as possible.

The "fixing," which took place in the smoky, incense-filled confines of Tsetsegmaa's hut, involved a long and elaborate series of prayers summoning White Tara, a prominent Buddhist goddess. Tsetsegmaa's monotonous recitation of prayers in the Tibetan language was only interspersed by occasional interludes during which she would hold up a golden bell over Kolya's head and make angry exclamations. The climax was reached when Tsetsegmaa shouted, as loud as she could and with her face turned toward the north (which is also where the souls of dead people go): "Kolyyyyaaaa, Kolyyyyaaaa, my son! Poor little one, afraid, afraid, come back, come back!" As she later explained, this was the key moment in the *zazal* when the *süld* is meant to return to the patient, who may for the same reason experience "a warm and strange feeling; many also start crying." While Kolya's eyes did not fill with tears, he did indeed experience a deep sense of relief in the aftermath of the ritual. Later the same day, following Tsetsegmaa's careful instructions, he climbed one of the foothills facing the sacred Bogd Khan mountains to the south of Ulaanbaatar to make offerings to the city's four mountain spirits (*ezed*), as Tsetsegmaa requested. "Now," he said in the taxi en route home, "The *ezed* of the city have acknowledged my worship, and will ensure that my luck [*hiimor'*] will rise."

Stories like this were by no means exceptional. Indeed, alongside problems involving money, trade and debt, concerns about alcohol, drunkenness and violence were some of the most common among Tsetsegmaa's clients. As she explained, "Both the victims and the perpetrators of violence come to me. A young man might tell me, 'I beat up someone badly. I drank vodka and acted thoughtlessly. Now, I am about to go to prison. Please save me from this.' Or a woman will come to see me and beg, 'My younger brother is an alcoholic. He

Making offerings (2004)

was born only in 1974. Please make him stop drinking.'" This, indeed, was what life boiled down to for a great many periurban households in Mongolia's times of transition: alcoholism and violence (Benwell 2006, 2009; Pedersen 2011). And while such symptoms of crisis are by no means unique to Mongolia, there is something characteristic about the manner in which they were conceptualized in Ulaanbaatar around the turn of the millennium.

As noted by a number of anthropologists (Heissig 1980; Humphrey 1996; Empson 2012; Pedersen and Willerslev 2012), Mongolians have recourse to an extraordinarily wide range of terms when communicating metaphysical aspects of themselves. Here, it will suffice to discuss four such concepts, namely *süns*, *süld*, *hiimor'*, and *javhaa*. Whereas the concept of *süns* may be translated as "soul" in the sense of "an overarching concept that implie[s] a human existence both in and beyond the confines of the body" (Humphrey 1996: 213), the other three concepts have less obvious English equivalents. The most difficult but perhaps also the most interesting is *süld*. Always a polysemic concept in Mongolian traditions,[2] *süld* in the present context may best be translated as "force" or "energy." The same goes for the concept *hiimor'*, which, although it has often been translated as "luck," is used more or less synonymously with *süld*, at least by our Ulaanbaatar friends. So, while *süns* is widely considered to be inalienable from the body (if you lose it, then you die), *süld* and *hiimor'* denote relative rather than absolute properties of the self (see also Empson 2011: 69–70).

As Tsetsegmaa reassured Kolya at their first meeting, when he told her about a nagging fear that his *süns* might have left him, "Relax, it is not your *süns* but your *süld* that is down. Without *süns* you would already be dead, whereas the *süld* is more like the *javhaa* of your *hiimor'*. If you become very afraid, if there is too much disorder [*hyamral*] in your life, then the *süld* gets startled [*tsochih*]. After some time, your work will become unsuccessful, you will feel uncomfortable, and [there will be] disease and suffering. But if I call it back, it will return to its proper channel." Instead of being a fixed and finite substance, as in the case of *süns*, then, *süld* is a proportional measure of the self that fluctuates or vibrates with varying intensity over time. The fact that the fourth term, *javhaa*, like *süld*, is commonly translated as "magnificence," "might" and "courage" not only further substantiates the complexity and fluidity of these concepts; it also illustrates the degree to which concepts of existential strength were imbricated with concepts of power in Ulaanbaatar around 2000 in the sense that in order for a given person to be lucky (to have *hiimor'*) and to have prominence (*süld*), he or she needed to be powerful (to have *javhaa*), and vice versa.

Against this backdrop we can compare the concept of *süld* (as well as *hiimor'* and *javhaa*) with Mongolian ideas about property, which, as we demonstrated in Chapter 3, also became increasingly relative, multiple and "fuzzy" (Verdery 1995a). To substantiate this crucial point, consider the following conversation that took place between Kolya and Tsetsegmaa a few weeks after his *süld* had been called back at their last meeting:

K: Things are still not good back home. Actually, nothing has gotten better. People who are visiting must think, "What kind of place is this? What a strange family is that?" My brothers are drinking. Every day. And many people follow them home, which makes my father nervous. So, he also drinks. I try telling them: "Stop! Think of your life, think of your household." I really want to be nice. But it doesn't work. We just argue and argue.

T: There is no *enyergi*?

K: No *enyergi*.

T: When your family is like that, it is a sign that something has entered from the outside. I have seen your father and your brother [in the photos]. The vodka is causing bad flows [*muu ursgal*] to enter. You must make them leave. Then things will become nice.

K: Also, that *ber* [daughter-in-law, here referring to Kolya's older brother's wife] is drinking all the time . . .

т: The drinking is making her heart cold [*hüiten setgel*]. The 404 diseases and the 1,080 obstacles are connected with the vodka. If a household has one alcoholic woman, then they all enter.

к: I come home, but immediately feel like leaving. If guests arrive with vodka, they are met with smiles. I cannot struggle on my own. It is too hard. My father kicked the *ber* out. "You are a drunk, you cannot clean, you are not doing any work," he shouted. There was a big argument. This is what makes me so worried. Whenever I come, she has been drinking.

т: You need to be as peaceful as you can. When you become upset, she will release a terrible charge of bad *enyergi*, which is then added to yours. You need to be positive [*eyereg*] in order to create the opposite charge [*esreg tseneg*]. To protect your own light you need to treat angry persons nicely. Then [the bad *enyergi*] will go away. If you look angrily at such a person, you will only receive more bad things. You will be punctured [*tsoorno*].

к: Perhaps you should come and perform a ritual back home. I told my brothers that I want to have them looked at by you. Things are going off course at the moment. Maybe you can make them stop drinking?

т: As long as there is just one person in the household who wants to move in the right direction, the bad flows will go away for sure. Whatever caused that *ber* to become alcoholic has to be cut away [*taslaad orhih*]. When I think back, you have improved since you came here first time. Your *hiimor'* has risen. You mentality is different now. It has become more centered [*tövlörsön*].

The terms used by Kolya to express his worries—as well as those used by Tset-segmaa to mitigate this nervousness—all express a characteristically leaky self. Like Kolya's land, his life-force (*süld*) and energy (*enyergi*) are at constant risk of being "punctured" and "startled" by various "flows" (*ursgal*) beyond his control. And, much as Kolya was struggling to make the plot of land his alone by curtailing different networks of obligation (see Chapter 5), he also engaged in a sustained attempt at "cutting away" (*taslaad orhichihoj*) the 404 diseases and 1,080 obstacles associated with the alcoholism of his sister-in-law.

This, then, could be what the growing demand for private lamas in Ulaan-baatar around the turn of the millennium was all about: the need to cut and contain the flow of spirit (in the dual sense of the word) in response to the ever mounting problems and uncertainties of the transition. As modes of being that are neither fully singular nor fully multiple, people's selves (just like their be-longings, cf. Chapter 3) are perceived to exist in a precarious state of dynamic equilibrium (*tövlörsön*), on either side of which lurks the ever imminent danger of being pushed too much toward one or the other side. Maintaining one's *süld*, *hiimor'* and *javhaa* becomes a matter of relentlessly subjecting oneself to flows (*ursgal*) and influences (*nölöölöl*), while at the same time cutting this infinite potentiality of social and spiritual relations down to size. If one is not able to perform this balancing act, one risks losing oneself too much into the disorder (*hyamral*) and becoming a prisoner of the excessive opportunities and freedoms of the age of the market (like Misha, Kolya's eldest brother, literally did when his failed attempts to become an entrepreneur put him in prison). Conversely, there is also the danger that one might fold in on oneself and extinguish all *enyergi*, as both Lyosha, the other older brother, did when he indulged in nostalgic memories of the socialist past, and Andrei, his younger brother, did by losing himself in private daydreams of a future in riches (see Chapter 1). As the most successful brother and breadwinner of the household, Kolya was straddling the ever lurking danger of being dragged into the flow of transition and ending up losing his *süld*, with the risk of fully containing himself and his property and thus ending up living a "boring" life. Sometimes this delicate balancing act worked, and he was able to contain the double flow of fuzzy property and fuzzy souls and channel it in ways that turned out to his advantage. At other times, as when Kolya came to visit Tsetsegmaa or when he lay idle in bed, the chaos impinging on him from all sides caught up with him, and he was overwhelmed by a deep sense of crisis.

A DAY IN THE CADILLAC

Hamid, Kolya and the rest, we have established so far in this chapter, were facing a truly baffling mixture of religious and economic imaginaries, as well as a multitude of spiritual and material flows from which their selves seemed to emerge as capricious assemblages of "souls," "luck" and "might." Accordingly, as the above examples also illustrated, it makes a lot of sense to say that they were part of a wider postsocialist "occult economy" (Comaroff and Comaroff 1998) at the time of our fieldwork. Yet, unlike the "economy of fortune" that anthropologists have described from a variety of Mongolian and Inner Asian rural settings (da Col and Humphrey 2012), this urban occult economy did not rely on any proper, fully fledged cosmology to work. Instead, as we wish to demonstrate in the rest of this chapter, our friends' calibration of the transition's relentlessly changing spiritual and economic trajectories involved not so much a cosmological framework as a hope. To make this point, we now return to the story with which we opened this book, when our friends were driving around Ulaanbaatar in Hamid's old Cadillac.

As Hamid, Kolya, Andrei and Erdenebold met that Tuesday morning, there was a sense that this was going to be a special—even a fortunate—day. For one thing, there was a feeling in the air that Erdenebold would finally manage to retrieve the large sum of money owed to him by a wealthy Ulaanbaatar businessman. This expectation was based on a series of promising verdicts reached by Tsetsegmaa, the Buddhist astrologer whom Erdenebold had consulted the previous day. Based on well-established astrological techniques, Tsetsegmaa, the astrologer, had "calculated Erdenebold's fate" (*huv' zayag n' tootsoh*) and predicted that, on this particular day, he stood a good chance of getting his money back as his *hiimor'* and *süld* were both at exceptionally high levels. Another, more prosaic reason that this was bound to be a "good day" was that, just that same morning, Hamid had pulled some strings with some "bosses" in Ulaanbaatar's shady underworld of private loans to apply new pressure on his own debtors, thus securing funds to obtain the missing engine parts for his car. Suddenly, for the first time in years, the Cadillac was working, and the five of us set out on a journey through Ulaanbaatar and its suburbs that was to last well into the night.

Although everyone was in high spirits, and although Hamid had made it clear that the many treats and pleasures of the coming hours were to be incurred at his expense alone, this was not considered to be a frivolous event like the Sunday picnics. On the contrary, there was a sense that the group was about to accomplish a day of hard but also profitable work. The following ten hours were spent driving around the city, interspersed by numerous stops of varying length and purpose, typically because someone was supposed to be there whose help, services or money was required. Because he found himself unable to participate in what seemed a pointless waste of time and phone units, Morten often found himself alone with Andrei in the backseat, while Kolya and Hamid were outside "doing business" on their fancy cell phones. Sometimes, a car would materialize as the outcome of these conversations, a vehicle that typically involved a new group of friends and another assemblage of transitional souls, as well as a different constellation of expectations and hopes. On these occasions, countless cigarettes and not a few beers were consumed in a mock-serious atmosphere in which the two sides could be heard complaining about their "businesses" while trying to extract money and favors from one another or, alternatively, making joint plans about how to make money out of nothing. For that is what they seemed to be hoping for, on this and all other days: the sudden manifestation of *ashig* (profit) out of half-existing and half-imagined chains of people that did not, at least from an outside perspective, offer much potential for much economic value.

The bulk of the day was spent visiting a series of bars, cafés and restaurants in pursuit of a rich Ulaanbaatar tycoon who owed Erdenebold some money that had been paid by Erdenebold in advance rent for his bar project. However, despite the fact that a considerable amount of time was spent tracking the man down, the group never managed to locate his whereabouts. The closest Erdenebold got was a phone conversation with him, which only confirmed his suspicions that he was deliberately withholding the money. As Erdenebold mumbled, as he lowered the cell phone from his ear:

> This guy has no intention whatsoever of returning the money. But he cannot tell me this. If he were to simply say no, then he knows I would begin using other means of fighting. I would then ask lawyers, important people I know, and different kinds of leaders to scold him—I would be doing things like that in order to have maximum pressure applied on him. This is why he keeps saying to me, "I will give the money back to you, I will." He is just making excuses. "Come again tomorrow," he says, and then disappears so I can't find him for weeks. All this to gain some more time for the money to circulate within his own company. After two weeks, he will have made a profit. Of course, an amount like MNT200,000 is a joke to him, but my money is still useful, as he can put it in circulation.

Strikingly, although this common game of hide-and-seek had at this point been going on for weeks, Erdenebold's expectations of getting the money back had not decreased. For the rest of the day in the Cadillac, as well as on the several other occasions during the following weeks when the issue of the debt was brought up, he continued to express a firm conviction that "one day, the loan will be returned"—even as he was being presented with what seemed to be ever mounting evidence to the contrary. What *was* subject to constant change, however, was Erdenebold's idea of how he was going to get the money back, as if one certainty about one future event could simply be substituted with a new certainty about another future event, rather than (as one might have expected) each failure building up more uncertainty until reaching a tipping point when hope flips into hopelessness.

At some point around sunset, events began taking an unfortunate turn. It was not just that Erdenebold was confirmed in his suspicions that this was, sadly, not turning out to be as "good" and "fortunate" a day as predicted by the astrologer. Indeed, while she did not find it necessary to answer why her first predictions had proved wrong, this was confirmed by Tsetsegmaa herself who, in response to Erdenebold's increasingly desperate phone calls, performed yet another divination on his behalf that revealed numerous remaining "obstacles" (*saaduud*) in relation to retrieving his money. These newly found "obstacles" were to mark the beginning of a series of setbacks that reached their culmination when, at a very late hour that same night, Hamid's financial situation had deteriorated to a point where it became increasingly obvious that his Cadillac was not going to remain a fully functioning vehicle for much longer. Indeed, by the next morning, he and his Russian partner Tanya found themselves so haunted by their own half-broken promises to creditors that they were forced to give away certain parts of the Cadillac's engine as collateral for an outstanding loan of their own, the return of which was also long overdue. And thus ended a summer's day in the Cadillac, which, in spite of all the events that might have made it into a day to remember, had, in fact, not been very different from most other days in the lives of Hamid and other people from this generation.

So what are we to make of the story? We can begin by noting that, unlike in certain rural Mongolian contexts (Kabzinska-Stawarz 1991; Empson 2006, 2011, 2012; High 2017), the concept of fortune (*hishig*) did not loom very large in Kolya's and the others' lives. Indeed, the story about Hamid and the others shows what happens when Inner Asian notions of fortune and luck are severed from their traditional rural context, where such "metaphysical concepts of the person" (Humphrey 1996) still seem to be quite widely known and shared (but see Højer 2009, 2019; Swancutt 2012). Certainly, Kolya and the others did not have recourse to any elaborate and coherent Buddhist or shamanic cosmology with which they could explain what looked like the uneven distribution of "portions" (*huv'*) of fortune (*hishig*) among themselves and others.

Being to a large extent forced to construct their cosmologies out of scattered phone calls to competing religious entrepreneurs and occult specialists, Kolya and his friends spent a lot of time and energy trying to figure out what kinds of invisible metaphysical capacities they might be imbued with (*süld*, *hiimor'*, etc.), and what the relative strength of these capacities might be vis-à-vis those of other people. Indeed, it cannot be emphasized enough how much Kolya and the others worried about invisible states of affairs hovering somewhere between the occult and the economic, or between flows of the soul and flows of the market, constantly speculating and endlessly discussing how best to calibrate and optimize these two equally important but seemingly disparate dimensions of life in transition. For, as Tsetsegmaa once reminded Kolya in response to what she considered to be his obsession with outward appearances, "If you have *javhaa*, then you will be successful. Outside form doesn't matter. It doesn't matter whether you are handsome or ugly. If there is *javhaa* behind the outside, you will have the magic of pulling people toward you." Indeed, she explained to Morten, this was what went wrong that day in the Cadillac: having started out the morning with his *hiimor'* and *süld* at their peak, these two relative metaphysical properties of Erdenebold's self gradually diminished in intensity as the day ticked by, possibly as a result of having been repeatedly

Burning incense (2006)

put in contact and therefore compared with the superior *hiimor'* and *süld* of the powerful tycoon.

Thus our friends' socioeconomic activities seemed to form part of a distinct social mathematics (Corsín-Jimenez 2007). Unlike the "economy of fortune" in rural Asian settings, however, their calculus of hope did not rely on a shared and stable cosmology to work.[3] Rather, for them, and probably for many other more or less dispossessed urban hunters in postsocialist Mongolia, it was the shared activity of hoping and dreaming that momentarily calibrated otherwise disparate realms and scales of their lives by cutting overstretched networks down to size. As such, we now show, one may thus think of hope as a prospective momentum or temporal attitude, which gathers into fragile assemblages otherwise heterogeneous entities, dimensions and affects. During the brief but recurring moments when everything adds up (as when, one morning, all the parts of the Cadillac were put together to make a functioning car), it is the work of hope (as we shall call it) that enables people to calibrate their dispersed inner capacities (souls, life-forces and luck) with their equally dispersed outer capacities (loans, credits and collateral). A poor man's fortune, hope is what people do when they have no firm ground, in the form of an economic, religious or political cosmos, on which to build their ideas of the future.

THE WORK OF HOPE

We can broadly distinguish between two different forms of hope in our friends' lives. One of these can in the above story be associated with Kolya, Hamid and Erdenebold, and the other with Kolya's brother Andrei. The second form of hope is captured by the term *möröödöl*, which refers to daydreams (and more generally desire and wish) that are not shared with and therefore cannot be contested by others. This passive, introspective and individualistic daydreaming is what Andrei—and Morten—were preoccupied with as they were waiting passively in the backseat of the Cadillac while Kolya, Hamid and the others were "working" (as they often insisted calling these and other activities of hustling and gathering), shouting into their cell phones or meeting with people. Yet the day in the Cadillac was also infused with another kind of hope, namely the more active, intersubjective and irreducibly social practice of hoping commonly referred to as *naidah*. In this other form—which was practiced, for instance, by Erdenebold in his doggedly optimistic pursuit of his tycoon debtor—hope always involves some sort of action in and on the world, an action that invariably takes place with and indeed *through* other people, and in that sense may be described as irreducibly social (indeed, *naidah* may also be translated as "to rely on," just as the nouns *naidlaga* and *naidvar* mean "trust" and "confidence," respectively).[4] This does not imply that hope is automatically part of the world. Rather, hope in the form of *naidah* must, like trust, continually be made in a collective effort. For Hamid and the others, then, hope amounted to a form of work (*ajil*) in its own right, for it was a necessary aspect of "doing business" during the postsocialist transition. As in other late capitalist contexts where the medium-term horizons of high-modernist economic planning and Keynesian financial politics had been "evacuated" into an unknown and abstract future (Guyer 2007), in Ulaanbataar around the millennium hope and other potentially "cruel" forms of optimism (Berlant 2011) had become a primary site of subjectivity and agency for not just the urban dispossessed but whole swathes or even generations of Mongolian people.

But what does this active "work of hope" consist of? Like fortune, hope involves a distinct orientation in time—a certain temporal attitude by which subjects, or collectivities of subjects, become suspended between the present and the future (what Ernest Bloch called the "intermediate future"). According to Hirokazu Miyazaki, who along with Vincent Crapanzano (2003) and Jarrett Zigon (2009) has spearheaded the anthropological literature on this topic, hope is an epistemological method, a certain way of knowing (Miyazaki 2004, 2006, 2013). Discussing the aspirations of Tada, a senior Japanese trader of financial securities, in terms of his prospects for future retirement, Miyazaki explores how Tada's failed aspirations come to have real effects on his and his colleagues' lives by allowing for the appearance of radically new alternatives that could never have been predicted or even *thought* within a conventional practical logic.

Against this backdrop the concept of hope takes center stage in our attempt to make sense of the "apparently irrational optimism" of our friends (cf. this book's Introduction). For according to this non-practice-theoretical interpretation, hope is not a practical sensibility that produces (more or less realistic) scenarios for the future, as in Bourdieu's Husserl-inspired phenomenology of temporal prospection and other anthropological studies of time navigation (Gell 1992; Vigh 2009). Instead, hope is a unique temporal attitude: "a method of radical temporal reorientation of knowledge" (Miyazaki 2004: 5), which appropriates the future as a "model for actions in a present moment" (Miyazaki 2006: 157). Notwithstanding numerous differences between Miyazaki's ethnography and our own, in both cases "failure is an endpoint" (Miyazaki and Riles 2005), for the point about hope is for things never to be completed (see also Jensen 2014).

This, we propose, is precisely what Hamid and the others were doing that day in the Cadillac: they were doing the work of hope. Their seemingly "irrational" optimism, then, was basically an alternative form of work. Instead of representing one mistaken attempt at anticipating the future after the other without drawing any lessons from it, the repeated failure of things to work out as planned for Kolya and the others was the result of a certain temporal orientation and social logic, *the purpose of which is the (re)production of social momentum and agency as such.*

Note that there is a crucial difference between Miyazaki's notion of hope and the one we are advancing here. In Miyazaki's case, hope is a private cognitive process that involves transforming the knowledge that one has in one's head with respect to the future in a novel way (the situation, however, is different in Miyazaki's other field site of Fiji [2004]). Conversely, among Kolya and his friends, epistemological questions do not rank above other questions in the pursuit of hope (questions of profit, as well as of women, or of simply "having fun," are just as important). Nor is hope a private activity here. On the contrary, as we saw, hope is here necessary for the very constitution and reality of social worlds, and is therefore also too important to be tucked away inside the insulated dreamscapes of a single mind. So, when we say that hope amounts to a kind of work, this is not just a metaphor: work is what hope *is*—a distinct and respectable form of labor that, via its creation of social t(h)rust, is necessary for the reproduction of social networks (see also Fox 2015).

Much like the divinatory practices and beliefs described earlier in this chapter, the work of hope and chance explored in its second part seem to pertain to a messy continuum between the so-called political-economic and the so-called cosmological; in fact, it is almost as if the more one seeks to locate a boundary between such purported "domains" or "arenas" of social life, the more they blur and mix up. For the same reason, the best solution may be to bite the bullet and do away with these and other ingrained and cherished social scientific ways of theorizing ethnographic realities, especially in contexts like the present one, where people were either reluctant or simply uninterested in doing so themselves (see also Pedersen 2011: 29–34). For Hamid and his friends, to work really is to hope—or, we could say, to hope really is to work—for only through the collective activity of shared dreaming was it possible to maintain the idea (or illusion) that people are connected and trust one another at all. In that sense, the value produced by the work of hope is the continued existence of the social network. Without hope in the deeply social form described here, it would not be possible to imagine a chain of business partners from which one might, on a "good day," carve out a "profit." And yet, such chains exist only as dormant futures; they have no reality outside sudden instances of hope, as that day in the Cadillac when everything, for a brief moment, seemed to add up.

Hope, then, is what people do when they have absolutely no firm ground on which to base their anticipations. More so than any other activity, the work of hope enabled people like Kolya and Hamid to assemble and apportion their dispersed "inner" economies (*süns, süld, javhaa*, etc.) with their no less dispersed "outer" economies (property, debt, collaterals, etc.) within a context of permanent transition. It was during moments of hope, and these moments only, that these hustlers were perceived, by themselves as much as by others, as complete persons imbued with social agency ("life-force," "might," etc.), much as the fragmented car pieces were only assembled into a real car on the particular day recounted above.

INCIDENTAL CONNECTIONS

Another good example of the work of hope was the way in which Kolya as well as other people tended to respond to phone calls or text messages that were mistakenly addressed to them. Consider, as an example of this seemingly peculiar practice (which could be said to represent yet another example of apparently irrational optimism), an incident that took place in Ulaanbaatar in the mid-1990s, during the days when phone ownership was still a rare and thus prestigious thing. Having just arrived in Mongolia for his doctoral research, Morten at this early point in his investigations was living in a rented flat, desperately spending his days trying to nurture a network of urban contacts before leaving for "the real field" up North. Unusually, the apartment had a phone line; alas, he had no one to call. But this did not stop the phone from ringing—not, however, because anyone wished to reach him but either because the caller was seeking a former resident of the flat, or because he or she had simply dialed the wrong number. Leaving aside what, to Morten, seemed to be a very high frequency of these incidents (he often received several calls a day), what struck him was that so many of them were treated as relations of chance. And although Morten never had any further interaction with any of the people he encountered in this way, he rarely put down the receiver without having exchanged a minimum of words with the stranger at the other end.

As became clear, as an increasing number of Mongolia's people gained access to land lines or cell phones over the coming years, actively pursuing such "incidental connections," as one might call them, was common practice. There were thus occasions during the time we spent with Kolya and the others just after the turn of the millennium when we observed them responding to text messages that had clearly been sent to them by mistake; indeed, it is telling that, on the handful of occasions where Morten himself texted a stranger by mistake, he *always* received a reply, typically in the form of what seemed to be a standard question like, "Hello, what's your name?" or "Hello there, who are you?" or "Hi there. How old are you?" On one occasion, Morten decided to do what his friends were doing all the time, namely to try to respond to the questions posed by the incidental connection at hand—"just to see what happens. Who knows, perhaps it is a beautiful girl," as Kolya and Sergei fantasized while assisting Morten in composing what they, after long and careful deliberations, agreed to be the right wording of his reply.

Now, while in the great majority of cases, the communication with the chance relationship in question quickly died out and was soon forgotten about, there were a couple of occasions when Sergei (a handsome and charming fellow) ended up having week- or monthlong exchanges with women he had established contact with in this way. And while he never met up with any of these flirting partners on a face-to-face basis, a strange but unmistakable sense of emotional intimacy and quasi-proximity was established through these incidental connections, not least when a young woman (or so she identified herself) kept on texting him with messages like, "Every morning I see you from the bus, and spend the rest of the day dreaming about you," or "You don't know what I look like, but I am watching you right now from the bus; oh my gosh, you are so handsome!"

Even during this digital stone age before Facebook, Snapchat and Tinder, then, cell phones gave urban hunters such as Kolya and his friends unprecedented opportunities for making new connections, the primary or perhaps only raison d'être of which was to facilitate the coming into being of as many potential social relations as possible. In fact, one might even go so far as to suggest that Mongolia's urban landscape to a significant extent comprised such relationships: a dormant social soup that was stirred, ever so slightly, every time a new incidental connection was made. Horst and Miller came to a similar conclusion in their study of cell phone use in Jamaica (2005). Contrary to what one might have expected, the "most important element [was] not the content of conversations but their use to maintain connections over time" (2005: 760). This "link-up" (as Horst and Miller call it) closely resembles how Kolya and the others used their phones. Also, in Mongolia, the performative force of texting or calling was more important than the propositional content, to borrow Austin's distinction (Austin 1962). And also, like in Jamaica, people in Mongolia put an enormous amount of effort into maintaining even the most ephemeral contacts by contacting their hundreds of "friends" via text messages (this was back when cell phones had a limited number of slots for contacts, sparking endless worried debates about who to delete to make space for new ones).

So why did Kolya and his friends, and many others from their generation, put such effort into making incidental connections? At first glance, the answer would appear to be clear enough: they did so because social networking is what people tend to revert to during difficult times of crisis and transition, especially when there is a lack of sociocultural institutions with accompanying rights and obligations on which to "hinge" one's existence (see also Introduction and Chapters 1 and 4). As Henrik Vigh, a Danish anthropologist working with ex-combatants in West Africa, has put it, during times of chronic crisis and deteriorating life chances, a common form of urban survival may be described as "throwing pebbles in the pond" (personal communication). It is tempting to interpret Kolya's propensity to follow up on chance encounters as a variation of the widely reported "pragmatic" attitude by which marginalized people in different contexts capitalize on every opportunity available to them.

And yet, on closer inspection, the ethnography suggests that something different was at stake during Mongolia's times of transition. It is true that our friends were happy to confirm our first impressions, namely that they were striving to "extend their social networks," including when indulging in the genesis of incidental connections of the sort we described earlier (see also Chapter 4). But the fact is that few of these potential social relations were ever activated again, and that, on the few occasions when that actually happened, it was by no means clear either to them or us who, if anyone, had gained or profited from it, at least as long as we take "gain" and "profit" to be the materialization and fulfillment of preexisting plans, goals and tactics. So, while there is no doubt that people harbored desires toward their incidental connections (indeed, as we saw, one of the main reasons for engaging in these encounters was to hunt and position oneself to be hunted by imaginary lovers), no elaborate scheming could be discerned from such attempts at extracting potential futures from incidental connections; in fact, if anything, Kolya and the rest gave the impression of being overly naive and optimistic. We have already seen many examples.

Much like the Jamaican men whose mobile phones are bursting with the numbers of young women they would like to sleep with but of whom they are perfectly aware they are never even going to see again (Horst and Miller 2005), we submit that the relations of chance established through misplaced text messages and other incidental connections in Ulaanbaatar were not considered real, at least not in the sense of being realistic. Just as Kolya and the others were all too aware that the "business proposals" they received in spam emails were scams, even if they still chose to reply to them "just to see what happens" (an issue to which we return in the Conclusion), they were also perfectly conscious of the fact that, when they received another flirtatious message from a contact first established via a mistaken attempt at texting someone else, it was highly unlikely, not to say downright impossible, that they were ever going to meet, let alone sleep with, this virtual lover. Indeed, we would go so far as to venture that it is the very existence of a gap between what is realistic and what is not (but which is nevertheless still real)—or, we could say, the void between what seems to happen with a purpose and what does not—that instilled a deep sense of satisfaction and, oddly enough, freedom in people.

LIVING FOR THE MOMENT

It is tempting to understand the story of Hamid, Kolya and the Cadillac in existentialist terms (Lucht 2012; cf. Jackson 2002). But although the day that Morten spent in the Cadillac with our friends comprised unconnected events, random stops, sudden beginnings and unexpected turns, as well as rash decisions, things did *not* turn out to be meaningful in the end. Instead of being established retrospectively, as in typical existentialist tales (whether fiction or nonfiction), meaning was here pushed ahead (without ever being quite established) by a future-oriented attitude that one might refer to as "prefigura-tion" (Maeckelbergh 2009),[5] or indeed hope in the sense suggested by us above. Whatever one chooses to call it, we are dealing with a continual colonization or expansion of "the present" by "the moment," understood as an instantaneous collapse or "folding" of the present and the future.

Thus, the work of hope does not imply that people are simply "living in the present, without any thought for either future or past," to paraphrase Day et al. (1999: 2). Following Henri Bergson (1990) and Gilles Deleuze (1994), we sug-gest that the temporality of "the moment" is not necessarily restricted to that of "the present." Instead, one might say that each moment overflows the pres-ent, as a "sign which creates itself out of the future" (Maurer 2002: 18; see also Hodges 2008; Nielsen 2011; Pedersen 2012; Pedersen and Nielsen 2013; Nielsen and Pedersen 2015). And crucially for our argument, this is a future that *cannot be planned or even anticipated*. We are here reminded about an argument made by Elisabeth Grosz, in which she contrasts the "possible" with the "virtual" (or, to use a less technical term, "the potential"). According to Grosz, the possible "is both more and less than the real." As she goes on to explain, "[i]t is more, insofar as the real selects from a number of coexisting possibilities, limiting their ramifying effects. But it is also less, insofar as the possible is the real minus existence . . . By contrast, the virtual cannot be opposed to the real: it is real. It is through its reality that existence is produced. Instead of an impoverished real (the possible), the virtual can be considered more a superabundant real that induces actualization" (1999: 25–27). This, we suggest, is what Kolya and his friends did when practicing the work of hope: they were tapping into a "super-abundant reality" (as opposed to anticipating a "number of possibilities") in order to actualize potentials that could, by definition, not be known by them in advance. For the object of their dreams was not *the future* as a spatialized hori-zon of tactical projection but *many futures* figured by, and made actual through, the present (cf. Krøijer 2015).

So this, we suggest, is what our friends were doing all those hours, days and weeks on end, which they seemed to be wasting on daydreaming about future riches and women galore: they were practicing an excessive interest in the "superabundant" potentials of their surroundings. By attending more in-tensively, or hopefully, to a given situation, they were able to extract from it a potential that was invisible to others. Indeed, is that not what the differ-ent practices that might be called hustling are essentially about—the capacity, and the will, to conjure, extract and share potential resources from the world? This, then, is why "living for the moment" is not the same as "living in the present." On the contrary, as argued in the Introduction, the more people are able to live "in the moment," the more they are also able to escape from "the present" as a subproletarian predicament.[6] Had Kolya, Hamid and the others been confined to the present, their situation would have resembled the predicament of so many marginalized postcolonial subjects from different places in the world, where the medium-term horizons of high-modernist economic planning have been "evacuated" into an abstract future dictated by neoliberal calculative fictions (Guyer 2007), leaving "cruel optimism" (Berlant 2011) and nihilism (Frederiksen 2013) as the only options available for muddling through.

Instead, by engaging with events of the future as if they have already happened, Kolya and his friends were firmly committed to a "forthcoming" and thus engaged in "protensive" anticipation in Husserlian terms (see Gell 1992: 211–228). Yet, this was an "impossible" (unrealizable) future that was subject to constant destruction, transformation and renewal, and not, as the story about the day in the Cadillac illustrated, a "practical logic" by which they made realistic projections from the present. Being sort of "trampoliners of time," Hamid, Kolya and the others performed the work of hope to "preexperience" what had not yet happened and thus to remain open to multiple futures at one and the same time. This, then, is why hope was a meaningful response to the challenges of the age of the market. It allowed our friends to deal with novelty not by trying to anticipate, predict or neutralize it but by accepting the inherently unpredictable nature of the transition from socialism to capitalism via a systematic unwillingness to plan, which, as we also discussed in the Introduction to this book, calls to mind the proclivity of hunter-gatherers and other marginal peoples to "live for the moment." Urban hunters, indeed.

CONCLUSION

We now understand why people like Hamid, Kolya, Hulan and Erdenebold refused to give up, despite the fact that they seemed to be going from one failure to the next. In fact, the apparently irrational optimism espoused in their hopes and dreams emerges as perfectly meaningful and sensible. Far from representing, in the manner of Bourdieu, one dodged attempt at applying a purportedly universal "practical sense" (*illusio*) after the other, the repeated failure of things to work out reflected an alternative temporal attitude and social practice, namely the work of hope. In fact, it might have been rather unhelpful for Hamid and Kolya to be practical in Bourdieu's sense (2000). Instead of being overwhelmed by the uncertainties of postsocialist life—an experience that could easily develop into passive resignation and aggressive nostalgia (see Højer 2018) or, perhaps, into a cynical attitude of reckless fatalism—Kolya and the others were "radically certain." This radical certainty—which, we emphasize, has nothing to do with an ability to predict the future, and everything to do with deliberately abstaining from even trying to do so—did not involve plotting a possible path from the present into the future, for there was no terrain, not even an imagined one, to be socially navigated (Vigh 2006). Had our friends been able and willing to form "realistic hopes" in the conventional practice-theoretical sense, they may have extinguished their hunter-like capacity for gauging the potentials of the moment by limiting themselves to the possibilities of the present.

This, we submit, is what urban hunting is all about in its purest form—the capacity, as well as (not to forget) the guts, to continue tapping into potential values from a perpetually changing milieu and resource horizon, even when that involves a constant flooding of all the many dreams of one moment by the next moment's new sea of potentialities. Far from being engaged in a fatalistic celebration of absolute chance, then, our friends were trampolining from one moment to the next, jumping into each new situation from a vantage that always disappeared at the moment of takeoff. Instead of neurotically trying to plan ahead or breezily taking things as they came, Kolya, Hamid and their friends were, so to speak, falling into the present from a semi-visible future, like raindrops from a clear sky.

Conclusion

In hindsight, it is striking just how much time we spent with our Ulaanbaatar friends in gritty, smoke-filled Internet cafés. Freed from the burden of low-paid and "boring" jobs, as they put it, Kolya and his male friends were spending a considerable amount of their time on the Internet: listening to and downloading music; scrolling through and contributing to news, chat and erotic websites; and, above all, checking their email accounts (all of them had several email addresses, partly because this seemed to be the norm in Mongolia in those years, but also because it allowed them to flirt with women unbeknownst to their partners). During one of these afternoons, Morten, in a carefully studied movement that had taken him months to perfect, gently rolled over to Kolya at the table across from him without rising from his office chair, using his own table as a launchpad for setting in train what might be called an act of routinized postsocialist laziness. Welcoming him with an inviting arm around his shoulder and gesturing that it was fine that he "spied" on him, Kolya kept tapping on the keyboard in what clearly amounted to a prolonged email exchange. It was at this point that Morten became worried. As he glanced at the long thread of text, he noticed the subject line "Business Opportunity: Terminally Ill African Prince" and realized what Kolya was up to. This sparked the following memorable dialogue between the pair of them:

MORTEN: Do you know what you are doing? That is spam email, a so-called Nigerian scam!

KOLYA: Aha, yes, I know. The man did write that he comes from somewhere in Africa . . .

MORTEN: But you are not supposed to answer such emails! No one does, you know. It is all a scam. It is all an attempt to trick you and cheat you!

KOLYA: Yes, but, ahem, it is still interesting to write to him.

MORTEN: No, don't do that! Have you not heard the stories? In Denmark, for example, there was an old woman who was asked to send her bank details, and her naivety ended up costing her all her savings!

KOLYA: Really? Well he did actually ask for my credit card details because he says he needs them to register a common company in our names in Nigeria.

MORTEN: Aha! There you go. I told you. That he's asking about your credit card proves my point! It is all a scam involving . . . [Morten was interrupted before finishing the sentence]

KOLYA: But actually I did send him the credit card details . . . [Now it was Kolya's turn to be interrupted]

MORTEN: You did *what*? That really wasn't very smart, you know. Why on earth did you do that?

KOLYA: Well, because I wanted to see what happened. And, indeed, he then sent a lot of new information about his own bank and the diamond mine he inherited from his father, the King.

MORTEN: [at this point, for one of the few times in his life, speechless]

KOLYA: Now he is keen to receive some money from us. Alex also sent his details to him. He wants 1,000 dollars. However, as we have told him, we don't have any money at the moment. But Alex and I have promised that we may be able to send ten dollars soon, providing that he tells us more about the business. In fact, that's what I was just doing, asking why he has not replied to our latest emails. He has become very silent as of late.

That same evening, as Kolya, Morten and the others were drinking beer at the Genghis Khan Beer Club, Morten asked Kolya and his friend Alex (who had now joined them) whether they really believed in their "African friend" and his emails. After all, Morten queried, "I cannot think of anyone as streetwise as you guys. Surely, there is no way you could be conned that easily and lamely—that man is obviously no match for a couple of seasoned postsocialist hustlers like yourselves [which was how they sometimes liked to characterize themselves]"? "Well, you see, Morten," responded Kolya, pausing to take a long drag of his counterfeit Lucky Strike, and also taking quite a while to blow out the smoke as if he needed to buy time to form a proper answer, "we don't really believe in him. But we still like doing it, just to see what happens. It is funny to be in contact with someone like that—we have been exchanging a lot of emails with him. Of course he is interested in our money, and he might even try to steal from our credit cards, but so what? There is nothing in our bank accounts. We never have any money and, even if we did, we would not be able to save it" (here Alex, who was running up a gambling debt and later ran into serious trouble from this, just nodded).

The above anecdote captures what has been our central matter of concern in this book. Perhaps more than any other incident that took place over the course of the several years we spent in the company of Kolya and the others between 1995 and 2010, it reminds us of what we have coined as the anthropological paradox of apparently irrational optimism. Just what kind of thinking and motivation could possibly lie behind Kolya's and Alex's decision to respond to such emails? Are we not here witnessing a tragic collapse of the "capacity to aspire" (Appadurai 2004)—of the very "disposition to see objective potentialities on the present structure," which Bourdieu found lacking in subproletarian subjects and other "annihilation of chances associated with crisis situations" (2000: 213)?

Our goal with this book has been to present not just an ethnography of urban hunting in postsocialist Mongolia but more generally also a new theory of human agency and social relations within contexts of permanent transition. There would seem to be considerable demand within the social and human sciences for such a study. Surely, judging from all the stories that we have told and everything else we have described in our seven chapters, there is more to our friends' thinking and acting than subproletarian suffering and marginalized victimhood. While we have tried hard not to paint an overly smug and rosy picture of everyday life in Mongolia's age of the market, we have also systematically sought to avoid presenting people as its more or less passive and mute slaves. Quite the contrary: in the above example and many others, Kolya and the others *deliberately* seemed to expose themselves to the intentions, manipulations and dreams of other people, as if doing otherwise would prevent something important from happening, even—and perhaps especially—in situations that would undoubtedly be dismissed as hoaxes or scams by most other people in Mongolia and elsewhere.

If by "radical change" we understand a situation whereby everything solid has melted into air (to paraphrase Marx and Engels), then radical change has become a way of life for many people in Mongolia. Leaving aside the minority of politicians, business tycoons and media stars who make up Ulaanbaatar's new elite, and notwithstanding the fact that a middle class has been emerging, the vast majority of Ulaanbaatar's inhabitants are still facing the social and existential uncertainties of radical socioeconomic change. Indeed, for Ulaanbaatar's "lost generation," we have argued, transition became a permanent way of life. As discussed in the Introduction to this book, instead of expressing a pervasive uncertainty, pessimism and nostalgia, as reported from so many postsocialist and indeed postcolonial contexts, Hamid, Kolya, Hulan and Erdenebold were acting as if they were strangely—if not downright irrationally—hopeful; they were, in Zigon's rather apt phrasing, "very interesting if not a bit over optimistic" (2009: 261). Because this apparently irrational optimism looks so accidental but is, in fact, imbued with a unique logic, it defies conventional social analysis. The analytical challenge is not only that Kolya and his friends jumped abruptly between different ideas and projects (as opposed to pursuing a single strategy or coherent plan); it is also that all sorts of unconnected events and circumstances made their social reality deeply irregular and inherently unpredictable. Our solution to this problem has been to propose that our friends' actions reflect a unique temporal attitude and social practice that is able to incorporate the unexpected not by anticipating and neutralizing it but by accepting the reality of perpetual rupture through a systematic unwillingness to plan.

But what kind of human agency and freedom is it—for a distinct kind of freedom and agency it surely is—that seems to be a function of the degree to which one cannot predict what is going to happen next? Quite clearly, it is not freedom in its vulgar voluntaristic sense as the exercise of maximal individual agency under the duress of minimum collective social, cultural and political constraint (see Laidlaw 2002; Mahmood 2001). If "individuality," as Caroline Humphrey suggests, is always "attained through decision: the 'plumping for' a specific way of being a person" (2009: 263) and by "leaping across what is not known—or not thought about" (2009: 269), then that is what Kolya's incidental encounter with the "African prince" was all about: "plumping for" and "leaping across" unknown social landscapes. Indeed, as we have shown, such jumping and jolting across the shifting sands of transition—whether it took place on the phone, over the Internet or via face-to-face encounters on street corners, in marketplaces or in people's homes—was treated with the same open-ended attitude in Ulaanbaatar around the turn of the millennium. Far from treating them as irritating or risky disturbances best ignored, such relations of chance for Kolya and the others provided a gateway to a vast sea of dormant relations stretching across the postsocialist city and beyond: an invisible social potentiality that each incidental encounter served to momentarily actualize and make visible. Indeed, we have argued, the very existence of a gap between what is real(istic) and what is not (but which is yet still real) or, one could say, the chasm between what seemed to happen with a purpose and what did not in postsocialist Mongolia instilled a deep sense of satisfaction and agency. Paradoxically, freedom and agency emerge as the transgression of choices and goals—it is, so to speak, an intrinsic property of life in transition as such.

In his famous essay *The Metropolis and Mental Life* from 1903, George Simmel wrote, "There is perhaps no psychic phenomenon which is so unconditionally reserved to the city as the blasé outlook. It is at first the consequence of those rapidly shifting stimulations of the nerves which are thrown together in all their contrasts and from which it seems to us the intensification of metropolitan intellectuality seems to be derived. If the unceasing external contact of numbers of persons in the city should be met by the same number of inner reactions as in the small town, in which one knows almost every person he meets and to each of whom he has a positive relationship, one would be completely atomized internally and would fall into an unthinkable mental condition" (2002 [1903]: 14–15). "Unthinkable" or not, this intensification and atomization in many ways seem to capture something about the "mental condition" of Kolya and the others at the time of our fieldwork. Yet at the same time, if there is one word with which the attitude of our friends could emphatically *not* be described, it is "blasé." Super cool they undeniably were, having grown up and (in many cases) having spent their entire lives hustling in the slowly crumbling concrete residue of a state socialist high-modernist utopia. But the urban suaveness and confidence displayed in their looks and in their actions were hardly signs of detached disinterest, as Simmel would have it.

Quite the contrary, as we have argued in this book, Kolya, Hulan and the others were practicing an *excessive* interest in their social and material surroundings. By attending more intensively—or more precisely, hopefully—to a given situation, they were able to tap into it and extract from it a potential that was and would remain invisible to others. It is in this sense that the apparently irrational optimism practiced by them when replying to spam emails and answering text messages sent to them by mistake represented no less than an alternative (non-practice-theoretical) practical sense: a strategically naive cultivation of an exalted awareness of the potentials of the present—in short, urban hunting. So, while our intention has emphatically not been to over-exoticize and essentialize our friends by claiming that "apparently irrational optimism" summed up their whole personalities and lives, we insist that to capture the complexities of life in Ulaanbaatar during the first decades after socialism it has been vital to home in on the sui generis logic of radical transition.

THE END OF TRANSITION?

So, when—if ever—does the transition come to an end? While it is tempting and in a sense accurate to answer, "Never," we would like to end this book with some broader reflections about the economic and political development that Mongolia, along with other former state socialist countries, has experienced over the last decade or so. This will also allow us to make some final observations about the ethnographic phenomenon we have called urban hunting, and about the empirical reach and scope of the theory of human agency and social time we have developed to account for this phenomenon.

While the bulk of this book has focused on life in the capital city of Mongolia between roughly 1995 and the mid-2010s, the late 2010s has in many ways been a different kettle of fish. To be sure, constant transition has been a persistent feature throughout all the years following the collapse of state socialism and the abrupt introduction of market capitalism in 1990/1991, and to this day returning locals and foreigners observe that "everything is changing in Ulaanbaatar." Still, there is a profound difference between then and now in the way in which change occurs.

The early 1990s were characterized by the effects of the democratic movement (the Mongolian People's Revolutionary Party, however, staying in power until 1996) and by the crumbling of a Mongolian economy that had, until then, been upheld with Soviet support amounting to about one-third of Mongolia's GDP (Sneath 2002: 194). Structural reforms and austerity measures meant that many people lost their jobs, Mongolian exports decreased dramatically (Sneath 2002: 194) and inflation skyrocketed. People were literally fighting for survival at this time, many by carrying out "suitcase trade" with China and Russia or otherwise entering the emerging informal economy, as we discussed in Chapters 2, 4 and 6. In 1996 the Democratic Union seized power in parliament for the first time, following the "democratic revolution," and while it seems that shifting governments over the years have meant little in terms of Mongolia's development—at least in comparison with larger forces such as the collapse of the Eastern bloc, the Chinese economy, foreign aid and loans and the investment of multinational mining companies—the democratic coalition introduced market economic reforms that, together with falling world market prices for cashmere and copper, meant that the economy did not stabilize over this period. Inflation was reduced to "only" 44.6 percent in 1996 and 10 percent in 1999 but a survey conducted by the World Bank and United Nations Development Programme showed that 35.6 percent of the population was still living below the poverty line in 1998 (Rossabi 2005: 138). Growing dissatisfaction and crises in the democratic coalition (Rossabi 2005: 95) thus eventually led to a landslide victory for the Mongolian People's Revolutionary Party in 2000.

While the first decade of the new millennium came to be characterized by shifting governments, there was a growing sense, partly due to the rapidly growing Mongolian mining economy, that change was itself now beginning to change. As Louis Vuitton shops began popping up along with French cuisine and an emerging Mongolian middle class, it was becoming clear that Kolya and the others were ahead of us in terms of knowing the newest global music and fashion trends, and not least in having acquired the newest and most advanced mobile phones and sometimes even cars. This was the time when the increasingly powerful and professionalized trading monopolies described in Chapter 2 were colonizing the informal markets, and when the "Hulans," so to speak, gave way to the "Ariunaas" (cf. Chapter 4). In 2001 a gold-copper deposit was found in the Gobi desert at Oyu Tolgoi, and by 2003 this site had become the biggest mining exploration site in the world. When the Oyu Tolgoi investment agreement between the Government of Mongolia and Ivanhoe Mines/Rio Tinto was signed in 2009, this event was felt to mark a new beginning for Mongolia. Oyu Tolgoi was predicted to be accounting for one-third of Mongolia's GDP by 2020, and Mongolia as a whole was facing the scenario of an imminent mining-based economic boom. The image of Mongolia, both domestically and internationally, had shifted from the democratic darling of Western aid within a sea of Eurasian authoritarianism (Tsedevdamba 2016) to a ripe fruit for foreign direct investment, which had hitherto remained hidden and undeveloped in the backwaters of Inner Asia (as a taxi driver told Morten in 2011, "I am feeling sorry for you Europeans: you are going down and we are just going up, up"). In 2012, commentators predicted that, within a few years, Mongolia would be the fastest-growing economy in the world. "Put together Mongolian supply and Chinese demand," *The Economist* wrote, "and Mongolia will be rich beyond the wildest dreams . . ." Economic promise, however, quickly turned into demise when the years following 2012 increasingly came to feature rising national debt, slumping mineral prices, lack of foreign investments and a stalled (mining) economy. And, with this, we might venture, "boom and bust" had essentially taken over from "radical transition" as the defining trope of Mongolian social life. The "wild east" (Haslund-Christensen 2002) had been tamed.

With all the reservations that come with making broad-stroked descriptions and sweeping claims, then, "postsocialist Mongolia" arguably ceased to exist by the late 2000s. Unlike the dramatic changes of the early 1990s—which, as we have argued in this book, in important ways assumed the form of a radical rupture with the political, social and economic forms of its late socialist past—Mongolia's path toward "post-postsocialist" society (to paraphrase Buyandelgeriyn 2008) was much more gradual, piecemeal and incremental. Yet it was as if, once the transformation had been completed, there was no way of denying it. Indeed, the signs seemed to be everywhere, ranging from the introduction of mortgage loans for the fast-growing segment of property owners in Ulaanbaatar's new Korean-built apartment towns through the opening of the Armani shop in the new Central Tower to the mushrooming boom in organic vegetarian restaurants, trendy coffee shops and posh wine bars catering to the desires of the first generation of Mongolian youth born into the age of the market. Equally significant but somewhat less visible (at least from the vantage of a still more gentrified, sanitized and commercialized city center) post-postsocialist signatures included the rise in ultranationalist xeno- and above all sino-phobic neo-Nazi groupings and movements (Billé 2014; Pedersen and Bunkenborg 2012; Højer 2018, 2019b), and what might best be described as the emergence of a periurban proletariat comprising impoverished rural migrants and failed urban hunters only barely capable of muddling through and making ends meet via endlessly shifting combinations of small-scale trade, low-paid jobs and increasingly strained family networks (see Nielsen and Pedersen 2015; Pedersen 2017a). In all likelihood, the severe economic downturn that Mongolia has suffered from since 2013 following a decade of rapid growth and an overheated property market[1] has only enhanced this regrettable process of increasing inequality and proletarization.

Or so, at least, is the shared sense that the two of us have been left with, having individually been returning to Ulaanbaatar over the last decade in conjunction with various new research projects in urban and rural Mongolia (Pedersen and Bunkenborg 2012; Bunkenborg and Pedersen 2012; Bunkenborg et al., forthcoming; Pedersen 2017b; Højer 2018, 2019b). While it is no coincidence that these impressions were imprinted on us concurrently with our own maturation into professional academics (as well as husbands and fathers), we are not alone in making the observation that Mongolia (or "Mine-golia" as some scholars and policy makers have dubbed it; see Bulag 2009) has been finding itself in a new situation, politically, socially, culturally and, above all, economically in recent years.

Needless to say, none of these developments and discourses went unnoticed by Kolya and the others. As we have sometimes mentioned and sometimes also explicitly discussed in the course of this book, there were both an individual and a shared sense that the transition was over—not in the sense that economic and political reforms were no longer taking place, nor in the sense that people's lives and domestic groups and institutions had necessarily become more stable, but in the sense that change itself now seemed to have acquired a degree of predict-ability that had not been the case since 1990. With this "change in the change of change" (the fact that change itself had stopped changing as much as it used to do, as it were; not the end of change, but the domestication, coagulation and institutionalization of the changes set in train by early market and democratic reform), it suddenly also became possible to act more strategically toward the fu-ture, hedging one's life chances and economic opportunities according to shared norms of economic exchange and moral obligation. In short, it was almost as if, with the advent of the new post-postsocialist age, the more conventional models of social practice and human agency began to apply again, including Bourdieu's theory of practice. People's horizons of expectation were now imbued with a different and (in our eyes) notably more recognizable (and for us, "reasonable" and "realistic") shape than had been the case a decade or so earlier.

Probably more realistically but arguably also more sadly, people now sud-denly seemed to know all the things they could not do, all the plans and goals that they would never be able to realize, precisely because it was now much clearer to them what they could do, both tactically in terms of optimizing pos-sibilities in the near future and more strategically by manipulating and enhanc-ing their positioning within a wider and only slowly changing social, economic and cultural order. So, in closing, it is worthwhile reminding ourselves of what we have already sought to stress in the Introduction to this book, namely that there were and still are two "times of transition" within which everyone lives their lives with a different emphasis, involvement and sense of predestination, and to which a distinct mode of social practice and kind of agency are associ-ated. This book has paid particular attention to the "hunting" variant of these, but that does not mean that our main protagonists did not relate to and were not part of the other temporalities, let alone were incapable of being practical in the more commonsensical, practice-theoretical sense. Nor, it is also worth not-ing, does this hunting- or hustling-centric focus mean that there were not many members belonging to Mongolia's first postsocialist cohort who were, and felt, significantly less lost and dispossessed at the time of our fieldwork, and who, for the same reason, spent much of their time thinking and discussing how best to cope with and manage, through tactical maneuvering and strategic planning, the uncertainties and the hardships of transition.

And yet, just as we do not wish to claim that some of our interlocutors were incapable of pursuing long-term goals, so, too, we do not wish to "bookend" the transition into "a contained ten-year saga" (as one anonymous reviewer aptly phrased it). As a matter of fact, when one of us (Lars) recently traveled in

Mongolia (2018), he got the feeling that the time of transition has never really ended after all. It may well be that we just have grown older, along with our now middle-aged informants; that the culture of radical change is still very much alive among the younger generations; and that the conclusions presented in this book are as pertinent as ever to life in Mongolia. Indeed, it could be that what we have called urban hunting is a recurrent phenomenon that always tends to appear during periods characterized by increasing uncertainty about what the future will bring, like years of economic stagnation, or, in the case of Kolya, the long winter season, when the tourists from whom he makes a living are absent. This, at least, was the conclusion that Lars reached during recent fieldwork. In a furniture shop in Züünharaa, some two hundred kilometers north of Ulaanbaatar, he was talking to an outspoken middle-aged man about the mining industry when the interviewee made an observation that almost eerily corroborated the central contention of this book:

> Most people have no job and no one has money. Mongolian businesses are like this: A person gets a loan from someone and lends the money to someone else. [Eventually] the bank owns everything . . . Do you know the profession of young people nowadays? They are doing *chavh* [a slingshot]. It means that they go here and there to confuse and trick people. That's their main job. They don't produce anything. They convince people and make them buy things. They trick companies and each other. For example, if the price of a thing is MNT10, then they go to people and try to convince them to buy it for 20. They just go around. They drive cars, go out and find people to confuse and trick. When there is work, they act quickly but otherwise they are just lying down watching TV. When there is something to do, they move very fast [*chavhdah*] [lit. "to slingshoot" or "to catapult"]. They are as fast as a slingshot. Then they make money for the next month. And then they lie down again. Ha ha ha.

It is hard to imagine a better image of the characteristic mode of subjectivity and the distinct temporal attitude that we have explored in this book, or indeed a more apt summary of the transitional context of unemployment, poverty and debt that rendered this form of agency a dominant and, as we have shown, quite logical response to not just a postsocialist but a global predicament. For this was arguably what Kolya, Hulan and our other Ulaanbaatar friends were excelling at in the heyday of radical transition: catapulting or slingshooting themselves from one moment of opportunity to the next, and between one group of new "friends" and "acquaintances" to a new one, in the stubbornly optimistic hope that, this time around, enough money and value would be generated to make them wealthy for at least just a moment.

Notes

1. In using the term "slum" as general designation for this vast periurban zone, we lump together a number of quite different Ulaanbaatar neighborhoods, some of which are significantly more developed than others when it comes to access to running water, public transport and other infrastructures.

2. It may still raise some eyebrows that we refer to some of our informants as our friends, or even family. Might this not imply an ethically and/or epistemologically problematic confusion of roles (Spradley 1979: 27–28; see also Hendry 1992)? Is friendship not an "odd term" that conceals an exploitative relationship and gives the fieldwork a phony romantic flavor (Crick 1992: 176)? While this may in some instances be correct, we find it hard to use any other word for people whom, in some instances, we have known for more than two decades and with whom we started to hang out for no other purpose other than simply having a time and a laugh. What is more, we find problematic the assumption that a distinction between the role of friend and informant can always be upheld (might our friends in Denmark not also be seen as informants in certain contexts?) and that friendship cannot develop across fields or "cultures," not to mention the odd and hypostasized concepts of "culture," "friend" and indeed "ethnographic method" that seem to be involved in such reified assumptions. Can friendship only develop within a culture? Are "objects" of anthropological

inquiry per definition not friends? And is "friendship" an unequivocal and unambiguous concept with only one meaning that under no circumstances cannot apply to fieldwork situations? We do not think so.

3. One of the reviewers of this book pointed out that this joke has also been rendered—perhaps more accurately!—as socialism being "the longest route from feudalism to feudalism."

4. There are clear parallels between our notion of a "transitional culture" and Lewis' famous but controversial "culture of poverty" (1968). "The culture of poverty," he writes, "in modern nations is not only a matter of economic deprivation, of disorganization or of the absence of something. It is also something positive and provides some rewards without which the poor could hardly carry on . . . [I]t transcends regional, rural-urban and national differences and shows remarkable similarities in family structure, interpersonal relations, time orientation, value systems and spending patterns . . . Indeed, many of the traits of the culture of poverty can be viewed as attempts at local solutions for problems not met by existing institutions and agencies because the people are not eligible for them, cannot afford them, or are ignorant or suspicious of them . . . Most frequently the culture of poverty develops when a stratified social and economic system is breaking down or is being replaced by another, as in the case of the transition from feudalism to capitalism or during periods of rapid technological change . . . The most likely candidates for the culture of poverty are the people who come from the lower strata of a rapidly changing society and are already partly alienated from it" (1965: xliii–xliv). Lewis has, on often-justifiable grounds, been criticized for essentializing and psychologizing (and thus ignoring) the structural asymmetries pertaining to the hegemonic organization and inherent inequalities of modern capitalist political-economies (e.g., Wasquant 2007). Nevertheless, his work deserves to be taken seriously by anyone with an interest in the nature of social agency in contexts of radical change. In particular, his bold attempt to synthesize a transspecific sociocultural form from across multiple empirical sites represents a refreshing analytical alternative to prevailing particularizing trends and anticomparative norms within anthropology. For is that not precisely what the social-scientific study of so-called postsocialist and (more broadly) "transitional" societies has been crying for some time now: that someone insists that it is possible to say something generic about what it means to live in transition, and about how one might best go about it, which exceeds the particular ethnographic instance?

5. This is somewhat akin to Benjamin's contention that "'the state of emergency' in which we live is not the exception but the rule" (Benjamin 1968: 248; see also Taussig 1992), and Vigh's Benjamin-inspired notion of "crisis as context" (2009), at least if we disregard the somewhat normative implications of Vigh's formulation (2009: 10) and the fact that his concept of "social navigation" is associated with hardship, insecurity, conflict, uncertainty and so forth (see Vigh 2009).

6. Indeed, this seemed to be a widespread sensation among people not just in Ulaanbaatar but elsewhere in Eurasia in the late 1990s: that life could not, indeed should not, be controlled, governed or planned given that an unbridgeable chasm between past, present and future existed. As Joma Nazpary reported from urban Kazakhstan based on fieldwork in the 1990s, "The feelings of a total void which permeates all aspects of life are commonplace. Not only [was] the present disconnected from the past, but the progression [had]

been cancelled altogether. There [was] no future. Such a description of chaos, although corresponding to real 'chaos,' reflect[ed] sudden emergence of the random and invisible logic of the market forces accompanied by the alienated greed and alienating greed for accumulation of capital, bolstered by enormous use of force, [and created] the experience of a very radical ontology of disruption [where] life and events bec[a]me *extremely* contingent and unpredictable" (2002: 4); see also Pedersen 2011).

7. In a similar manner, the constant introduction of reforms and new legislation in post-socialist Georgia meant that "NGOs simply stopped planning ahead" (Frederiksen 2013: 8).

8. As one of the anonymous peer reviewers of this book pointed out, the fact it was only a generation ago that many Mongolians had known greater stability might help explain why it was easier for them to imagine the return of socialism, and why hope was a common response. This picture differs from other anthropological accounts of life in chronic transition like Povinelli's work (2008, 2011) on hardship among various marginalized groups, who have been economically, politically and culturally repressed for so long that there are few options left than to endure and recognizing the effort of others who also do so. Conversely, according to the other reviewer, our friends' apparently irrational optimism might rather be seen as a reflection of a larger postsocialist promise: the rhetoric and the wishful thinking, so widespread among politicians and economists in the 1990s, that Mongolia was en route to becoming "the next Asian Tiger" (see also Bruun and Odgaard 1995; Rossabi 2005).

9. As Matt Hodges notes (2008), the problem with many anthropological accounts of social practice and human agency is that an oftentimes "tacit unspecified temporal ontology" is "evoked through a common root vocabulary of process, flow or flux—itself implying, and facilitating in an unspecified way the notion that time involves 'change'" (2008: 402). Here, time is assumed to constitute "a universal property of human societies and culture" (Harris cited in Hodges 2008: 402) that remains detached from and is thus not influenced by the "concrete multiplicity of differential times" (2008: 403) that ethnographers encounter in the field and which, in Hodges' view, should represent the point of departure for a more robust anthropological theorization of temporal phenomena. (For related critiques of prevailing concepts and accounts of time within anthropology, see also Corsín-Jimenez 2003; Nielsen 2009; Pedersen and Nielsen 2013; Pedersen 2012b.)

10. In that sense, as Rakowski puts it, one "might say that beyond the 'private,' 'state,' and 'welfare' Polands, there existed another, fourth dimension of making do in the new reality—'ecological' strategies and activities, or, to phrase it differently, 'hunter-gatherer Poland'" (2016: 38).

11. In coining this apt term, Peterson sought to capture a social institution reported by ethnographers from hunter-gatherers across the world, namely the obligation if not the injunction to share one's hunting spoils with the rest of one's group. Thus, as Peterson writes, "[w]hile both ethnographers and Aboriginal people emphasize the positive moral imperative of the ethic of generosity as the principal dynamic, observation and ethnographic evidence suggest that much giving and sharing is in response to direct verbal and/or nonverbal demands . . . Such demand sharing, or mutual taking, is widespread in Australia and, it seems, hunter-gatherers more generally . . . [D]emands can be refused [but] only through hiding, secretive behaviour, and lying" (Peterson 1993: 860–861, 864).

12. Indeed, is there not something rather sedentary or even Fordist about Bourdieu's concept of practice and the associated trope of the seasoned and reasoned farmer originating from the deep margins of the Mediterranean, who is all too aware that he does not control time fully and therefore cannot plan too far ahead, but who has learned sufficiently from many years of his own experience (and, before that, parental guidance) to minimize his and his household's risks as much as possible by strategically hedging on his life chances? Whence Bourdieu's aversion to risk-taking, and living one's life as "a game of chance'" (2000: 221): it goes against the grain of an implicit sedentary, and indeed Fordist, temporal ontology that appears built into the edifices of his social theory, and that dictates that time is (within certain and, crucially, unequally distributed limits) manageable and, for the same reason, should be spent wisely and under constant supervision of its effects.

13. "Hunting and gathering," Ingold thus goes on to argue, "represent alternating phases in that continuous task which, for the hunter-gatherers, is no less than life itself" (1986: 79–80). In the same way as human gathering "exceeds foraging" as a biological and momentary extraction of resources from an environment, the temporality of hunting "exceeds predation. The difference is that whereas with hunting this extension *precedes* the extractive situation, with gathering it *follows on*" (1986: 90). This is so, Ingold argues, because "one does begin to gather until the resource has been located, yet the activity only qualifies as gathering because it is motivated by an intention to distribute the produce for consumption by dependants at a later time" (1986: 91). Conversely, when it comes to the hunting, the "intention to procure game precedes the encounter with prey" (ibid.; see also Ingold 1980). Notwithstanding the modifications that this account has been subject to in hunter-gatherer studies (including not least by Ingold himself [2000]; see also Guenther 2007), the deceptively simple point that we wish to make here is that this description offers a surprisingly precise depiction of the daily struggle for resources we witnessed during several years of fieldwork among dispossessed young (and not so young) men in the Mongolian capital of Ulaanbaatar.

14. To paraphrase Mittermaier, "[day] dreams *matter[ed]* in [Ulaanbaatar] in the sense of having significance in people's lives and, more literally, in the sense of having an impact on the visible, material world . . . *not* because they provide[d] [day]dreamers with a protective blanket of false consciousness or hallucinatory wish fulfillment, but because they insert[ed the] [day]dreamer into a wider network of symbolic debts, relationships, and meanings" (2011: 2–3).

CHAPTER 1. LOST IN TRANSITION?

1. From the 1960s to the late 1980s, the USSR maintained a force of one hundred thousand soldiers in Mongolia (Rossabi 2005: 8, 33).

2. MNT is an abbreviation of *Tögrög*, the Mongolian national currency.

3. In order to substantiate this point, it is helpful to discuss different Mongolian ideas and concepts of friendship. One can broadly distinguish between two categories of friends in postsocialist Mongolia. On the one hand, people involved in nonkinship patron-client relationships may refer to one another as *huurai ah düü* ("dry" elder / younger siblings). While sympathy and empathy may feature, such relationships are fundamentally asym-

metrical modes of conduct (the junior person will speak to the senior person in a formal way, always addressing him or her by the respectful term for seniors (*ah/egch* depending on gender), and in terms of the rights and obligations of the two sides. The senior is expected to help the junior, either directly through downward allocations of valuables (money, livestock, etc.) or indirectly by exercising influence to the junior's benefit. In exchange, the junior partner must respect (*hündleh*) his senior and is expected to do favors and carry out petty jobs and tasks for him or her (like acting as a driver for the senior friend). As argued by several anthropologists (Sneath 1993; Pedersen 2006, 2007a), such patron-client relationships play an even greater role in postsocialist society than they did during the heyday of state socialism. Not that traditional age hierarchies were ignored during the socialist period, but in the age of the market, being under the protection of one or more patrons became a matter of sheer economic survival for many people.

The second variety of friends, who are referred to as *naiz*, are those who, like our friends in their internal relationships (barring siblings), relate to one another on more egalitarian terms. Unlike asymmetrical patron-client friendships, symmetrical friendships between parties who consider themselves equal are particularly associated with specific periods in a person's life (school, army, etc.). Indeed, in a society where hierarchy is still the norm, it is especially within such institutions that people meet peers considered a priori equal to them (as captured in the term *chatsuu*, which is used to denote the relationship—if not bond—understood to exist between two persons of the same age). While people also use these more symmetrical friends (*naizuud*) to achieve things and obtain resources when in need (as we will see numerous illustrations of in the chapters to come), there is nevertheless an underlying ideal of a pure friendship that is unsoiled by any instrumental concerns. Certainly, for our Ulaanbaatar friends [*sic*], "real friends" (*jinhene naiz*) are "people who respond to their internal, spontaneous sentiments rather than the demands or expectations placed on them by the demands of kinship, trade, propinquity, interest or the like" (Carrier 1999: 22). Be that as it may, perhaps especially for people from working-class or ethnically mixed backgrounds, tight networks of "dry brothers" and close "friends" (*dotno naiz*) were primary sources of scarce goods and services that could not be obtained through official channels (in the Soviet Union, this reliance on "friends" was widely referred to as *blat*; Ledeneva 1998).

4. Especially during the period of our fieldwork carried out between 1995 to 2000, it was common for clients to change allegiance from one patron-friend to another. This happened (1) when debtors disappeared from one social-economic network only to abruptly enter, as if jumping between networks, another social arena and new setting, and (2) when juniors concluded that they might be offered better "protection" (*hamgaalal*) and support from other seniors. Apparently, these asymmetrical relationships did not require a protracted span of time to work; it was, it seemed, perfectly acceptable to "leap" in and out of such relations. Indeed, patron-client relationships have sometimes been reported to *thrive* during times of radical change, both in the postsocialist world (Sneath 1993; Nazpary 2002) and in sub-Saharan Africa (Vigh 2006; Bach and Gazibo 2012).

CHAPTER 2. MARKET SUBJECTS

1. Cited in Anderson 1998: 30.
2. As Alan Wheeler explains (2004: 224), "during the Soviet years, [trading] was prohibited . . . among private individuals and institutions since it was seen as counter to the collective goals of building a socialist society." Yet, "[t]he government allowed people to buy and sell their personal used and unwanted items at the 'black market' (*har zah*), although this was frowned upon." During late socialism, some of these flea-market-like sites developed into permanent enterprises located on the outskirts of towns and cities, where an increasing number and diversity of scarce commodities and food products were bartered and otherwise transacted. Ulaanbaatar's Black Market was a case in point.
3. During fieldwork in Kyrgyzstan in 2008, for example, Lars was told that trade had been considered an extremely low-status activity and was almost only carried out by women in the early postsocialist period. Similar conclusions have been reached in other studies of postsocialist contexts, such as Heyat's study of entrepreneurship in Soviet and post-Soviet Caucasus (2002).
4. Saraa's background was not as unique as she herself took it to be. Mongolia's "informal sector" was full of people with long educations in the late 1990s (for example, 25 percent had a university degree; Morris 2001: 37).
5. According to the World Bank report, "Importers who wish[ed] to park their containers [paid] 9,000 togrogs per day. Trucks pa[id] 6,000 togrogs per day. Individual vendors pa[id] varying fees, from 300 togrogs to 3,500 togrogs per day, depending on the volume of business they d[id], although the management [had] difficulty, understandably, getting honest participation from vendors" (Anderson 1998: 30).
6. The term "Valley of Drunks" was not just used to denote a place inside the Harhorin Market. It was also used as a more generic term for "all those places in the city where many drunks gather," as Morten's research assistant once explained, such as for instance a pedestrian street in the Ulaanbaatar city center with many market stalls. But of course, this only underscores the observation made above, namely that the whole plethora of dispossessed and deprived outcasts found in Ulaanbaatar around the turn of the millennium was strongly associated with market venues.
7. In medieval Mongolia, markets flourished along the porous borders between nomadic polities, and the unstable boundaries between nomadic and sedentary states (Lattimore 1962). It was only later, following the loss of Mongolian independence to, first, the Qing empire and, later, the Soviet Union that trading became associated with being "Chinese" and thus non-Mongolian (Sanjdorj 1980; Bulag 1998; Wheeler 2004; Pedersen 2007a).
8. As Wheeler notes (2004), *zah* not only refers to the periphery of cities on whose outskirts the first semi-illicit markets emerged in the late 1980s. It also denotes a sort of absolute exteriority, namely the marginal position occupied by unmarried women from the gendered perspective of the male household head (*geriin ezen*). Similarly, the word "trade"— *hudaldaa*—is etymologically linked to a root occasionally used to classify male affines in marital contexts (*hud-*), affirming a notion of material, matrimonial and monetary transactions across the margin between two patriarchal centers.

CHAPTER 3. ELUSIVE PROPERTY

1. Our notion of property-as-assemblage derives from our ethnography—as when Hulan was struggling to hold on to her piece of land by "assembling" a fence, a group of workers, enough funds, etc.—but it also draws on recent theories of emergence, notably the concept of "assemblage" formulated by Manuel DeLanda (2006) on the basis of Deleuzian philosophy (e.g., Deleuze and Guattari 1987), as well as the concept of "association" that has been advanced by Bruno Latour (e.g., 2005) and other actor-network theorists (Verdery and Humphrey also use the notion of assemblage in their approach to property, but they do so without further theorizing it and only as assemblages of "social" relations [Verdery and Humphrey 2004: 7–8]). While these approaches are both concerned with the general issue of how to create momentary stabilizations between dynamic and heterogeneous elements, this chapter explores how they may be particularly apt prisms for understanding the specificity of the bricoleur-like activities of urban hunters (cf. Lévi-Strauss 1966).

2. The only exception was that "[h]ousing cooperative members who supplied the money could build or buy an apartment and received 'cooperative tenure' as a joint title to the building. Through the cooperative association they could lease or sell their apartments" (Bauner and Richter 2006: 9).

3. Mongolia thus differs from many other postsocialist countries in that the country's economy has been based mainly on pastoral nomadism rather than agriculture, and because there has been no issue of restituting property rights to previous presocialist landowners in the postsocialist privatization process.

4. This does not include pastureland, which cannot be privatized, according to the constitution (Hanstad and Duncan 2001: 10). The Land Law passed in 1994, however, did authorize the leasing of pastoral resources such as pasture and camp sites, but local understandings (of officials and herders alike) and an unclear legal framework strongly limit its implementation (Fernandez-Gimenez and Batbuyan 2004), as does "a deeply rooted ethic of open access among Mongolian herders" (Mearns 2004: 141).

5. The Law on Allocation of Land to Citizens of Mongolia for Ownership was promulgated in 2003.

6. A USAID report from 2004 states that "[t]o date, there has not been a strong push to acquire private land title outside of the nation's capital" (Myers and Hetz 2004: 11).

7. The 2002 Law of Mongolia on Land states only the following about fencing, in Article 48.1: "If land in possession or in use is not specifically protected by erected fences or posted warning signs prohibiting entering and crossing, any person may enter or cross this land without causing damage to the land" (Government of Mongolia 2002).

8. This situation may be compared to postsocialist Romania, where conceptions of owning fields are similarly based on visibility and tangibility: "The goal of village elites was not simply to have land but to have it worked [. . .] Land had to be concrete, particular, bounded, and recognizably distinct from everyone else's. It and its products had to be visible—and visibility linked to their particular holding. In short, land had to be property as a concrete physical object, not as abstract shares in some state farm" (Verdery 2004: 150).

9. The need to legitimize such settlements is recognized, for example, in a report submitted to USAID: "Land titling in the Ger districts can also be interpreted as part of a long-needed move to legitimize [the] 'land squatting and land grabbing' that has gone on over the last 14 years" (Myers and Hetz 2004: 12). In the same report, the existence of an informal land market is similarly acknowledged: "Residential land markets, however, are emerging on a non-formal basis. Evidence was provided to indicate that Ger district land plots were being acquired, bought, and sold. The volume of these transactions is unclear . . ." (Myers and Hetz 2004: 12–13; cf. Bauner and Richter 2006: 19).

10. This might explain why our friends were dogmatically apolitical (see Chapter 1). After all, as Strum and Latour write, politics "is what allows many heterogeneous resources to be woven together into a social link that becomes increasingly harder and harder to break" (1987: 797).

11. It is impossible to say exactly how many people were living in the flat, as relatives and friends were moving in and out all the time.

12. We do not wish to imply that everyone in Ulaanbaatar or elsewhere in Mongolia followed these "rules," but this is how Kolya explained it. Actually, our impression was that the tradition of ultimogeniture was still widely practiced.

13. In line with this, Alexander argues that the privatization processes in the postsocialist world taught us that "the temporal context of property mattered" (2004: 252).

CHAPTER 4. HUSTLING AND CONVERSION

1. One of the basic premises of network and commodity chain studies is thus that they do not focus on isolated individuals or firms but rather on "economic units" that are conceived of as "networks of firms linking interdependent assets across formal organizational boundaries" (Grabher and Stark 1997: 3). While such connections, chains or links obviously exist (e.g., meat networks, vegetable networks or car networks), in such studies they seem to be defined simply by the commodity in question (meat, vegetables, cars) in the case of commodity chains (which may be defined as "the sequence of activities through which raw materials or components are transformed into final products" [Bair 2008: 15]) or—in the case of social networks—by the fact that they "organize," however informally.

2. She used the expression *nüdend örtöh*, literally meaning "to strike the eye." The meaning of *örtöh* hovers between perception and tactility. Dictionaries translate it as "to be affected by" and "fall victim to" (Ganhuyag 2005: 730), or "to be perceived," "to be felt" and "to be touched" (Bawden 1997: 281).

3. This might not apply to other changers. Vegetable changers, for example, seemed to be working in a more organized environment of open trade.

4. *TÜTS* is an abbreviation of *Türgen Üilchilgeenii Tseg* (literally meaning "fast service spot").

5. Inflation fell from 325.5 percent in 1992 to 44.6 percent in 1996, and then to 1.6 percent in 2002, rising again to 9.5 percent in 2005 (National Statistical Office of Mongolia 2005: 122).

CHAPTER 5. THE SPIRIT OF DEBT

1. Indeed, the Mongolian expression for market economy is *zah zeel*, the meaning of *zeel* being loan or credit. See Wheeler 2004 for an illuminating discussion of the etymology and contemporary meaning of *zah zeel*.

2. Interestingly, the popularity of "fringe banking" was not limited to the postsocialist world in the 1990s. In 1994, Caskey wrote that "[t]here are more pawnshops today, both in absolute numbers and on a per capita basis, than at any time in United States history" (1).

3. In terms of specifically financing business startups in the informal sector, pawnshops, according to a survey of the Mongolian informal sector, only financed 0.95 percent of loans in Ulaanbaatar in 1999. According to this survey, business startups were mainly financed by individual or family savings or by loans from other individuals (Bikales et al. 2000: 17–18).

4. As objects influence what they come into contact with, whether people or other objects, this might also explain why money earned from gold should be spent as quickly as possible (Mette High, personal communication; see also High 2008) and why goldsmiths are often in a terrible state (see quote above).

5. The link between product or business activity and personal trajectory is common—for example, in contexts of trading in meat and vodka (other businesses associated with immorality and danger include environmental exploitation, such as mining and forestry). Like pawnbroking, vodka trade is neither virtuous nor secure, and Bayarmaa told that when she traded in vodka in Western Mongolia as a student, she only did so in small quantities. Her ex-husband, conversely, traded in vodka on a larger scale, and later on, she whispered, his father and younger siblings all died. The pawnbroker does not deal in meat and alcohol, but it is common for Mongolians—as for the Kenyan Luo (Shipton 1989)—to associate money with the quality of its (im)moral source. The money becomes tainted with the way in which it was earned: if earned in a proper way, it is good money, but if earned in an improper way, it may bring bad luck. Another informant was once involved in blackmailing someone, and she recounted how she felt remorse and later on wasted the money on nothing. What would you expect, she said, when the money was earned like that (cf. Shipton 1989; Zelizer 1989; High 2013)?

6. There was, however, one pawnbroker for whom this and other conversions were simply presented as trivial "business as usual." "There are no arguments with customers," she explained, for "everything is clear and written down on a piece of paper." But then again, it turned out that this young female informant—unlike our other informants—was only an employee at a pawnshop and not the pawnbroker herself, and the shop had just been renovated and now had the clinical look of a small bank. Some of her customers remarked that, before, the shop looked like a jail (i.e., like other *protected* pawnshops) but that now it was really looking nice. Two uniformed guards were standing outside. This, it would seem, is one way to effect a further separation of gifts and commodities. The black energies of customers and pawned items were held at a safe physical distance, and the customers were not in contact with the pawnbroker herself. And interestingly, banks, as opposed to pawnshops, may be thought of by Mongolians as being the most commodifying and "alienating" of Mongolian credit institutions because, unlike pawnshops, they do not physically collect their customers' personal belongings and, hence, are not hubs of misfortune.

CHAPTER 6. MARKET TRICKSTERS

1. Tellingly, it is commonly assumed, both within the academy and beyond, that the Mongolian word for "trade" is etymologically related to Mongolians' terms for deception and dishonesty. Certainly, Wheeler points out, "Mongols . . . are quick to point out the similarity between *hudaldaa*, or 'trade,' and *hudal*, which is the word for 'deceit' or 'lie.' Indeed, Jagchid and Hyer write that "the root" of trade (*hudaldaa*) is the word '*hudal*' which 'has the connotation of cheating or lying, indicating the Mongol attitude toward merchants" (1979: 304). Similarly, according to Uradyn Bulag, "[i]n the Mongol language, commerce or business—*hudaldaa*, means cheating" (2000: 193, cited in Wheeler 2004: 219–220).

2. One may object (as did one of the peer reviewers of this book) that this point is self-evident, and that the idea that economic (specifically trading) practices are less socially embedded than other practices plays the role of a strawman in our argument. To be sure, it is hard to find an anthropologist (and, increasingly, an economist) who is still wedded to the neoclassical notion of "economic man" (cf. Gudeman 1986; Dilley 1992; Carrier 1997). Still, by stressing that economic actors are always socialized into specific "contexts," do anthropologists not inadvertently also imply that, hidden deep within them, there is a kernel of asocial self-interest?

3. Ulaanbaatar's changers, it would thus seem, are perceived by themselves and by others to be in ontological continuity with their wares. As such, the case of the *chenjüüd* might be seen to represent an ultimate example of commodity fetishism. And yet, we suggest, the particular "grammar of surfaces" (Lemon 2000: 28) found on Ulaanbaatar's markets, where the materiality of goods is perceived to index people's innermost being, is a characteristic postsocialist phenomenon, which cannot be explained by conventional theories of commodity fetishism, where commodities are defined as alienable objects and gifts as inalienable ones (cf. Gregory 1982). For if, according to Marx's theory of commodity fetishism, goods are desired not due to their "material particularity but as 'supra sensible' value" (Stallybrass 1998: 184), in the case of the changers it is the other way around. In line with Marx's notion of fetishism—the sensuous worshipping of unique objects (Stallybrass 1998: 184; Graeber 2005)—the goods that are displayed on the changers' bodies are "material presence[s] that [do] not represent but tak[e] one's fancy" (Pels 1998). As in our analysis of pawned objects in Chapter 5, the concept of commodity here reaches a limit, for the goods at hand are not perceived as *more* but rather as *less* abstract than other objects.

4. Such economic middlemen are not unique to capitalism, even if they do seem to be particularly ubiquitous to certain postsocialist or postcolonial contexts. Various changer-like personae already operated in the cracks of the planned economy in places like Mongolia and the USSR during the socialist period. In Eastern Siberia in the 1980s, for example, collective farms each had "a 'pusher' (*tolkach*). Thus in areas where fodder is scarce, kolkhozy have their pushers traveling around the district or even the region looking for farms with spare hay. Or, if buying organisations are slow in paying up, it may be necessary to station a *tolkach* with them to ensure payment . . . [A] *tolkach* may find it necessary to impress a supplier, for instance by putting on some kind of uniform, and efficient 'pushers' make card indexes of important people in the district, noting their birthdays and anniversaries, as well as their soft spots" (Humphrey 1998: 223; see also Pedersen 2011: 94–101, for the tragicomic story about three generations of economic/shamanic tricksters in Northern Mongolia).

CHAPTER 7. THE WORK OF HOPE

1. Of course, it was still possible for clients to rank their diviners in terms of their capacity to make accurate predictions, in the sense that diviners were perceived to be equipped with different capacities (inherited abilities, divinatory tools, acquired knowledge, etc.) which enabled them to reveal the relative nature of the cosmos with differing degrees of fine-tuning. But, as the example of the imperfect calculators at the Black Market suggests, it was not just the diviners who could not be 100 percent precise in Mongolia at the turn of the millennium, but the reality of transition itself. Perhaps "80 percent accurate" was simply as good as things got in the age of the market; it was impossible to ask for and expect more. Thus understood, the pervasive uncertainty widely reported from postsocialist (and postcolonial) contexts is not just "epistemological"—an inability for humans to make complete sense of the world. It is also a sort of "ontological uncertainty": not in the existentialist sense suggested by Anthony Giddens (1991) and taken up by a number of anthropologists, but in the sense of a radically changing cosmos' limited capacity for making sense of *itself* (Pedersen 2014).

2. For instance, *süld* was traditionally used to refer to tutelary deities and protective geniuses in Buddhist and folk-religious contexts (Heissig 1980), and is still used for politico-religious talismans such as the state emblem (*töriin süld*).

3. The analogy between a "traditional" economy of fortune revolving around concepts such as *süld*, *hishig* and *hiimor'* on the one hand and a "modern" economy of hope associated with concepts like *möröödöl* and *naidvar* on the other, is an imperfect one. For example, whereas the former can be described as vernacular religious and as such derives partly from Buddhist theories of selfhood, the latter is less spiritual and much more directly preoccupied with gauging future temporal horizons.

4. Jarrett Zigon (2009) also distinguishes between two forms of hope, one predominantly passive and individual, and another active and social. On the one hand, as he put it, hope is "an existential stance of being-in-the-world. In this way, hope can be thought of as the temporal structure of the background attitude that allows one to keep going or persevere through one's life. This aspect of hope can be seen as similar to what is often characterized as the passive nature of hope. On the other hand, hope is the temporal orientation of conscious and intentional action in . . . those moments when social and moral life is reflectively and consciously called into question and posed as a problem. This aspect of hope is similar to what is often called the active nature of hope" (258).

5. "Why . . . does strategy necessarily have to be singular?" Marianne Maeckelbergh asks in her study of left-wing radical youth in the United Kingdom (2009: 92). The same question may be posed with respect to Hamid, Kolya and our other Ulaanbaatar friends: "perhaps [their] rejection of strategy means no singular goal, but does a rejection of a singular goal therefore mean no strategy?" (Maeckelbergh 2009: 93). Could we then consider the apparently irrational optimism of our Ulaanbaatar friends, and indeed many other aspects of what we have called the culture of transition, as an economic analogue to the anarchist political practice of prefiguration studied by Maeckelbergh and other anthropologists working on left-wing activists—a distinctly postsocialist "figuration of future" (Krøijer 2015), as it were?

6. And this, then, is also the way in which our friends' attitude to life in transition could be described as alternatively practical as opposed to nonpractical in Bourdieu's terms (see Introduction). Far from "living in the present," they were inhabiting a sort of "deep moment" that contained multiple potential futures—which, indeed, is the general problem with practice theories: they rest on an over-spatialized temporal ontology that, among other problems (Hodges 2008; Laidlaw 2014) reduces "the potential" to "the possible," and "the moment" to "the present."

CONCLUSION

1. Since the Mongolian economy follows the ups and downs of the global commodities market and the Chinese economy, the country did not experience any big bust during the global financial crisis of 2007–2008. Instead, the crisis was, so to speak, postponed half a decade until the Chinese economy and the commodities market began to come under increasing stress.

Bibliography

Abrahms-Kavunenko, Saskia. "Spiritually Enmeshed, Socially Enmeshed: Shamanism and Belonging in Ulaanbaatar." *Social Analysis* 60, no. 3 (2016): 1–16.

Addo, Ping-Ann, and Niko Besnier. "When Gifts Become Commodities: Pawnshops, Valuables and Shame in Tonga and the Tongan Diaspora." *Journal of the Royal Anthropological Institute* (N.S.) 14 (2008): 39–59.

Agamben, Giorgio. *Homo Sacer: Sovereign Power and Bare Life.* Stanford, CA: Stanford University Press, 1998.

Agamben, Giorgio. *State of Exception.* Chicago: University of Chicago Press, 2005 (2003).

Alexander, Catherine. "Value, Relations and Changing Bodies: Privatization and Property Rights in Kazakhstan." In C. Humphrey and K. Verdery (eds.), *Property in Question: Value Transformation in the Global Economy*, pp. 251–273. Oxford: Berg, 2004.

Anderson, James H. "The Size, Origins and Character of Mongolia's Informal Sector during the Transition." World Bank Policy Research Working Paper 1916. Washington, DC: World Bank, May 1998.

Ansell Pearson, Keith. *Germinal Life: The Difference and Repetition of Deleuze.* London: Routledge, 1999.

Appadurai, Arjun (ed.). *The Social Life of Things.* Cambridge: Cambridge University Press, 1986.

Appadurai, Arjun. "Disjuncture and Difference in the Global Economy." *Public Culture* 2, no. 2 (1990): 1–24.

Appadurai, Arjun. "The Capacity to Aspire: Culture and the Terms of Recognition." In V. Rao and M. Walton (eds.), *Culture and Public Action*, pp. 59–84. Stanford, CA: Stanford University Press, 2004.

Apte, Mahedev L. *Humor and Laughter: An Anthropological Approach.* Ithaca, NY: Cornell University Press, 1985.

Asian Development Bank. *Mongolia: Cadastral Survey and Land Registration Project.* Completion Report, Asian Development Bank, 2010.

Astuti, Rita. "At the Center of the Market: A Vezo Woman." In S. Day, E. Papataxiarchis and M. Stewart (eds.). *Lilies of the Field: Marginal People Who Live for the Moment*, pp. 83–95. Oxford: Westview Press, 1999.

Atwood, Christopher P. *Encyclopedia of Mongolia and the Mongol Empire.* New York: Facts on File, 2004.

Austin, John L. *How to Do Things with Words.* 2nd ed. Edited by J. O. Urmson and M. Sbisá. Cambridge: Cambridge University Press, 1962.

Bach, Daniel C., and Marmodou Gazibo (eds.). *Neopatrimonialism in Africa and Beyond.* London: Routledge, 2012.

Bair, Jennifer. "Global Commodity Chains: Genealogy and Review." In J. Bair (ed.), *Frontiers of Commodity Chain Research*, pp. 1–34. Stanford, CA: Stanford University Press, 2008.

Balog, Mátyás. "Contemporary Shamanisms in Mongolia." *Asian Ethnicity* 11, no. 2 (2010): 229–238.

Bareja-Starzynska, Agata, and Hanne Havnevik. "A Preliminary Study of Buddhism in Present-Day Mongolia." In O. Bruun and L. Narangoa (eds.), *Mongols from Country to City: Floating Boundaries, Pastoralism and City Life in the Mongol Lands*, pp. 212–236. Copenhagen: NIAS Press, 2006.

Barth, Frederik. "Economic Spheres in Darfur." In F. Barth (ed.), *Process and Form in Social Life*, pp. 157–178. London: Routledge and Kegan Paul, 1981 (1967).

Baudelaire, Charles. *The Painter of Modern Life.* New York: Da Capo Press, 1964 (1863).

Bauner, Saskia, and Bodo Richter. *Real Estate Market, Mortgage Market and Cadastre in Ulaanbaatar and Darhan-City, Mongolia.* Eschborn: Deutsche Gesellschaft für Technische Zusammenarbeit (GTZ) GmbH, Division Agriculture, Fisheries and Food Sector Project Land Management, 2006.

Bawden, Charles R. "The Supernatural Element in Sickness and Death According to the Mongol Tradition—Part I." *Asia Major* (N.S.) 8, no. 2 (1963): 215–257.

Bawden, Charles R. *The Modern History of Mongolia.* London: Kegan Paul International, 1989.

Bawden, Charles R. *Mongolian-English Dictionary.* London: Kegan Paul International, 1997.

Bear, Laura, Ritu Birla and Stine Simonsen Puri. "Speculation: Futures and Capitalism in India." *Comparative Studies of South Asia, Africa and the Middle East* 35, no. 3 (2015): 387–391.

Bell, Sandra, and Simon Coleman. "The Anthropology of Friendship: Enduring Themes and Future Possibilities." In S. Bell and S. Coleman (eds.), *The Anthropology of Friendship*, pp. 1–19. Oxford: Berg, 1999.

Benjamin, Walter. *Illuminations.* New York: Schocken Books, 1968.

Benjamin, Walter. *Charles Baudelaire: A Lyric Poet in the Era of High Capitalism.* Brooklyn, NY: Verso Classics, 1997.

Benwell, Ann Fenger. "Facing Gender Challenges in Post-Socialist Mongolia." In O. Bruun and L. Narangoa (eds.), *Mongols from Country to City: Floating Boundaries, Pastoralism and City Life in the Mongol Lands*, pp. 110–139. Copenhagen: Nordic Institute of Asian Studies, 2006.

Benwell, Ann Fenger. *Keeping Up Appearances: Gender and Ideal Womanhood in Postsocialist Mongolia.* Unpublished PhD thesis, Department of Anthropology, University of Copenhagen, 2009.

Berdahl, Daphne. "'(N)Ostalgie' for the Present: Memory, Longing and East German Things." *Ethnos* 64, no. 2 (1999): 192–211.

Berdahl, Daphne. "Introduction: An Anthropology of Postsocialism." In D. Berdahl, M. Bunzl and M. Lampland (eds.), *Altering States: Ethnographies of Transition in Eastern Europe and the Former Soviet Union*, pp. 1–13. Ann Arbor: University of Michigan Press, 2000.

Berdahl, Daphne, and Matti Bunzl. *On the Social Life of Postsocialism: Memory, Consumption, Germany.* Bloomington: Indiana University Press, 2010.

Bergson, Henri. *Matter and Memory.* London: Zone Books, 1990.

Berlant, Lauren. *Cruel Optimism.* Durham, NC: Duke University Press, 2011.Biehl, João. "Life of the Mind: The Interface of Psychopharmaceuticals, Domestic Economies and Social Abandonment." *American Ethnologist* 31, no. 4 (2004): 475–496.

Biehl, João. *Vita: Life in a Zone of Social Abandonment.* Berkeley: University of California Press, 2005.

Bikales, Bill, Chimed Khurelbaatar and Karin Schelzig. "The Mongolian Informal Sector: Survey Results and Analysis." Economic Policy Support Project DAI (2000). www.forum.mn.

Billé, Franck. *Sinophobia: Anxiety, Violence and the Making of Mongolian Identity.* Honolulu: University of Hawaii Press, 2014.

Bird-David, Nurit. "The Giving Environment: Another Perspective on the Economic Systems of Gatherer-Hunters." *Current Anthropology* 31, no. 2 (1990): 189–196.

Bird-David, Nurit. "Beyond 'The Original Affluent Society': A Culturalist Reformulation." *Current Anthropology* 33, no. 1 (1992): 25–34.

Bird-David, Nurit. "'Animism' Revisited: Personhood, Environment and Relational Epistemology." *Current Anthropology* 40, no. 1 (1999): 67–91.

Bloch, Maurice. "The Past and the Present in the Present." *Man* (N.S.) 12 (1977): 278–292.

Bockman, Johanna, and Gil Eyal. "Eastern Europe as a Laboratory for Economic Knowledge: The Transnational Roots of Neoliberalism." *American Journal of Sociology* 108, no. 2 (2002): 310–352.

Bohannan, Paul. "Some Principles of Exchange and Investment among the Tiv." *American Anthropologist* (N.S.) 57, no. 1 (1955): 60–70.

Bourdieu, Pierre. *Outline of a Theory of Practice.* Cambridge: Cambridge University Press, 1977.

Bourdieu, Pierre. *Algeria 1960: The Disenchantment of the World: The Sense of Honour: The Kabyle House or the World Reversed: Essays.* Cambridge: Cambridge University Press, 1979.

Bourdieu, Pierre. *Pascalian Meditations.* London: Polity Press, 2000.

Bourgois, Philippe. *In Search of Respect: Selling Crack in El Barrio.* Cambridge: Cambridge University Press, 2003.

Boym, Svetlana. *Common Places: Mythologies of Everyday Life in Russia.* Cambridge, MA: Harvard University Press, 1994.

Bradach, Jeffrey L., and Robert G. Eccles. "Price, Authority and Trust: From Ideal Types to Plural Forms." *Annual Review of Sociology* 15 (1989): 97–118.

Brightman, Robert. *Grateful Prey: Rock Cree Human-Animal Relationships.* Los Angeles: University of California Press, 1993.

Bruun, Ole. *Precious Steppe: Mongolian Nomadic Pastoralists in Pursuit of the Market.* Oxford: Lexington Books, 2006.

Bruun, Ole, and Li Narangoa. "A New Moment in Mongol History: The Rise of the Cosmopolitan City." In O. Bruun and L. Narangoa (eds.), *Mongols from Country to City: Floating Boundaries, Pastoralism and City Life in the Mongol Lands*, pp. 1–20. Copenhagen: NIAS Press, 2006.

Bruun, Ole, and Li Narangoa (eds.). *Mongols from Country to City: Floating Boundaries, Pastoralism and City Life in the Mongol Lands.* Copenhagen: NIAS Press, 2006.

Bruun, Ole, and Ole Odgaard (eds.). *Mongolia in Transition.* Richmond, Surrey: Curzon Press, 1995.

Buck-Morss, Susan. *Dreamworld and Catastrophe: The Passing of Mass Utopia in East and West.* Cambridge, MA: MIT Press, 2002.

Bulag, Uradyn E. *Nationalism and Hybridity in Mongolia.* Oxford: Clarendon Press, 1998.

Bulag, Uradyn E. "Mongolia in 2008: From Mongolia to Mine-golia." *Asian Survey* 49 (2009): 129–134.

Bunkenborg, Mikkel, and Morten A. Pedersen. "The Ethnographic Expedition 2.0: Resurrecting the Expedition as a Social Scientific Research Method." In K. H. Nielsen, M. Harbsmeier and C. J. Ries (eds.), *Scientists and Scholars in the Field: Studies in the History of Fieldwork and Expeditions*, pp. 415–429. Aarhus: Aarhus University Press, 2012.

Bunkenborg, Mikkel, Morten Nielsen and Morten A. Pedersen. *Collaborative Damage: A Comparative Ethnography of Chinese Globalization.* Forthcoming.

Burawoy, M., and Katherine Verdery (eds.). *Uncertain Transition: Ethnographies of Change in the Postsocialist World.* Oxford: Rowman and Littlefield, 1999.

Buyandelger, Manduhai. *Tragic Spirits: Shamanism, Socialism and the State of Neoliberalism in Mongolia.* Chicago: University of Chicago Press, 2013.

Buyandelgeriyn, Manduhai. "Dealing with Uncertainty: Shamans, Marginal Capitalism, and the Remaking of History in Postsocialist Mongolia." *American Ethnologist* 34, no. 1 (2007): 127–147.

Buyandelgeriyn, Manduhai. "Post-Post-Transition Theories: Walking on Multiple Paths." *Annual Review of Anthropology* no. 37 (2008): 235–250.

Campi, Alicia. "The Rise of Cities in Nomadic Mongolia." In O. Bruun and L. Narangoa (eds.), *Mongols from Country to City: Floating Boundaries, Pastoralism and City Life in the Mongol Lands*, pp. 21–55. Copenhagen: NIAS Press, 2006.

Carrier, James G. (ed.). *Meanings of the Market: The Free Market in Western Culture.* Oxford: Berg, 1997.

Carrier, James G. "People Who Can Be Friends: Selves and Social Relationships." In S. Ball and S. Coleman (eds.), *The Anthropology of Friendship*, pp. 21–38. Oxford: Berg, 1999.

Caskey, John P. *Fringe Banking: Check-Cashing Outlets, Pawnshops and the Poor.* New York: Russell Sage Foundation, 1994.

Castoriadis, Cornelius. *The Imaginary Institution of Society* (trans. K. Blamey). London: Polity Press, 1987.

Chaussonnet, V. "Needles and Animals: Women's Magic." In W. Fitzhugh and A. Crowell (eds.), *Crossroads of Continents: Cultures of Siberia and Alaska*, pp. 209–226. New York: Smithsonian Institution Press, 1988.

Chua, Liana. "To Know or Not to Know? Practices of Knowledge and Ignorance among Bidayuhs in an 'Impurely' Christian World." *Journal of the Royal Anthropological Institute* (N.S.) no. 15 (2009): 332–438.

Chuluunbat, Narantuya, and Rebecca Empson. "Networks and the Negotiation of Risk: Making Business Deals and People among Mongolian Small and Medium Businesses." *Central Asian Survey* 37, no. 3 (2018): 419–437.

Coleman, Rebecca. "'Things That Stay': Feminist Theory, Duration and the Future." *Time and Society* 17, no. 1 (2008): 85–102.

Collier, Stephen J. *Post-Soviet Social: Neoliberalism, Social Modernity, Biopolitics.* Princeton, NJ: Princeton University Press, 2011.

Comaroff, Jean, and John Comaroff. "Occult Economies and the Violence of Abstraction: Notes from the South African Postcolony." *American Ethnologist* 26, no. 3 (1998): 279–301.

Corsín-Jimenez, Alberto. "On Space as a Capacity." *JRAI* (N.S.) 9, no. 1 (2003): 137–153.

Corsín-Jimenez, Alberto. "Well-Being in Anthropological Balance: Remarks on Proportionality as Political Imagination." In A. Corsín-Jimenez (ed.), *Culture and Well-Being. Anthropological Approaches to Freedom and Political Ethics*, pp. 180–200. London: Pluto Press, 2007.

Crapanzano, Vincent. "Reflections on Hope as a Category of Social and Psychological Analysis." *Cultural Anthropology* 18, no. 1 (2003): 3–32.

Crick, Malcolm. "Ali and Me: An Essay in Street-Corner Anthropology." In J. Okely and H. Callaway (eds.). *Anthropology and Autobiography*, pp. 175–192. London: Routledge, 1992.

Da Col, Giovanni, and Caroline Humphrey (eds.). "Cosmologies of Fortune: Luck, Vitality and Uncontrolled Relatedness." Special Issue of *Social Analysis* 56, no. 1 (2012).

Dalaibuyan, Byambajav. "Formal and Informal Networks in Post-Socialist Mongolia: Access, Uses, and Inequalities." In J. Dierkes (ed.), *Change in Democratic Mongolia*, pp. 31–54. The Netherlands: Brill, 2012.

Das, Veena, and Deborah Poole (eds.). *Anthropology on the Margins of the State.* Santa Fe, NM: School of American Research Press, 2004.

Day, Sophie, Evthymios Papataxiarchis and Michael Stewart (eds.). *Lilies of the Field: Marginal People Who Live for the Moment.* Oxford: Westview Press, 1999.

De Boeck, Filip. "Inhabiting Ocular Ground: Kinshasa's Future in the Light of Congo's Spectral Urban Politics." *Cultural Anthropology* 26, no. 2 (2011): 263–286.

de Certeau, M. *The Practice of Everyday Life.* Berkeley: University of California Press, 1984.

DeLanda, Manuel. *A New Philosophy of Society: Assemblage Theory and Social Complexity.* London: Continuum Books, 2006.

Deleuze, Gilles. *Difference and Repetition.* London: Athlone Press, 1994.

Deleuze, Gilles, and Félix Guattari. *A Thousand Plateaus: Capitalism and Schizophrenia*. Minneapolis: University of Minnesota Press, 1987.

Dilley, Roy (ed.). *Contesting Markets: Analyses of Ideology, Discourse and Practice*. Edinburgh: Edinburgh University Press, 1992.

Dunn, Elizabeth C. *Privatizing Poland: Baby Food, Big Business and the Remaking of Labor*. Ithaca, NY: Cornell University Press, 2004.

Dunn, Elizabeth C., and Katherine Verdery. "Dead Ends in the Critique of (Post)Socialist Anthropology: Reply to Thelen." *Critique of Anthropology* 31, no. 3 (2011): 251–255.

Ellis, Joe. "Assembling Contexts: The Making of Political-Economic Potentials in Shamanic Workshop in Ulaanbaatar." *Inner Asia* no. 17 (2015): 52–76.

Empson, Rebecca (ed.). *Time, Causality and Prophecy in the Mongolian Cultural Region*. Kent, UK: Global Oriental, 2006.

Empson, Rebecca. "Separating and Containing People and Things in Mongolia." In A. Henare, M. Holbraad and S. Wastell (eds.), *Thinking through Things: Theorising Artefacts Ethnographically*, pp. 113–140. London: Routledge, 2007.

Empson, Rebecca. *Harnessing Fortune: Domestic Animals and Mountain Ceremonies*. Oxford: Oxford University Press, 2011.

Empson, Rebecca. "The Dangers of Excess: Accumulating and Dispersing Fortune in Mongolia." *Social Analysis* 56, no. 1 (2012): 117–132.

Empson, Rebecca. "Portioning Loans: Cosmologies of Wealth and Power in Mongolia." In A. Abrahamson and M. Holbraad (eds.), *Framing Cosmologies: The Anthropology of Worlds*, pp. 182–198. Manchester: Manchester University Press, 2014.

Englund, Harri, and James Leach. "Ethnography and the Meta-Narratives of Modernity." *Current Anthropology* 41, no. 2 (2000): 225–239.

Ericksen, Annika. "Depend on Each Other and Don't Just Sit: The Socialist Legacy, Responsibility, and Winter Risk among Mongolian Herders." *Human Organization* 73, no. 1 (2014): 38–49.

Fehérváry, Krisztina. "American Kitchens, Luxury Bathrooms and the Search for a 'Normal' Life in Postsocialist Hungary." *Ethnos* 67, no. 3 (2002): 369–400.

Ferguson, J. (1997). "Anthropology and Its Evil Twin: 'Development' in the Constitution of a Discipline." In F. Cooper and R. Packard (eds.), *International Development and the Social Sciences: Essays on the History and Politics of Knowledge*, pp. 150–175. Berkeley: University of California Press.

Ferguson, James. *Expectations of Modernity: Myths and Meanings of Urban Life on the Zambian Cobberbelt*. Berkeley: University of California Press, 1999.

Fernandez-Gimenez, Maria E. "Sustaining the Steppes: A Geographical History of Pastoral Land Use in Mongolia." *Geographical Review* 89 (1999): 315–341.

Fernandez-Gimenez, Maria E. "Land Use and Land Tenure in Mongolia: A Brief History and Current Issues." *Rangelands of Central Asia: Proceedings of the Conference on Transformations, Issues, and Future Challenges*. Salt Lake City, Utah, January 27, 2004. Department of Agriculture, Forest Service, Rocky Mountain Research Station, 2006.

Fernandez-Gimenez, Maria E., and B. Batbuyan. "Law and Disorder: Local Implementation of Mongolia's Land Law." *Development and Change* 35, no. 1 (2004): 141–165.

Fox, Elizabeth. "Making Cashmere, Making Futures: The Work of Hope and the Materialisation of Dreams in a Mongolian Cashmere Factory." *Inner Asia* no. 17 (2015): 77–99.

Frederiksen, Martin D. *Young Men, Time and Boredom in the Republic of Georgia*. Philadelphia: Temple University Press, 2013.

Friedman, Jonathan. "The Political Economy of Elegance: An African Cult of Beauty." *Culture and History* 7 (1990): 101–125.

Friedman, Jonathan R. "The Political Economy of Elegance." In J. Friedman (ed.), *Cultural Identity and Global Process*, pp. 147–166. London: Sage, 1994.

Friedman, Jonathan R. "Shock and Subjectivity in the Age of Globalization: Marginalization, Exclusion, and the Problem of Resistance." *Anthropological Theory* 7, no. 4 (2007): 421–448.

Fukuyama, Francis. "The End of History." *National Interest* 16 (Summer 1989): 3–18.

Ganhuyag, Chuluunbaatar. *Mongolian-English Dictionary*. Ulaanbaatar: Project Monendic, 2005.

Gell, Alfred. *The Anthropology of Time: Cultural Constructions of Temporal Maps and Images*. Oxford: Berg, 1992.

Gell, Alfred. *Art and Agency: An Anthropological Theory*. Oxford: Clarendon Press, 1998.

Gell, Alfred. "The Market Wheel: Symbolic Aspects of an Indian Tribal Market." In E. Hirsch (ed.), *The Art of Anthropology: Essays and Diagrams*, pp. 107–135. London: Athlone Press, 1999.

Ghodsee, Kristen. *Lost in Transition: Ethnographies of Everyday Life after Communism*. Durham, NC: Duke University Press, 2011.

Giddens, Anthony. "The Self: Ontological Security and Existential Anxiety." In A. Giddens, *Modernity and Self-Identity: Self and Society in the Modern Age*, pp. 35–69. Stanford, CA: Stanford University Press, 1991.

Godelier, Maurice. *The Enigma of the Gift*. Cambridge: Polity Press, 1999.

Government of Mongolia. Law of Mongolia on Land. Ulaanbaatar, 2002.

Grabher, Gernot, and David Stark. "Organizing Diversity: Evolutionary Theory, Network Analysis, and Post-Socialism." In G. Grabher and D. Stark (eds.), *Restructuring Networks in Post-Socialism*, pp. 1–32. Oxford: Oxford University Press, 1997.

Graeber, David. *Debt: The First 5,000 Years*. Brooklyn, NY: Melville House, 2011.

Graeber, David. "Fetishism as Social Creativity; or, Fetishes Are Gods in the Process of Construction." *Anthropological Theory* 5, no. 4 (2005): 407–438.

Grant, Bruce. *In the Soviet House of Culture*. Princeton, NJ: Princeton University Press, 1995.

Greenberg, Jessica. *After the Revolution: Youth, Democracy, and the Politics of Disappointment in Serbia*. Stanford, CA: Stanford University Press, 2014.

Gregory, Christopher A. *Gifts and Commodities*. London: Academic Press, 1982.

Grosz, Elizabeth (ed.). *Becomings, Explorations in Time, Memory and Futures*. Ithaca, NY: Cornell University Press, 1999.

Grosz, Elizabeth. "Feminism, Materialism, and Freedom." In D. Coole and S. Frost (eds.), *New Materialisms: Ontology, Agency, and Politics*, pp. 139–157. Durham, NC: Duke University Press, 2000.

Gudeman, Stephen. *Economics as Culture: Models and Metaphors of Livelihood*. London: Routledge, 1986.

Guenther, Mathias G. "Current Issues and Future Directions in Hunter-Gatherer Studies." *Current Anthropology* 102, no. 2 (2007): 371–388.

Guyer, Jane. "Prophecy and the Near Future: Thoughts on Macro-Economic, Evangelical and Punctuated Time." *American Ethnologist* 34, no. 3 (2007): 409–421.

Haas, Paula. "Contradictory Moralities: Alcohol Consumption in Inner Mongolia." *Asian Anthropology* 13, no. 1 (2014): 20–35.

Hamayon, Roberte. *La chasse à l'âme. Esquisse d'une théorie du chamanisme sibérien.* Nanterre: Société d'ethnologie, 1990.

Han, Clara. *Life in Debt: Times of Care and Violence in Neoliberal Chile.* Berkeley: University of California Press, 2012.

Hann, Christopher M. (ed.). *Property Relations: Renewing the Anthropological Tradition.* Cambridge: Cambridge University Press, 1998.

Hann, Christopher M. "Anthropology's Multiple Temporalities and Its Future in Central and Eastern Europe." Max Planck Institute for Social Anthropology, Working Papers no. 90 (2007): 1–11.

Hann, Christopher M. (ed.). *Postsocialism: Ideals, Ideologies and Practices in Eurasia.* London: Routledge, 2002.

Hanstad, Tim, and Jennifer Duncan. *Land Reform in Mongolia: Observations and Recommendations.* RDI Reports on Foreign Aid and Development 109, 2001.

Hart, Keith. "Heads or Tails? Two Sides of the Coin." *Man* (N.S.) 21, no. 4 (1986): 637–656.

Hart, Keith. "Marcel Mauss: In Pursuit of the Whole. A Review Essay." *Comparative Studies in Society and History* 49, no. 2 (2007): 473–485.

Haslund-Christensen, Michael. *The Wild East: Portrait of an Urban Nomad.* Copenhagen: Haslund Film, 2002.

Heissig, Walter. *The Religions of Mongolia.* London: Routledge, 1980.

Henare, Amira, Martin Holbraad and Sari Wastell (eds.). "Introduction: Thinking through Things." In A. Henare, M. Holbraad and S. Wastell (eds.), *Thinking through Things: Theorising Artefacts Ethnographically,* pp. 1–31. London: Routledge, 2007.

Hendry, Joy. "The Paradox of Friendship in the Field: Analysis of a Long-Term Anglo-Japanese Relationship." In J. Okely and H. Callaway (eds.), *Anthropology and Autobiography,* pp. 163–174. London: Routledge, 1992.

Henig, David, and Gareth E. Hamilton (eds.). "Beyond Postsocialism? Creativity, Moral Resistance and Change in the Corners of Eurasia." Special edition of *Durham Anthropology Journal* 17, no. 1 (2010).

Hertz, Ellen. *The Trading Crowd: An Ethnography of the Shanghai Stock Market.* Cambridge: Cambridge University Press, 1998.

Heyat, Farideh. "Women and the Culture of Entrepreneurship in Soviet and Post-Soviet Azerbaijan." In C. Humphrey and R. Mandel (eds.), *Markets and Moralities: Ethnographies of Postsocialism,* pp. 19–31. Oxford: Berg, 2002.

High, Holly. "Re-Reading the Potlatch in a Time of Crisis: Debt and the Distinctions That Matter." *Social Anthropology* 20, no. 4 (2012): 363–379.

High, Mette M. "Wealth and Envy in the Mongolian Gold Mines." *Cambridge Anthropology* 27, no. 3 (2008): 1–19.

High, Mette M. "Polluted Money, Polluted Wealth: Emerging Regimes of Value in the Mongolian Gold Rush." *American Ethnologist* 40, no. 4 (2013): 676–688.

High, Mette. *Fear and Fortune: Spirit Worlds and Emerging Economies in the Mongolian Gold Rush.* Ithaca, NY: Cornell University Press, 2017.

Hodges, Mark. "Rethinking Time's Arrow: Bergson, Deleuze and the Anthropology of Time." *Anthropological Theory* 8, no. 4 (2008): 399–429.

Hohnen, Pernille. *A Market out of Place? Remaking Economic, Social and Symbolic Boundaries in Post-Communist Lithuania*. Oxford: Oxford University Press, 2005.

Højer, Lars. *Dangerous Communications: Enmity, Suspense and Integration in Postsocialist Northern Mongolia*. PhD thesis, Department of Social Anthropology, University of Cambridge, 2003.

Højer, Lars. "The Anti-Social Contract: Enmity and Suspicion in Northern Mongolia." *Cambridge Anthropology* 24, no. 3 (2004): 41–63.

Højer, Lars. "Troubled Perspectives in the New Mongolian Economy." *Inner Asia* 9, no. 2 (2007): 261–273.

Højer, Lars. "Absent Powers: Magic and Loss in Postsocialist Mongolia." *Journal of the Royal Anthropological Institute* (N.S.) 15, no. 3 (2009): 575–591.

Højer, Lars. "The Spirit of Business: Pawnshops in Ulaanbaatar." *Social Anthropology* 20, no. 1 (2012): 34–49.

Højer, Lars. "Apathy and Revolution: Temporal Sensibilities in Contemporary Mongolia." In J. Laidlaw, B. Bodenhorn and M. Holbraad (eds.), *Recovering the Human Subject: Freedom, Creativity and Decision*, pp. 74–94. Cambridge: Cambridge University Press, 2018.

Højer, Lars. *The Anti-Social Contract: Injurious Talk and Dangerous Exchanges*. New York: Berghahn Books, 2019a.

Højer, Lars. "Patriots, Pensioners and Ordinary Mongolians: Deregulation and Conspiracy in Mongolia." *Ethnos*, 2019b.

Holbraad, Martin. "Expending Multiplicity: Money in Cuban Ifá Cults." *Journal of the Royal Anthropological Institute* (N.S.) 11 (2005): 231–254.

Holbraad, Martin. *Truth in Motion: The Recursive Anthropology of Cuban Divination*. Chicago: University of Chicago Press, 2012.

Holbraad, Martin, and Morten A. Pedersen. *The Ontological Turn: An Anthropological Exposition*. Cambridge: Cambridge University Press, 2017.

Horst, Heather A., and Daniel Miller. "From Kinship to Link-Up: Cell Phones and Social Networking in Jamaica." *Current Anthropology* 46, no. 5 (2005): 755–778.

Humphrey, Caroline. "The Moral Authority of the Past in Post-Socialist Mongolia." *Religion, State and Society* 20, nos. 3–4 (1992): 375–389.

Humphrey, Caroline. "Remembering an Enemy: The Bogd Khaan in Twentieth-Century Mongolia." In R. Watson (ed.), *Memory, History and Opposition under State Socialism*, pp. 21–44. Santa Fe, NM: School of American Research, 1994.

Humphrey, Caroline. "Creating a Culture of Disillusionment: Consumption in Moscow, a Chronicle of Changing Times." In D. Miller (ed.), *Worlds Apart: Modernity through the Prism of the Local*, pp. 43–68. London: Routledge, 1995.

Humphrey, Caroline, with Urgunge Onon. *Shamans and Elders: Experience, Knowledge and Power among the Daur Mongols*. Oxford: Clarendon Press, 1996.

Humphrey, Caroline. *Marx Went Away—but Karl Stayed Behind*. Ann Arbor: University of Michigan Press, 1998.

Humphrey, Caroline. *The Unmaking of Soviet Life: Everyday Economies after Socialism*. Ithaca, NY: Cornell University Press, 2002a.

Humphrey, Caroline. "Rituals of Death as a Context for Understanding Personal Property in Socialist Mongolia." *Journal of the Royal Anthropological Institute* (N.S.) no. 8 (2002b): 65–87.

Humphrey, Caroline. "Ideology in Infrastructure: Architecture and Soviet Imagination." *Journal of the Royal Anthropological Institute* 11, no. 1 (2005): 39–58.

Humphrey, Caroline. "The 'Creative Bureaucrat': Conflicts in the Production of Soviet Communist Party Discourse." *Inner Asia* 10, no. 1 (2008a): 5–35.

Humphrey, Caroline. "Reassembling Individual Subjects: Events and Decisions in Troubled Times." *Anthropological Theory* 8, no. 4 (2008b): 357–380.

Humphrey, Caroline, and Stephen Hugh-Jones. "Introduction: Barter, Exchange and Value." In C. Humphrey and S. Hugh-Jones (eds.), *Barter, Exchange and Value: An Anthropological Approach*. Cambridge: Cambridge University Press, 1992.

Humphrey, Caroline, and Ruth Mandel (eds.). *Markets and Moralities: Ethnographies of Post-socialism*. Oxford: Berg, 2002.

Humphrey, Caroline, and Vera Skvirskaja. "Trading Places: Post-Socialist Container Markets and the City." *Focaal* no. 55 (2009): 61–73.

Humphrey, Caroline, and Vera Skvirskaja (eds.). *Post-Cosmopolitan Cities: Explorations of Urban Coexistence*. Oxford: Berghahn Books, 2012.

Humphrey, Caroline, and David Sneath. *The End of Nomadism? Society, State and the Environment in Inner Asia*. Cambridge, UK: White Horse Press, 1999.

Humphrey, Caroline, and Katherine Verdery. "Introduction: Raising Questions about Property." In K. Verdery and C. Humphrey (eds.), *Property in Question: Value Transformation in the Global Economy*, pp. 1–25. Oxford: Berg, 2004.

Ingold, Tim. *Hunters, Pastoralists and Ranchers*. Cambridge: Cambridge University Press, 1980.

Ingold, Tim. *The Appropriation of Nature: Essays on Human Ecology and Social Relations*. Manchester: Manchester University Press, 1986.

Ingold, Tim. "Hunting and Gathering as Ways of Perceiving the Environment." In R. Ellen and K. Fukui (eds.), *Redefining Nature: Ecology, Culture and Domestication*. Oxford: Berg, 1996.

Ingold, Tim. *The Perception of the Environment: Essays in Livelihood, Dwelling and Skill*. London: Routledge, 2000.

Jackson, Michael. *The Politics of Story Telling: Violence, Transgression, and Intersubjectivity*. Copenhagen: Museum Tusculanum Press, 2002.

Jagchid, Sechin, and Paul Hyer. *Mongolia's Culture and Society*. Boulder, CO: Westview, 1979.

James, Deborah. *Money from Nothing: Indebtedness and Aspiration in South Africa*. Stanford, CA: Stanford University Press, 2014.

Jensen, Casper Bruun. "Experiments in Good Faith and Hopelessness: Toward a Post-Critical Social Science." *Common Knowledge* 20, no. 2 (2014): 337–362.

Kabzinska-Stawarz, Iwona. *Games of Mongolian Shepherds*. Warsaw: Polish Academy of Sciences, 1991.

Kamata, Takuya, James A. Reichert, et al. *Mongolia: Enhancing Policies and Practices for Ger Area Development in Ulaanbaatar*. Ulaanbaatar: World Bank, 2010.

Kandiyoti, Deniz. "How Far Do Analyses of Postsocialism Travel?" In C. M. Hann (ed.), *Postsocialism: Ideals, Ideologies and Practices in Eurasia*, pp. 238–257. London: Routledge, 2002.

Kapferer, Bruce. *A Celebration of Demons: Exorcism and the Aesthetics of Healing in Sri Lanka.* Oxford: Berg, 1991.

Kaplonski, Christopher. "Creating National Identity in Socialist Mongolia." *Central Asian Survey* 17, no. 1 (1998): 35–49.

Kaplonski, Christopher. *Truth, History and Politics in Mongolia.* London: Routledge, 2004.

Kideckel, David A. "Getting By in Postsocialism: Labor, Bodies, Voices." In D. A. Kideckel (ed.), *Getting By in Postsocialist Romania: Labor, the Body and Working-Class Culture,* pp. 1–28. Bloomington: Indiana University Press, 2008.

Konstantinov, Yulian, Gideon M. Kressel and Trond Thuen. "Outclassed by Former Outcasts: Petty Trading in Varna." *American Ethnologist* 25, no. 4 (1998): 729–745.

Korsby, Trine M. *Hustlers of Desire: Transnational Pimping and Body Economies in Eastern Romania.* PhD dissertation, Department of Anthropology, University of Copenhagen, 2015.

Kristensen, Benedikte M. "The Human Perspective." *Inner Asia* 9, no. 2 (2007): 275–289.

Kristensen, Benedikte M. *Returning to the Forest: Shamanism, Landscape and History among the Duha of Northern Mongolia.* PhD dissertation, Center for Comparative Culture Studies, Department of Cross-Cultural and Regional Studies, University of Copenhagen, 2015.

Krøijer, Stine. *Figurations of the Future: Forms and Temporality of Left Radical Politics in Northern Europe.* Oxford: Berghahn Books, 2015.

Kruglova, Anna. *Anything Can Happen: Everyday Morality and Social Theory in Russia.* PhD dissertation, Department of Anthropology, University of Toronto, 2016.Laidlaw, James. "For an Anthropology of Ethics and Freedom." *Journal of the Royal Anthropological Institute* 8, no. 2 (2002): 311–332.

Laidlaw, James. *The Subject of Virtue: An Anthropology of Ethics and Freedom.* Cambridge: University Press, 2014.

Lampland, Martha. *The Object of Labor: Commodification in Socialist Hungary.* Chicago: University of Chicago Press, 1995.

Latour, Bruno. *Reassembling the Social: An Introduction to Actor-Network-Theory.* Oxford: Oxford University Press, 2005.

Lattimore, Owen. *Inner Asian Frontiers of China.* Boston: Beacon, 1962.

Law, John. "Notes on the Theory of the Actor-Network: Ordering, Strategy and Heterogeneity." *Systems Practice* 5 (1992): 379–393.

Leach, Edmund. *Culture and Communication: The Logic by Which Symbols Are Connected: An Introduction to the Use of Structuralist Analysis in Social Anthropology.* Cambridge: Cambridge University Press, 1976.

Ledeneva, Alena V. *Russia's Economy of Favours: Blat, Networking and Informal Exchange.* Cambridge: Cambridge University Press, 1998.

Ledeneva, Alena V. *How Russia Really Works: Informal Practices in the 1990s.* Ithaca, NY: Cornell University Press, 2006.

Lemon, Alaina. "'Your Eyes Are Green Like Dollars': Counterfeit Cash, National Substance, and Currency Apartheid in 1990s Russia." *Cultural Anthropology* 13, no. 1 (1998): 22–55.

Lemon, Alaina. "Talking Transit and Spectating Transition: The Moscow Metro." In D. Berdahl, M. Bunzl and M. Lampland (eds.), *Altering States: Ethnographies of Transition in Eastern Europe and the Former Soviet Union,* pp. 14–39. Ann Arbor: University of Michigan Press, 2000.

Lévi-Strauss, Claude. *The Savage Mind.* Chicago: University of Chicago Press, 1966.

Lévi-Strauss, Claude. *The Elementary Structures of Kinship*. Boston: Beacon Press, 1969.

Lewis, Oscar. *La Vida: A Puerto Rican Family in the Culture of Poverty*, 2nd ed. New York: Knopf, 1968.

Lindquist, Galina. *Conjuring Hope: Healing and Magic in Contemporary Russia*. Oxford: Berghahn Books, 2005.

Lucht, Hans. *Darkness before Daybreak: African Migrants Living on the Margins in Southern Italy Today*. Berkeley: University of California Press, 2012.

Maeckelbergh, Marianne. *The Will of the Many: How the Alterglobalization Movement Is Changing the Face of Democracy*. New York: Pluto Press, 2009.

Mahmood, Saba. "Feminist Theory, Embodiment and the Docile Agent: Some Reflections on the Egyptian Islamic Revival." *Cultural Anthropology* 6, no. 2 (2001): 202–236.

Marsden, Magnus. *Trading Worlds: Afghan Merchants across Modern Frontiers*. London: Hurst & Co., 2016.

Marsh, Peter K. "Beyond the Soviet Houses of Culture: Rural Responses to Urban Cultural Policies in Contemporary Mongolia." In O. Bruun and L. Narangoa (eds.), *Mongols from Country to City: Floating Boundaries, Pastoralism and City Life in the Mongol Lands*, pp. 290–304. Copenhagen: NIAS Press, 2006.

Marsh, Peter K. "Our Generation Is Opening Its Eyes: Hip-Hop and Youth Identity in Contemporary Mongolia." *Central Asian Survey* 29, no. 3 (2010): 345–358.

Maurer, Bill. "Repressed Futures: Financial Derivatives' Theological Unconscious." *Economy and Society* 31, no. 1 (2002): 15–36.

Mauss, Marcel. *The Gift: The Form and Reason for Exchange in Primitive Societies*. London: Routledge, 1990 (1923–1924).

Meagher, Kate. "Culture, Agency and Power: Theoretical Reflections on Informal Economic Networks and Political Process." DIIS Working Paper 27. Copenhagen: DIIS, 2009.

Mearns, Robin. "Decentralisation, Rural Livelihoods and Pasture-Land Management in Post-Socialist Mongolia." *European Journal of Development Research* 16, no. 1 (2004): 133–152.

Meillassoux, Claude. "On the Mode of Production of the Hunting Band." In P. Alexandre (ed.), *French Perspectives in African Studies*, pp. 187–203. London: Oxford University Press, 1973.

Merli, Laetitia. "Shamanism in Transition: From the Shadow to the Light." In O. Bruun and L. Narangoa (eds.), *Mongols from Country to City: Floating Boundaries, Pastoralism and City Life in the Mongol Lands*, pp. 254–271. Copenhagen: NIAS Press, 2006.

Miller, Danny. "Consumption as the Vanguard of History: A Polemic by Way of an Introduction." In D. Miller (ed.), *Acknowledging Consumption: A Review of New Studies*, pp. 1–57. London: Routledge, 1995.

Mittermaier, Amira. *Dreams That Matter: Egyptian Landscapes of the Imagination*. Berkeley: University of California Press, 2011.

Miyazaki, Hirokazu. *The Method of Hope: Anthropology, Philosophy and Fijian Knowledge*. Stanford, CA: Stanford University Press, 2004.

Miyazaki, Hirokazu. "Economy of Dreams: Hope in Global Capitalism and Its Critiques." *Cultural Anthropology* 21, no. 2 (2006): 147–172.

Miyazaki, Hirokazu. *Arbitraging Japan: Dreams of Capitalism at the End of Finance*. Berkeley: University of California Press, 2013.

Miyazaki, Hirokazu. "Insistence and Response." *Common Knowledge* 20, no. 3 (2014): 518–526.

Miyazaki, Hirokazu, and Annelise Riles. "Failure as an Endpoint." In A. Ong and S. J. Collier (eds.), *Global Assemblages: Technology, Politics, and Ethics as Anthropological Problems*, pp. 320–332. Oxford: Blackwell, 2005.

Morgan, Lewis Henry. *Ancient Society.* Tucson: University of Arizona Press, 1985 (1877).

Morris, Elizabeth. *The Informal Sector in Mongolia: Profiles, Needs and Strategies.* Bangkok: International Labour Office, 2001.

Myers, Gregory, and Peter E. Hetz. *Property Rights and Land Privatization: Issues for Success in Mongolia.* Mongolia: USAID, 2004.

National Statistical Office of Mongolia. *Mongolian Statistical Yearbook 2005.* Ulaanbaatar, 2005.

Nazpary, Joma. *Post-Soviet Chaos: Violence and Dispossession in Kazakhstan.* London: Pluto Press, 2002.

Nielsen, Finn Sivert. *The Eye of the Whirlwind: Russian Identity and Soviet Nation-Building. Quests for Meaning in a Soviet Metropolis.* Oslo: Department of Social Anthropology, 1987, www.anthrobase.com.

Nielsen, Morten. *In the Vicinity of the State: House Construction, Personhood, and the State in Maputo, Mozambique.* PhD thesis, Department of Anthropology, University of Copenhagen, 2008.

Nielsen, Morten. "Futures Within: Reversible Time and House-Building in Maputo, Mozambique." *Anthropological Theory* 11, no. 4 (2011a): 397–423.

Nielsen, Morten. "Inverse Governmentality: The Paradoxical Production of Peri-Urban Planning in Maputo, Mozambique." *Critique of Anthropology* 31, no. 4 (2011b): 329–358.

Nielsen, Morten, and Morten A. Pedersen. "Infrastructural Imaginaries: Collapsed Futures in Mozambique and Mongolia." In M. Harris and N. Rapport (eds.), *Reflections on Imagination: Human Capacity and Ethnographic Method*, pp. 237–262. Surrey: Ashgate, 2015.

Odgaard, Ole. "Living Standards and Poverty." In O. Bruun and O. Odgaard (eds.), *Mongolia in Transition*, pp. 103–134. Richmond, Surrey: Curzon, 1996.

Ortner, Sherry B. "Theory in Anthropology since the Sixties." *Comparative Studies in Society and History* 26, no. 4 (1984): 126–166.

Oushakine, Serguei A. *The Patriotism of Despair: Nation, War and Loss in Russia.* Ithaca, NY: Cornell University Press, 2009.

Papailias, Penelope. "Beyond the 'Greek Crisis': Histories, Rhetorics, Politics." Hot Spots, Cultural Anthropology website, 2011, www.culanth.org.

Park, Hwan-Young. "Metaphorical and Ideological Concepts of Post-Socialist Mongolian Kinship." *Inner Asia* 5, no. 2 (2003): 143–162.

Parry, Jonathan. "The Gift, the Indian Gift and the 'Indian Gift.'" *Man* (N.S.) 21 (1985): 453–473.

Parry, Jonathan, and Maurice Bloch. "Introduction: Money and the Morality of Exchange." In M. Bloch and J. Parry (eds.), *Money and the Morality of Exchange*, pp. 1–32. Cambridge: Cambridge University Press, 1989.

Patico, Jennifer, and Melissa L. Caldwell (eds.). Special Issue on Postsocialist Consumption. *Ethnos* 67, no. 3 (2002).

Pedersen, Morten Axel. "Totemism, Animism and North Asian Indigenous Ontologies." *Journal of the Royal Anthropological Institute* 7, no. 3 (2001): 411–427.

Pedersen, Morten Axel. "Where Is the Centre? The Spatial Distribution of Power in Post-Socialist Rural Mongolia." In O. Bruun and L. Narangoa (eds.), *Mongols from Country to City: Floating Boundaries, Pastoralism and City Life in the Mongol Lands*, pp. 82–109. Copenhagen: Nordic Institute of Asian Studies, 2006.

Pedersen, Morten Axel. "From 'Public' to 'Private' Markets in Postsocialist Mongolia." *Anthropology of East Europe Review* 25, no. 1 (2007a): 64–72.

Pedersen, Morten Axel. "Talismans of Thought: Shamanist Ontologies and Extended Cognition in Northern Mongolia." In A. Henare, M. Holbraad and S. Wastell (eds.), *Thinking through Things: Theorising Artefacts Ethnographically*, pp. 141–166. London: Routledge, 2007b.

Pedersen, Morten Axel. "At Home away from Homes: Navigating the Taiga in Northern Mongolia." In P. Kirby (ed.), *Boundless Worlds: An Anthropological Approach to Movement*, pp. 135–152. Oxford: Berghahn Books, 2009.

Pedersen, Morten Axel. *Not Quite Shamans: Spirit Worlds and Political Lives in Northern Mongolia*. Ithaca, NY: Cornell University Press, 2011.

Pedersen, Morten Axel. "The Task of Anthropology Is to Invent Relations: For the Motion." *Critique of Anthropology* 32, no. 1 (2012a): 59–65.

Pedersen, Morten Axel. "A Day in the Cadillac: The Work of Hope in Urban Mongolia." *Social Analysis* 56, no. 2 (2012b): 136–151.

Pedersen, Morten Axel. "The Fetish of Connectivity." In P. Harvey, E. C. Casella, et al. (eds.), *Objects and Materials: A Routledge Companion*, pp. 197–207. London: Routledge, 2013.

Pedersen, Morten Axel. "Shamanic Spirits in Transition: Postsocialism as Political Cosmology." In A. Abrahamson and M. Holbraad (eds.), *Contemporary Cosmologies: The Anthropology of Worlds*, pp. 161–184. Manchester: Manchester University Press, 2014.

Pedersen, Morten Axel. "Debt as an Urban Chronotope in Ulaanbaatar." *Ethnos* 82, no. 3 (2017a): 475–491.

Pedersen, Morten Axel. "The Vanishing Power Plant: Infrastructures and Ignorance in Ulaanbaatar." *Cambridge Journal of Anthropology* 35, no. 2 (2017b): 79–95.

Pedersen, Morten Axel. "Incidental Connections: Freedom and Urban Life in Mongolia." In J. Laidlaw, B. Bodenhorn and M. Holbraad (eds.), *Recovering the Human Subject: Freedom, Creativity and Decision*, pp. 115–130. Cambridge: Cambridge University Press, 2018.

Pedersen, Morten Axel, and Mikkel Bunkenborg. "Roads That Separate: Sino-Mongolian Relations in the Inner Asian Desert." *Mobilities* 7, no. 4 (2012): 554–569.

Pedersen, Morten Axel, and Lars Højer. "Lost in Transition: Fuzzy Property and Leaky Selves in Ulaanbaatar." *Ethnos* 73, no. 1 (2008): 73–96.

Pedersen, Morten Axel, and Morten Nielsen. "Transtemporal Hinges: Reflections on a Comparative Ethnographic Study of Chinese Infrastructural Projects in Mozambique and Mongolia." *Social Analysis* 57, no. 1 (2013): 122–142.

Pedersen, Morten Axel, and Rane Willerslev. "'The Soul of the Soul Is the Body': Rethinking the Soul through North Asian Ethnography." *Common Knowledge* 18, no. 3 (2012): 464–486.

Peebles, Gustav. "The Anthropology of Credit and Debt." *Annual Review of Anthropology* no. 39 (2010): 225–240.

Peebles, Gustav. "Whitewashing and Leg-Bailing: On the Spatiality of Debt." *Social Anthropology* 20, no. 4 (2012): 429–443.

Pelkmans, Mathijs (ed.). *Conversion after Socialism: Disruptions, Modernisms and Technologies of Faith in the Former Soviet Union*. Oxford: Berghahn, 2009.

Pels, Peter. "The Spirit of Matter: On Fetish, Rarity, Fact, and Fancy." In P. Spyer (ed.), *Border Fetishisms: Material Objects in Unstable Spaces*, pp. 91–122. London: Routledge, 1998.

Peterson, Nikolas. "Demand Sharing: Reciprocity and the Pressure for Generosity among Foragers." *American Anthropologist* 95, no. 4 (1993): 860–873.

Pine, Frances. "Incorporation and Exclusion in the Podhale." In S. Day, E. Papataxiarchis and M. Stewart (eds.), *Lilies of the Field: Marginal People Who Live for the Moment*, pp. 45–61. Oxford: Westview Press, 1999.

Piot, Charles. *Nostalgia for the Future: West Africa after the Cold War*. Chicago: University of Chicago Press, 2010.

Polanyi, Karl. *The Great Transformation*. Boston: Beacon Press, 1957.

Povinelli, Elisabeth A. "The Child and the Broom Closet: States of Killing and Letting Die." *South Atlantic Quarterly* 107, no. 3 (2008): 509–530.

Povinelli, Elizabeth A. *Economies of Abandonment: Social Belonging and Endurance in Late Liberalism*. Durham, NC: Duke University Press, 2011.

Plueckhahn, Rebekah. "The Power of Faulty Paperwork Bureaucratic Negotiation, Land Access and Personal Innovation in Ulaanbaatar." *Inner Asia* 19, no. 1 (2017): 91–109.

Plueckhahn Rebekah, and Terbish Bayartsetseg. "Negotiation, Social Indebtedness, and the Making of Urban Economies in Ulaanbaatar." *Central Asian Survey* 37, no. 3 (2018): 438–456.

Plueckhahn, Rebekah, and Bumochir Dulam. "Capitalism in Mongolia: Ideology, Practice and Ambiguity." *Central Asian Survey* 37, no. 3 (2018): 341–356.

Pusca, Anca. "Shock, Therapy and Postcommunist Transitions." *Alternatives* 32 (2007): 341–360.

Rabinow, Paul. *Reflections on Fieldwork in Morocco*. Berkeley: University of California Press, 1977.

Radcliffe-Brown, Alfred R. *Structure and Function in Primitive Society: Essays and Addresses*. London: Cohen and West, 1952.

Rakowski, Tomasz. *Hunters, Gatherers and Practitioners of Powerlessness: An Ethnography of the Degraded in Postsocialist Poland*. Oxford: Berghahn, 2016.

Raman, Parvathi, and Harry G. West. "Poetries of the Past in a Socialist World Remade." In H. G. West and P. Raman (eds.), *Enduring Socialism: Explorations of Revolution and Transformation, Restoration and Continuation*, pp. 1–28. New York: Berghahn Books, 2009.

Remme, Jon Henrik Z. "A Dispositional Account of Causality: From Herbal Insecticides to Anthropological Theories on Emergence and Becoming." *Anthropological Theory* 14, no. 4 (2014): 405–421.

Ries, Nancy. "'Honest Bandits' and 'Warped People': Russian Narratives about Money, Corruption and Moral Decay." In C. J. Greenhouse, E. Mertz and K. B. Warren (eds.), *Ethnography in Unstable Places: Everyday Lives in Contexts of Dramatic Political Change*, pp. 276–315. Durham, NC: Duke University Press, 2002.

Robbins, Joel. "Continuity Thinking and the Problem of Christian Culture: Belief, Time, and the Anthropology of Christianity." *Current Anthropology* 48, no. 1 (2007): 5–38.

Robbins, Joel, Bambi B. Schieffelin and Aparecida Vilaça. "Evangelical Conversion and the Transformation of the Self in Amazonia and Melanesia: Christianity and the Revival of

Anthropological Comparison." *Comparative Studies in Society and History* 56, no. 3 (2014): 559–590.

Rogers, Douglas. "Moonshine, Money and the Politics of Liquidity in Rural Russia." *American Ethnologist* 32, no. 1 (2008): 63–81.

Rossabi, Morris. *Modern Mongolia: From Khans to Commissars to Capitalists*. Berkeley: University of California Press, 2005.

Rothschild, Emma. *Economic Sentiments: Adam Smith, Condorcet and the Enlightenment*. Cambridge, MA: Harvard University Press, 2001.

Rouner, Leroy S. *The Changing Face of Friendship*. Notre Dame, IN: University of Notre Dame Press, 1994.

Ruel, Malcolm. "Christians as Believers." In J. Davis (ed.), *Religious Organization and Religious Experience*, pp. 9–31. London: Academic Press, 1982.

Sahlins, Marshall. *Stone Age Economics*. London: Tavistock Publications, 1974.

Sahlins, Marshall. *Culture and Practical Reason*. Chicago: University of Chicago Press, 1976.

Sampson, Steven. "Money without Culture, Culture without Money: Eastern Europe's Nouveau Riches." *Anthropological Journal on European Cultures* 3, no. 1 (1994): 7–29.

Sanjdorj, M. *Manchu Chinese Colonial Rule in Northern Mongolia*. Translated and annotated by U. Onon. London: C. Hurst, 1980.

Shrader, Heiko. *Lombard Houses in St. Petersburg: Pawning as a Survival Strategy of Low-Income Households?* Hamburg: LIT, 2000.

Scott, James C. *Seeing Like a State: How Certain Schemes to Improve the Human Condition Have Failed*. New Haven, CT: Yale University Press, 1998.

Schubert, Jon. "'A Culture of Immedialism': Co-optation and Complicity in Postwar Angola." *Ethnos* 83, no. 1 (2018): 1–18.

Shevchenko, Olga. *Crisis and the Everyday in Postsocialist Moscow*. Bloomington: Indiana University Press, 2009.

Shipton, Parker. *Bitter Money: Cultural Economy and Some African Meanings of Forbidden Commodities*. American Ethnological Society Monograph Series no. 1. Washington, DC: American Anthropological Association, 1989.

Simmel, Georg. "The Metropolis and Mental Life." In G. Bridge and S. Watson (eds.), *The Blackwell City Reader*, pp. 103–111. Malden, MA: Wiley-Blackwell, 2002 (1903).

Slocum, Sally. "Woman the Gatherer: Male Bias in Anthropology." In R. R. Reiter (ed.), *Toward an Anthropology of Women*, pp. 36–50. New York: Monthly Review Press, 1975.

Smith, Eric A. "Anthropological Applications of Optimal Foraging Theory: A Critical Review." *Current Anthropology* 24, no. 5 (1983): 625–651.

Sneath, David. "Social Relations, Networks and Social Organisation in Post-Socialist Rural Mongolia." *Nomadic Peoples* no. 33 (1993): 193–207.

Sneath, David. *Changing Inner Mongolia: Pastoral Mongolian Society and the Chinese State*. New York: Oxford University Press, 2000.

Sneath, David. "Mongolia in the 'Age of the Market': Pastoral Land-Use and the Development Discourse." In C. Humphrey and R. Mandel (eds.), *Markets and Moralities: Ethnographies of Postsocialism*, pp. 191–210. Oxford: Berg, 2002.

Sneath, David. "Lost in the Post: Technologies of Imagination, and the Soviet Legacy in Post-Socialist Mongolia." *Inner Asia* 5, no. 1 (2003): 39–52.

Sneath, David. "Property Regimes and Sociotechnical Systems: Rights over Land in Mongolia's 'Age of the Market.'" In K. Verdery and C. Humphrey (eds.), *Property in Question: Value Transformation in the Global Economy*, pp. 161–182. Oxford: Berg, 2004.

Sneath, David. "The 'Age of the Market' and the Regime of Debt: The Role of Credit in the Transformation of Pastoral Mongolia." *Social Anthropology* 20, no. 4 (2012): 458–473.

Spencer, Herbert. "The Social Organism." In *Essays: Scientific, Political and Speculative*, vol. 1. New York: D. Appleton and Company, 1904 (1860).

Spradley, James. *The Ethnographic Interview*. Belmont, CA: Wadsworth, 1979.

Spyer, Patricia. "Introduction." In P. Spyer (ed.), *Border Fetishisms: Material Objects in Unstable Places*, pp. 1–12. London: Routledge, 1998.

Spyer, Patricia. *The Memory of Trade: Modernity's Entanglements on an Eastern Indonesian Island*. Durham, NC: Duke University Press, 2000.

Ssorin-Chaikov, Nikolai. *The Social Life of the State in Subarctic Siberia*. Stanford, CA: Stanford University Press, 2003.

Stallybrass, Peter. "Marx's Coat." In Patricia Spyer (ed.), *Border Fetishisms: Material Objects in Unstable Spaces*, pp. 183–206. London: Routledge, 1998.

Stark, David. "Recombinant Property in East European Capitalism." In G. Grabher and D. Stark (eds.), *Restructuring Networks in Post-Socialism: Legacies, Linkages and Localities*, pp. 35–69. Oxford: Oxford University Press, 1997.

Stengers, Isabelle. "A 'Cosmo-Politics': Risk, Hope, Change." In Mary Zournazi (ed.), *Hope: New Philosophies for Change*, pp. 244–274. New York: Routledge, 2002.

Stewart, Michael. *The Time of the Gypsies*. Oxford: Westview Press, 1997.

Strathern, Marilyn. *The Gender of the Gift*. Berkeley: University of California Press, 1988.

Strathern, Marilyn. "For the Motion (1) [The Concept of Society Is Theoretically Obsolete]." In T. Ingold (ed.), *Key Debates in Anthropology*, pp. 60–66. London: Routledge, 1996 (1989).

Strathern, Marilyn. *Property, Substance and Effect: Anthropological Essays on Persons and Things*. London: Athlone Press, 1999.

Strum, Shirley S., and Bruno Latour. "Redefining the Social Link: From Baboons to Humans." *Social Science Information* 26, no. 4 (1987): 783–802.

Sturgeon, Janet C., and Thomas Sikor. "Post-Socialist Property in Asia and Europe: Variations on 'Fuzziness.'" *Conservation and Society* 2, no. 1 (2004): 1–17.

Suzman, James. *Affluence without Abundance: The Disappearing World of the Bushmen*. London: Bloomsbury, 2017.

Swancutt, Katherine. *Fortune and the Cursed: The Sliding Scale of Time in Mongolian Divination*. Oxford: Berghahn Books, 2012.

Szynkiewicz, Slawoj. "Mongolia's Nomads Build a New Society Again: Social Structures and Obligations on the Eve of the Private Economy." *Nomadic Peoples* 33 (1993): 163–192.

Taussig, Michael. *The Devil and Commodity Fetishism in South America*. Chapel Hill: University of North Carolina Press, 1980.

Taussig, Michael. *Shamanism, Colonialism and the Wild Man: A Study in Terror and Healing*. Chicago: University of Chicago Press, 1987.

Taussig, Michael. *The Nervous System*. New York: Routledge, 1992.

Thelen, Tatjana. "Shortage, Fuzzy Property and Other Dead Ends in the Anthropological Analysis of (Post)Socialism." *Critique of Anthropology* 31, no. 1 (2011): 43–61.

Todorova, Maria. "Introduction: From Utopia to Propaganda and Back." In M. Todorova and Z. Gille (eds.), *Post-Communist Nostalgia*. New York: Berghahn, 2010a.

Todorova, Maria. "Introduction: The Process of Remembering Communism." In M. Todorova (ed.), *Remembering Communism: Genres of Representation*, pp. 9–34. New York: Social Science Research Council, 2010b.

Tökés, Rudolf L. "'Transitology': Global Dreams and Post-Communist Realities." *Central Europe Review* 2, no. 10 (2000), www.ce-review.org.

Tsing, Anna L. *In the Realm of the Diamond Queen: Marginality in an Out-of-the-Way Place.* Princeton, NJ: Princeton University Press, 1993.

Tsing, Anna L. *Friction: An Ethnography of Global Connection.* Princeton, NJ: Princeton University Press, 2005.

Tsedevdamba, O. "The Secret Driving Force behind Mongolia's Successful Democracy." *PRISM* 6, no. 1 (2016): 140–152, www.inclusivesecurity.org.

Turnbull, Colin M. *The Forest People.* London: Simon and Schuster, 1961.

Verdery, Katherine. "Theorizing Socialism: A Prologue to the 'Transition.'" *American Anthropologist* 18, no. 3 (1991): 419–439.

Verdery, Katherine. *National Ideology under Socialism: Identity and Cultural Politics in Ceausescu's Romania.* Berkeley: University of California Press, 1995a.

Verdery, Katherine. "'Caritas' and the Conceptualization of Money in Romania." *Anthropology Today* 11, no. 1 (1995b): 3–7.

Verdery, Katherine. *What Was Socialism and What Comes Next?* Princeton, NJ: Princeton University Press, 1996.

Verdery, Katherine. "Fuzzy Property: Rights, Power and Identity in Transylvania's Decollectivization." In M. Burawoy and K. Verdery (eds.), *Uncertain Transition: Ethnographies of Change in the Postsocialist World*, pp. 53–81. Oxford: Rowman and Littlefield, 1999.

Verdery, Katherine. *The Vanishing Hectare: Property and Value in Postsocialist Transylvania.* Ithaca, NY: Cornell University Press, 2003.

Verdery, Katherine. "The Obligation of Ownership: Restoring Rights to Land in Postsocialist Transylvania." In K. Verdery and C. Humphrey (eds.), *Property in Question: Value Transformation in the Global Economy*, pp. 139–159. Oxford: Berg, 2004.

Verdery, Katherine, and Caroline Humphrey (eds.). *Property in Question: Value Transformation in the Global Economy.* Oxford: Berg, 2004.

Vigh, Henrik. *Navigating Terrains of War: Youth and Soldiering in Guinea-Bissau.* Oxford: Berghahn Books, 2006.

Vigh, Henrik. "Motion Squared: A Second Look at the Concept of Social Navigation." *Anthropological Theory* 9, no. 4 (2009): 419–438.

Vitebsky, Piers. *Reindeer People: Living with Animals and Spirits in Siberia.* London: HarperCollins, 2005.

Volkov, Vadim. *Violent Entrepreneurs: The Use of Force in the Making of Russian Capitalism.* Ithaca, NY: Cornell University Press, 2002.

Vreeland, Herbert H. *Mongol Community and Kinship Structure.* New Haven, CT: Human Relations Area Files, 1962.

Wasquant, Loïc. *Urban Outcasts: A Comparative Sociology of Advanced Marginality.* Boston: Polity Press, 2007.

Waters, Hedwig A. "The Financialization of Help: Moneylenders as Economic Translators in the Debt-Based Economy." *Central Asia Survey* 37 (2018): 403–418.

Watson, Conrad W. "Autobiography, Anthropology and the Experience of Indonesia." In J. Okely and H. Callaway (eds.), *Anthropology and Autobiography*, pp. 134–146. London: Routledge, 1992.

Watson, Ruby S. (ed.). *Memory, History, and Opposition under State Socialism*. Santa Fe, NM: School of American Research, 1994.

Weber, Max. *The Protestant Ethic and the Spirit of Capitalism*. New York: Oxford University Press, 2011 (1904–1905).

Weiner, Anette. *Inalienable Possessions: The Paradox of Keeping-While-Giving*. Berkeley: University of California Press, 1992.

West, Harry G., and Parvathi Raman (eds.). *Enduring Socialism: Explorations of Revolution and Transformation, Restoration and Continuation*. New York: Berghahn Books, 2009.

Wheeler, Alan. "Moralities of the Mongolian 'Market': A Genealogy of Trade Relations and the Zah Zeel." *Inner Asia* 6, no. 2 (2004): 215–238.

Whelan, T. S. *The Pawnshop in China*. Ann Arbor: Center for Chinese Studies of the University of Michigan, 1979.

Whyte, Susan R. *Questioning Misfortune: The Pragmatics of Uncertainty in Eastern Uganda*. Cambridge: Cambridge University Press, 1997.

Willerslev, Rane. "Not Animal, Not Not-Animal: Hunting, Imitation and Empathetic Knowledge among the Siberian Yukaghirs." *Journal of the Royal Anthropological Institute* 10 (2004a): 629–652.

Willerslev, Rane. "Spirits as 'Ready to Hand': A Phenomenological Analysis of Yukaghir Spiritual Knowledge and Dreaming." *Anthropological Theory* 4, no. 4 (2004b): 395–418.

Willerslev, Rane. *Soul Hunters: Hunting, Animism and Personhood among the Siberian Yukaghirs*. Berkeley: University of California Press, 2007.

Woodburn, James. "Egalitarian Societies." *Man* (N.S.) 17, no. 3 (1982): 431–451.

Woodburn, James. "African Hunter-Gatherer Organization: Is It Best Understood as a Product of Encapsulation?" In T. Ingold and J. Woodburn (eds.), *Hunters and Gatherers*, Vol. 1: *History, Social Change and Evolution*, pp. 31–64. Oxford: Berg, 1988.

Woodburn, James. "Sharing Is Not a Form of Exchange: An Analysis of Property-Sharing in Immediate-Return Hunter-Gatherer Societies." In C. M. Mann (ed.), *Property Relations: Renewing the Anthropological Tradition*, pp. 48–63. Cambridge: Cambridge University Press, 1998.

Yurchak, Alexei. "The Cynical Reason of Late Socialism: Power, Pretense, and the Anekdot." *Public Culture* 9, no. 2 (1997): 161–188.

Yurchak, Alexei. "Soviet Hegemony of Form: Everything Was Forever, until It Was No More." *Comparative Studies in Society and History* 45, no. 3 (2003): 480–510.

Yurchak, Alexei. *Everything Was Forever, until It Was No More: The Last Soviet Generation*. Princeton, NJ: Princeton University Press, 2006.

Zaloom, Caitlyn. *Out of the Pits: Traders and Technology from Chicago to London*. Chicago: University of Chicago Press, 2006.

Zelizer, Viviana A. "The Social Meaning of Money: 'Special Monies.'" *American Journal of Sociology* 95, no. 2 (1989): 342–377.

Zigon, Jarrett. "Hope Dies Last: Two Aspects of Hope in Contemporary Moscow." *Anthropological Theory* 9, no. 3 (2009): 253–271.

Zimmermann, Astrid E. "Enacting the State in Mongolia: An Ethnographic Study of Community, Competition and 'Corruption' in Postsocialist Provincial State Institutions." PhD thesis, Department of Social Anthropology, University of Cambridge, 2011.

Index

active person(s) (*hödölgööntei*; *idevhtei*): admiration for, in Mongolian culture, 116; urban hunters as, 27, 49, 73, 128; women as, 69, 73, 128, 130

actor-network theory, 121, 231n1

actual(ization), 25, 206, 211, 217–218

agency: apparently irrational optimism and, 21, 22, 216–218; postsocialist transition and divestment of, 35, 37. *See also* social agency

ah (elder brother): "dry" (*huurai ah*), 83, 228n3; Kolya as, 54, 107, 108; in market relations, 71, 83, 84

alcoholics (*arhichid*): as market outcasts, 85–86, 87–89. *See also* drinking/alcoholism

Alex (informant), and "African prince" email, 215, 216

ancestral spirits, in shamanic ceremonies, 138–139

Andrei (informant), 38, 53–54, 110; cruising with, 201–203, 205; response to transition, 54, 89, 200; ultimogeniture tradition and, 107

anticipation, 24, 207, 212

apartment(s), state-allocated, 106–109; emergent property relations and, 107–109; mortgaging of, 51, 109

apathy, postsocialist transition and, 38, 54, 56, 117

Ariunaa (informant), 129–141; ancestral spirits and, 138–139; as antihunter, 117, 129, 136, 139, 141; brother of, 137–138; conversion to Christianity, 134–136; detachment from postsocialist transition, 137, 139–141; on energy of objects, 158, 160; as language teacher, 131, 132–133, 137; as meat trader, 131; as shopkeeper, 130, 131–132

ashig. See profit